AF600230

THE CATHOLIC UNIVERSITY OF AMERICA
CANON LAW STUDIES
Number 117

CANONICAL PROVISIONS FOR CATHOLIC SCHOOLS

(Elementary and Intermediate)

A DISSERTATION

Submitted to the Faculty of Canon Law of the Catholic University of America in Partial Fulfillment of the Requirements for the Degree of

DOCTOR OF CANON LAW

BY

CONRAD HUMBERT BOFFA, J.C.L.
PRIEST OF THE ARCHDIOCESE OF CINCINNATI

THE CATHOLIC UNIVERSITY OF AMERICA PRESS
WASHINGTON, D. C.
1939

Nihil obstat

EDUARDUS ROELKER, S. T. D., J. C. D.
Censor Deputatus

Washingtonii, die 31 Maii, 1939

Imprimatur

✠ JOANNES T. MCNICHOLAS, O. P., S. T. M.
Archiepiscopus Cincinnatensis

In urbe Cincinnati, die 31 Maii, 1939

THE DOLPHIN PRESS
PHILADELPHIA · PENNSYLVANIA

To

THE MEMORY

OF

MY MOTHER

CALLED BY GOD TO HIMSELF

ON THE DAY OF MY EXAMINATION

MAY 31, 1939

FOREWORD

THE purpose of the present discussion is to study the subject of schools according to the rules laid down in the Code of Canon Law. The matter, therefore, is considered strictly from the canonical point of view, without prejudice to the principles and practice of pedagogy.

In the old canonical legislation, the question of schools is found in the fifth book of the Decretals, dealing with penalties and penal procedures, title V *De magistris et ne aliquid exigatur pro licentia docendi*. No doubt this constitutes an amplification of title III *De simonia*, since the content of title V has primarily in view the suppression of abuses that had originated among certain ecclesiastics and teachers, the former of whom demanded a fee for the granting of the permission to teach, and the latter, a payment for the teaching imparted. The Decretalists followed in this, as well as in other matters, the order of the Decretals.[1] Among the more modern authors who before the Code adopted a systematic order more or less logical, some treated this question under the heading *De minoribus institutis ecclesiasticis*,[2] while others connected it with the section *De locis et bonis ecclesiasticis*.[3] Wernz, adopting a better order, studies the question of schools under the section *De administratione magisterii ecclesiastici* and the title *De scholis*.[4] Finally the present Code of Canon Law includes the

[1] Cf. Schmalzgrueber, *Jus Ecclesiasticum Universum* (Romae, 1843-1845), lib. V, tit. V; Reiffenstuel, *Jus Canonicum Universum* (Parisiis, 1864-1870), lib. V, tit. V.

[2] Aichner, *Compendium Juris Ecclesiastici* (6th ed., Brixinae, 1887), § 146.

[3] Zech, *De Iure Rerum Ecclesiasticarum* (Ingolstadii, 1758), pars I, sect. I, tit. 10, *de academ.*; tit. 11, *de seminariis cler.*, § 145; Lämmer, *Institutionen des katholischen Kirchenrechts* (2nd ed., Freiburg im Breisgau, 1892), § 188.

[4] *Ius Decretalium* (Romae et Prati, 1906-1913), III, pars I, n. 66.

whole legislation governing schools in the third book *De rebus,* fourth part *De magisterio ecclesiastico*, twenty-second title *De scholis.* It is intimately connected with the twentieth title *De divini verbi praedicatione* and the twenty-first title *De seminariis*. This order is logical, for the *magisterium ecclesiasticum* is one of those means necessary for the Church in the attainment of her end, and she exercises it not only through the preaching of the Word of God and the formation of her ministers, but also through the school as an ordinary instrument of teaching.

The subject of schools as treated in the Code of Canon Law is more extended than the mere title seems to indicate. The legislator, in fact, while formulating precise regulations concerning the institutions of learning as such, sets down, at the same time, positive rules affecting Christian education at large. As the goal of Christian education is primarily a thorough training and formation in what concerns religion and morality, no education is complete and no school can carry on the task for which it is meant unless the very principles animating it rest on religion. Hence the need of Catholic training and of Catholic schools.

The present study of the canonical legislation on schools is divided into two parts and is restricted to primary and intermediate schools.

The first part of this dissertation is historical. Its purpose is to trace the manner in which the Church, through her legislation, has fulfilled Christ's injunction "to teach all nations" by establishing and controlling schools. The method employed has been demonstrative, so as to show the nature of this legislation, and to indicate its development up to the form treated in the present Code.

A commentary of the various canons relating to schools follows. These canons define the duties of all the faithful, parents and those who hold the place of parents, in reference to the religious training of youth. They also deal with the following topics: the necessity of similar training in any grade of schools; attendance at non-Catholic institutions by Catholic youth; the right of the Church to have her own system of schools, and the obligation of establishing them whenever the institutions already existing do not fulfil her desire concerning the religious formation of youth; finally, the exclusive authority of the Church in matters of religious instruction and morality, and the particular obligations of the local ordinaries together with their right of visitation. These canons for the most part are general in nature, as their particular application must be adapted to conditions as they exist in various localities. Attention has also been given to those enactments of the Plenary Councils of Baltimore which are still in force in the United States; and, because of the importance today of the question of control of schools by the family, the Church, and the State, a chapter has been added determining the rôle and the sphere of action of each.

The matter treated is by no means new, but it is, as it were, clothed in a new dress intentionally expressive of its juridical significance.

The author takes occasion here sincerely to thank His Excellency, the Most Rev. John T. McNicholas, O.P., S.T.M., Archbishop of Cincinnati, for the opportunity of advanced study, the Faculty of Canon Law for their helpful direction, and all who in any way contributed to the preparation of this work for their interest and aid.

TABLE OF CONTENTS

PART ONE

PRELIMINARY DISCUSSION
HISTORICAL SYNOPSIS

CHAPTER I

Preliminary Discussion

ORIGIN, DEFINITION, AND DIVISIONS OF SCHOOLS

By the divine ordination of Jesus Christ the Church is vested with a twofold power, that of Orders and that of Jurisdiction. Each has for its purpose the sanctification and salvation of men. The immediate object of the power of Orders is the administration of the Sacraments and Sacramentals (*potestas ministrandi*); the power of Jurisdiction, on the other hand, is concerned with the guidance and government of the members of the Church (*potestas regendi*). As such it comprises a double function, government (*imperium*) and teaching (*magisterium*).[1] It is with the teaching office of the Church that the subject of schools is associated.

The institution which is known today as the school was known among the Greeks as the διδασκαλεῖον and among the Latins as the *ludus*. The term σχολή, which transcription converted into *schola,* etymologically means an intellectual leisure; it is the discipline freely undertaken and methodically pursued with the view of acquiring superior knowledge. The term itself was never applied to all branches of instruction. It was restricted rather to those of higher standing.[2] The term *schola* appeared for the first time in the writings of Cicero. In Christian literature the most ancient testimony is offered by the Acts of the Apostles which relate that St. Paul, refusing to carry

[1] Ottaviani, *Institutiones Iuris Publici Ecclesiastici* (2nd ed., Typis Polyglottis Vaticanis, 1935-1936), I, 245; De Hammerstein, *De Ecclesia et Statu Juridice Consideratis* (Treviris, 1886), p. 155.

[2] Cf. Pliny, *Epistolae,* lib. VIII, ep. VII, 1; Jullien, *Les professeurs de littérature dans l'ancienne Rome et leur enseignement depuis l'origine jusqu'à la mort d'Auguste* (Paris, 1885), p. 114.

on his teaching in the temple of Ephesus, devoted his time to the instruction of disciples in the school of a certain Tyrannus: καθ' ἡμέραν διαλεγόμενος 'εν τῇ σχολῇ Τυράννου.[3] In the Roman usage, therefore, the term *schola* signified higher learning, grammar and rhetoric—in a word, the precious heritage which the Romans owed to Greek influence. The true term, used to designate the place and the subject of instruction, was for them that of *ludus*, which comprised various grades of teaching, such as the work of *primus magister, grammaticus, rhetor*. Because of the increasing extension of the word *schola*, the application of the term *ludus* was gradually restricted to express primary education. According to the general usage of today, the word "school" has a more generic meaning and designates any institution which has for its purpose the methodical apprehension of knowledge in different degrees. Specifically, it is defined as the institution in which doctrines and truths are expounded for the purpose of enlightening the minds of men.[4]

Among the most important classifications of schools is that regarding their origin or efficient cause. Thus classified, schools may be either private or public. The former are founded and owned by private individuals or groups of individuals, and maintain their character of private institutions even when they are recognized or endowed by public authority. The latter, on the contrary, are entirely dependent on public authority, which may be either ecclesiastical or civil, according to whether these schools come under the control of the Church or of the State.[5]

[3] Acts, XIX, 9.

[4] "Institutum in quo proponuntur doctrinae ac scientiae ad mentes hominum erudiendas." — Cocchi, *Commentarium in Codicem Iuris Canonici* (Taurinorum Augustae: Marietti, 1922-1930), VI, 116; cf. also Vermeersch-Creusen, *Epitome Iuris Canonici* (4th ed., Mechliniae et Romae: Dessain, 1930-1931), II, n. 709.

[5] Cf. Vermeersch-Creusen, *Epitome*, II, n. 709; Wernz, *Ius Decretalium*, III, pars I, n. 74. Some of the authors still give further divisions of schools which, however, are not fundamental and will be treated in the

The schools erected by the Church whether through a bishop, a pastor, or a religious community, are improperly called private institutions in the canonical sense. In fact, they rest on the Church which is a perfect society, and are erected in virtue of the ecclesiastical authority which is public.[6] These schools form the Catholic School System properly so-called. It must be noted, however, that the term "Catholic School" as used by the Code of Canon Law is more extensive in concept. Besides the schools which come directly under the control of the Church, it includes all other public and private institutions of learning which teach Religion and impart a Catholic education under competent ecclesiastical authority.[7]

proper place in the course of this study. Briefly they are: a) on the basis of attendance, obligatory and optional, according to whether attendance is compulsory by law or not. Such a distinction *per se* touches only elementary schools, and would hardly be applied to schools of higher learning unless in an indirect way, namely, in consideration of the amount of knowledge or credits required for the holding of certain offices; b) on the basis of religion, denominational, mixed, neutral or lay. Denominational schools are for pupils of a certain religious belief, while schools of mixed attendance are open to students of any religious denomination. In both types of schools religious instruction is a real part of the curriculum, but in the mixed schools religious instruction is taught separately, according to the different beliefs of the students. In the neutral or lay schools, religion is regarded only as an optional part of the curriculum, and often it is simply omitted or excluded. Cf. Cocchi, *Commentarium*, VI, 117; Blanco Nájera, *Derecho Docente de la Iglesia, la Familia y el Estado* (Linares: "El Noticiero," 1934), p. 6.

[6] In the American legal system there is no little confusion regarding a constant definition of "public" and "private" in reference to schools. Cf. Gabel, *Public Funds for Church and Private Schools* (Toledo, 1937), pp. 1-21. In most cases, however, one can say that it is neither tax support, nor gratuity of instruction, nor general admission to all pupils of a district, locality or state that differentiates the public from the private institutions, but rather ownership, to which may be joined historical origin and control. Cf. Hill, *Control of Tax-Supported Higher Education in the United States* (New York: The Carnegie Foundation for the Advancement of Teaching, 1934), p. 374; *Board of Regents of the Kansas State Agricultural College v. Hamilton*, 28 Kans. 377.

[7] Cf. Canons 1379 and 1373; Creusen, "L'École catholique," *NRT*, LIII (1926), 187, 195; Monti, *La Libertà della Scuola* (Milano: Società "Vita e Pensiero," 1928), p. 21.

One can define a Catholic school, therefore, as an institution wherein, under the supervision of the Church, children and youths are trained with a view to cultivating the higher faculties of the soul — the intellect and the will — in the light of Christian revelation.[8]

According to the more or less advanced grade of education which is imparted, a threefold division is furthermore recognized: elementary, intermediate, and superior. There is quite a divergence of opinion as to what degree of education is considered elementary. For instance, one could contrast the branches as taught by the priest Protogenes in the fourth century at Antinone, on the right bank of the Nile, reading, writing, and the rudiments of Christian doctrine,[9] with the requirements of a modern curriculum as set forth by Dr. Johnson: "The elementary curriculum should include all those things which are essential to a democratic living. Its function is to prepare the child for effective participation in the affairs of life, whether he goes on to a higher school or not. Hence it should present such information concerning God, man and nature, and cultivate such knowledge, build up such habits, foster such attitudes, interests and ideals, as will enable the child at the completion of his course to take his place in life, a thorough Catholic and an efficient member of society, truly Christian in his own individual character, able to maintain himself economically, realizing his duties as a good citizen, prepared to make the proper use of the goods of life."[10]

In the accepted canonical sense elementary education undertakes to provide for children an education fundamentally moral and religious together with that secular knowledge which the character and the exigencies of the times demand.[11]

[8] Demeuran, *L'Église* (Paris, 1914), p. 197.

[9] Theodoret, *Historia Ecclesiastica*, IV, 15—*MPG*, LXXXII, 1158.

[10] *The Curriculum of the Catholic Elementary School* (Washington: The Catholic University of America, 1919), p. 114.

[11] Wernz, *Ius Decretalium*, III, pars I, n. 73; Cavagnis, *Institutiones Iuris Publici Ecclesiastici* (Romae, 1882-1883), III, 16-18.

In the intermediate or secondary schools, popularly known in America as high schools and occasionally as colleges, that moral and religious training of the adolescent youth is continued, while through the study of letters and the sciences he is prepared to enter upon the study of his chosen profession in the university or superior school.[12]

The traditional division of schools into elementary, secondary, and schools of higher learning, as already hinted, is not an innovation of Christian times. Even in the Graeco-Roman period there could be distinguished three types of schools corresponding to the stages in a boy's training. Such a division had probably come about through custom, which had found the arrangement well suited to the needs of education. It could hardly have come through legislation, as the Roman schools were generally free of state control.[13]

The *ludus litterarum*,[14] or elementary school, accepted the Roman child at the age of six or seven years, and after a fundamental training in reading, writing, simple arithmetic and the Twelve Tables of the law,[15] graduated him into the *grammar school*. This furnished secondary education and received the child at about the age of twelve. Here, during the years of adolescence the youth was given a practical training in grammar and literature, arithmetic, music, and gymnastics, and at the conclusion of his course was ready to take up military service, follow his calling as a farmer, or continue his

[12] Wernz, *op. cit.*, III, pars I, n. 78; Vermeersch-Creusen, *Epitomė*, II, n. 709. For a clear distinction between a university and a college in English-speaking countries, cf. *The Irish University Question—The Catholic Case* (Dublin, 1897), pp. 5, 15, 17.

[13] Cicero, *De re publica*, IV, 3; Monti, *La Libertà della Scuola*, pp. 88-90.

[14] Plautus, *Mercat.*, II, ii, 32; Titus-Livy, *Hist.*, lib. III, cap. XLIV, n. 6; lib. VI, cap. XXV, n. 9.

[15] At the time of Cicero the custom of learning by heart the XII Tables was becoming obsolete. Cicero, *De Legibus*, II, 23, 59.

studies in one of the schools of rhetoric in preparation for his professional life.[16]

With the doctrine of Christ a new era began in the history of education. It is not claimed, however, that Christ intended to found a new method of education that was to supersede the customs of Greece and Rome. His contribution consisted rather in the infusion of a new spirit and of new ideals.[17] Thus, while the Roman system of education was undeniably efficient, it met with the denunciation of the early Fathers of the Church, who warned parents against placing their children under pagan tutelage.[18] For the Christian concept of education is indeed something infinitely higher than that of pagan Greece and Rome.

> The proper and immediate end of Christian education is to co-operate with divine grace in forming the true and perfect Christian, that is, to form Christ Himself in those regenerated by Baptism, according to the emphatic expression of the Apostle: " My little children, of whom I am in labour again, until Christ is formed in you " (Gal., IV, 19). For the true Christian must live a supernatural life in Christ: " Christ who is your life " (Col., III, 4), and display it in all his actions: " That the life also of Jesus may be made manifest in our mortal flesh " (II Cor., IV, 11).[19]

In keeping with the lofty aims of Christian education, all ecclesiastical legislation regarding schools rests on the fundamental principle that the training given Catholic youth must

[16] Cf. Apuleius, *Florida*, XX; Leclarcq, "École," *Dictionnaire d'Archéologie Chrétienne et de Liturgie* (Paris: Librairie Letouzey et Ané, 1924—), IV, part 2, 1730-1746; McCormick, *History of Education* (Washington, 1915), pp. 56-58.

[17] Cf. I Corinthians, I, 17, 20; II, 12.

[18] Cf. St. John Chrysostom, *Adversus oppugnatores eorum qui ad monasticam vitam inducunt. Ad patrem fidelem*—*MPG*, XLVII, 349; St. Jerome, *Ad Laetam*, ep. 107—*MPL*, XXII, 867.

[19] Pius XI, litt. encycl. *Divini illius Magistri*, 31 dec. 1929—*AAS*, XXII (1930), 83.

primarily and essentially be religious and moral in character. In this basic principle is to be found the reason for Catholic schools, and the history as well as the enactments of canonical legislation on the subject, are simply the development and application of the same principle.

CHAPTER II

1. Catholic Schools in the First Centuries of the Church

There is no legislation extant on the subject of Catholic schools during the formative stages of Christianity, presumably because schools did not exist in those early days under the supervision of the Church. Besides, the foundation of educational institutions directly under the control of the Church would indeed have presupposed a degree of organization which was not a fact in the very beginning of the Christian era. The Church, having set out to convert the world to the teaching of Christ, centered her activities about the New Dispensation and the moral obligations it implied. Since Baptism was instituted as a necessary means of salvation, it became necessary to prepare adequately candidates for the reception of that Sacrament. Thus Theophilus [1] and Apollo [2] were instructed in the words and in the ways of the Lord. In like manner, Jesus and the way of the Lord were preached unto the eunuch from Ethiopia [3] and to the gaoler at Philippi.[4]

As a consequence of this preparation the catechumenate gradually developed as an institution which was intended to test as well as to prepare those who wished to enter the Church. Although the instruction given to catechumens was of an entirely religious character, it was the most comprehensive kind of instruction that could be undertaken, and it well fulfilled the

[1] Luke, I, 4.

[2] Acts, XVIII, 25.

[3] Acts, VIII, 35.

[4] Acts, XVI, 31, 33.

needs of the family and of religion in a Christian community.[5] For the most part it was given to adults and had to be suited to their particular needs, needs which differed according to whether they were Jews or pagans. This recruiting of Christians from among adults did not prevent the early Church from being also solicitous for the young. Even Celsus, the bitter critic of all things Christian, could, in one of his most satirical passages, call attention to the solicitude with which Christians in the second century provided for the religious instruction of children.

> We see, indeed [says Celsus], in private houses, workers in wool and leather, and fullers, and persons of the most uninstructed and rustic character, not venturing to utter a word in the presence of their elders and wiser masters; but when they get hold of the children privately, and certain women as ignorant as themselves, they pour forth wonderful statements, to the effect that they ought not to give heed to their father and to their teachers, but should obey them; that the former [father and teachers] are foolish and stupid, and neither know nor can perform anything that is really good, being preoccupied with empty trifles; that they [the Christians] alone know how men ought to live, and that, if the children obey them, they will both be happy themselves, and will make their home happy also. And while thus speaking, if they see one of the instructors of youth approaching, or one of the more intelligent class, or even the father himself, the more timid among them become afraid, while the more forward incite the children to throw off the yoke, whispering that in the presence of father and teachers they neither will nor can explain to them any good thing, seeing they turn away with aversion from the silliness and stupidity of such persons as being altogether corrupt, and far advanced in wickedness, and such as would inflict punishment upon them; but that if they [the children] wish (to avail themselves of their aid,) they

[5] Lalanne, *Influence des Pères de l'Église sur l'éducation publique pendant les cinq premiers siècles de l'ere chrétienne* (Paris, 1850), p. 10.

> must leave their father and their instructors, and go with the women and with their play-fellows to the women's apartments, or to the leather shop, or to the fuller's shop, that they may attain to perfection;—and by words like these they gain them over.[6]

After due allowance has been made for the distortion and injustice with which Celsus views all Christian activities, enough truth remains in what he asserts to show that the education of youth was not neglected. Perhaps a better picture of what was the normal way of imparting instruction to children in these early times is found in the case of Origen. "Besides giving him the usual liberal education," Origen's father, Leonidas, "kept urging him . . . to drill himself in the sacred studies, requiring him to learn and recite every day." Thus "in the study of the faith" Origen "had already laid down a good foundation, having been trained in the divine Scriptures from the time that he was still a boy." But his father had also "brought him forward in secular studies," and after his father's death "he applied himself wholly with renewed zeal to the literary training." [7]

In spite of these occasional references to education in the second century, little is known about the manner in which the training of children was undertaken, and, as has been said above, there is no evidence of legislation on the part of the Church concerning any organized system of general instruction for youth.[8] The youth of that time attended the schools already established by Roman, Greek or Oriental teachers; and their faith was preserved by the instruction that they received at home as well as through the religious affiliations which bound

[6] Origen, *Contra Celsum*, III, 55—*MPG*, XI, 994. Tr. *The Ante-Nicene Fathers*, IV, 486.

[7] Eusebius, *Historia Ecclesiastica*, VI, 2—*MPG*, XX, 523, 526. Tr. by Oulton, *Loeb Classical Library*, II, 10, 15.

[8] Cf. Bardy, "L'Église et l'enseignement pendant les trois premiers siècles," *RSR*, XII (1932), 27.

them so closely to the Church. Occasionally, too, Christians held the office of teachers in the common schools, and the spiritual as well as the intellectual welfare of the pupils was thus safeguarded against the influences of pagan and skeptical thought.[9]

As Christianity spread, however, and as the number of converts increased, a corresponding need was felt for placing the training of Christian youth on a better organized basis. Historians point out that bishops found themselves obliged to commit the office of teaching to priests, who gathered about them the children of the various communities, and instructed them in the Christian truths as well as in the elementary branches of knowledge.[10] This practice of gathering the children of the different communities about the priests, and of instructing them, may be regarded as the first attempt to establish Christian elementary schools, where children had the opportunity to develop the higher faculties of the soul—the intellect and the will—under the supervision of the Church. The many persecutions to which Christianity was subjected during these centuries rendered it impossible, however, to have a sufficient number of priests or clerics. In many places their number was

[9] Cf. De Rossi, *La Roma Sotterranea* (Roma, 1867), II, 310; *Tavole*, II, tavola XLV-XLVI, n. 43; Prudentius, *Liber Peristephanon*, Hymnus IX—*MPL*, LX, 432.

It may be noted here that the Church, in making use of home instruction for children, followed the custom generally in vogue. Pliny describes the long-lived custom of home training in the following words: "Erat autem antiquitus institutum, ut a majoribus natu non auribus modo, verum etiam oculis disceremus, quae facienda mox ipsi ac per vices quasdam tradenda minoribus haberemus. . . . Suus cuique parens pro magistro aut, cui parens non erat, maximus quisque et vetustissimus pro parente."—*Epistolae*, lib. VIII, ep. XIV, 4, 6 (ed. Mueller, Lipsiae, 1903), p. 206. Cf. also Plutarch, *Cato major*, c. XX; *Scipio*, I, XXII, 36; Plautus, *Mostellaria*, vs. 126; Cornelius Nepos, *Atticus*, 1; Cicero, *Ad Atticum*, lib. VIII, ep. IV, 1.

[10] Denk, *Geschichte des Gallo-Frankischen Unterrichts und Bildungswesens, von den ältesten Zeiten bis auf Karl den Grossen* (Mainz, 1892), p. 183.

usually very small.[11] Hence the development of these schools was hindered to a great extent, but by no means totally impeded. They continued their work even during the times of persecution, and with varying fortunes were to lead up to the parochial schools of the Middle Ages. Theodoret expressly mentions the school established by the priest Protogenes at Antinone after he had been banished from Edessa in the latter part of the fourth century: "Admiramus vero Protogenes, et legitimis litteris instructus, et velocis scripturae peritus, loco reperto idoneo, ludum aperuit litterarium, puerorumque magister factus est, una illos et celeriter scribere docens, et in divinis eloquiis erudiens. Nam et Davidica illis carmina dictabat, et ex Apostolica doctrina, quae maxime congruebant, ediscenda proponebat." [12]

The rise of the catechetical schools marked a development in general education, and proved a valuable opportunity to Christians and others who desired a more advanced training. The curriculum was well rounded and full. It called for a comprehensive scheme of instruction which included the various branches of secular learning together with the study of religion. Grammar, rhetoric, the arts, dialectics and philosophy all found a place in the teachers' program and were brought into close relationship with the truths of the Gospel.[13] The principal catechetical schools were founded at important centers of cul-

[11] Cf. Thomassinus, *Vetus et Nova Ecclesiae Disciplina circa Beneficia et Beneficiarios* (Moguntiaci, 1787), pars I, lib. III, c. 2, n. 2.

[12] Theodoret, *Hist. Eccl.*, IV, 15—*MPG*, LXXXII, 1158. Stöckl (*Geschichte der Pädagogik* [Mainz, 1876], p. 78) and Denk (*op. cit.*, p. 183) refer to a school held by Protogenes at Edessa, and date it as far back as the middle of the second century. However, according to historical data Theodoret, describing the persecution of Edessa, mentions Protogenes as being contemporaneous with the Emperor Valens; and Valens was co-emperor with Valentinian I and Gratian, and ruled from the year 364 to 378.

[13] Cf. Clement of Alexandria, *Stromatum*, VI, 10—*MPG*, IX, 299-303; Gregory Thaumaturgus, *Oratio Panegyrica*—*MPG*, X, 1051-1103, especially chapters VII, IX, XIII, XIV, XV; Pius XI, const. ap. *Deus scientiarum Dominus*, 24 maii 1931—*AAS*, XXIII (1931), 241.

ture, such as Alexandria, Caesarea in Palestine, Syde in Pamphylia, Antioch, Edessa, and Nisibis.[14] However, while these institutions undoubtedly afforded an opportunity for intellectual progress, their importance as lower schools should not be exaggerated. They retained their main character as centers of theological discussion, where the weapons of controversy were forged for battle with pagans and heretics.[15] Though at times they provided a study of matters which would today be contained in an intermediate curriculum,[16] they remained only an extraordinary means for the attainment of knowledge. Christian pupils desiring an education were ordinarily compelled to attend the common schools, or the schools which in some places were kept by priests or clerics in major orders.[17]

2. Monastic, Episcopal, and Parochial Schools

The dawn of the fourth century inaugurated a new era in the history of the Christian Church. Under the aegis of imperial toleration conditions became much more favorable for the propagation of the faith and the founding of Christian institutions.[18] The activities of the Church received a wider scope, and a greater impetus was given the establishment of schools. This movement in the Church was called forth particularly by the fact that pagan society and environment had so affected the Christian home, that the care and diligence of former times in instructing the children in virtue had disappeared to an alarming extent. St. John Chrysostom furnishes evidence of the decline of the primitive fervor in the Christian family of the fourth century by his assertion that the domestic

[14] Albers, *Manuale di Storia Ecclesiastica* (tr. of the 2nd Dutch ed. by Berardo, Torino, 1913), I, 103.

[15] Eusebius, *Hist. Eccl.*, VI, 3; V, 10 — *MPG*, XX, 454, 526.

[16] Eusebius, *Hist. Eccl.*, VI, 15, 18 — *MPG*, XX, 554, 559-562.

[17] Langasco, *De Institutione Clericorum in disciplinis inferioribus* (Typis Polyglottis Vaticanis, 1936), p. 62.

[18] Lactantius, *De mortibus persecutorum*, XLVIII — *MPL*, VII, 267-270; Eusebius, *Hist. Eccl.*, X, 5—*MPG*, XX, 879-886.

circle was no longer capable of supplying the proper religious and moral training for the children. Under the circumstances attendance at the pagan schools was unquestionably fraught with the greatest danger to Christian faith and morals. Though he and others of the Fathers had studied under pagan masters, he directed parents to send their children to those who would diligently serve their spiritual as well as their intellectual wants.[19] To respond to this need of the time, several systems of schools developed. In the early Middle Ages three types of schools already flourishing may be distinguished: the monastic, the episcopal, and the parochial.

Monasticism, which had originated toward the end of the third century in the deserts of Egypt, was brought to the West by St. Athanasius,[20] and reached its full development with St. Benedict, who in 529 promulgated the constitution of monasticism, the Benedictine rule. Long before the pagan schools disappeared [21] the cenobites and the monks had engaged in educational pursuits. They not only taught those who were to recruit their own numbers, but also received into their communities the children of the people who lived about the monasteries. Some of them were orphans who were given the saving protection of Christian surroundings; others were sent by their parents that they might be instructed in Christian virtue.[22] The primary purpose of monasticism was the development and cultivation of spirituality by means of prayer and seclusion, but in time provision was likewise made for the systematic instruction of youth. Thus, the educational activities of the monks soon rendered their schools important factors in supplying the means of education for the laity. The most illustrious ex-

[19] *Adversus oppugnatores eorum qui ad monasticam vitam inducunt. Ad patrem fidelem*—*MPG*, XLVII, 349.

[20] Montalambert, *Monks of the West* (Boston, 1872), I, 225, 286.

[21] Cf. C. (1. 11) 2.

[22] Cf. St. Basil, *Regulae fusius tractatae*, interrogatio 15—*MPG*, XXXI, 951; St. Benedict, *Regula commentata*, caput 59—*MPL*, LXVI, 839.

amples of this religious education are found in the monastic institutions of Gaul. In that territory where the pagan schools had reached their highest development, the Christian schools of the fifth and sixth centuries grew in power, and increased in number in a degree proportionate to the decline of the schools of their antagonists. Although Gaul was a soil favorable to the seed of monasticism, its growth was not restricted to that country alone. The monastic movement extended to other countries, such as Spain, Italy, Africa, England and Ireland, where it produced its schools and scholars.[23]

There were two classes of monastic schools: the *interior* or conventual school, in which the aspirants to the monastic life were educated, and the *exterior* or secular school, in which students who generally contemplated a return to the world were taught. The pupils of the interior school were called *oblati*, those of the exterior school *nutriti*.[24]

Provision was also made in these ancient schools for the education of girls. The monasteries for women, following the example of those for men, contained schools in which were trained not only future novices, but also numbers of young girls destined for life at court or in the world. Daughters of the nobility and of the poor attended these schools for purely educational purposes, and many of them at the completion of their studies returned to their homes. They came at times in great numbers, and their formation consumed nearly the entire time of the religious. Muteau says that at Arles, where two hundred nuns were occupied in copying manuscripts, open school was kept for the neighborhood (écoles ouvertes). At

[23] Cf. Marion, *Histoire de l'Église* (Paris, 1905-1906), I, 573; Drane, *Christian Schools and Scholars* (London, 1867), I, 48; Healy, *Insula Sanctorum et Doctorum: Ireland's Ancient Schools and Scholars* (Dublin, 1893), p. 102.

[24] Mabillon, *Traité des études monastiques* (Bruxelles, 1672), pp. 88-93; cf. also Conventus abbatum Franciae cum monachis suis, c. 45—Hardouin, *Acta Conciliorum et Epistolae Decretales ac Constitutiones Summorum Pontificum* (Parisiis, 1715), IV, 1231.

Lâon also the learned abbess, St. Austrude, "est representée comme ayant consacré sa vie à la culture des lettres, 'exercens se etiam in magisterio doctrinae.'"[25]

Of singular importance is the Council of Cloveshoe, in England, held in the year 747. While the canons of this council aimed at the correction of abuses and the restoration of ecclesiastical discipline, the interests of learning and of the schools were foremost in the minds of the bishops who attended. The comprehensive nature of the educational uplift intended by the bishops can be seen especially from the text of canon seven. All schools are included—those for boys and those for girls—and a strong warning is given abbesses to cultivate in the hearts of their subjects a devotion to study and teaching.[26]

Simultaneously with the development of the monastic schools there appeared another sign of progress in education, namely the establishment of episcopal or cathedral schools, so called because they were originally maintained in the household of the bishop, and later at the cathedral of the diocese.[27] These schools undertook in a special manner the training of young men for the various clerical offices. The clerics lived in common, either in the episcopal residence or nearby,[28] and were taught by the bishop himself or by someone appointed by him. A school of

[25] *Les écoles et collèges en Provence* (Dijon, 1882), p. 14; cf. St. Caesarius of Arles, *Regula ad Virgines*, c. 17—*MPL*, LXVII, 1109.

[26] "Septimo decreverunt condicto, ut episcopi, abbates, atque abbatissae . . . studeant, et diligenti cura provideant, ut per familias suas lectionis studium indesinenter in plurimorum pectoribus versetur."—Mansi, *Sacrorum Conciliorum Nova et Amplissima Collectio* (Parisiis, 1901-1927), XII, 397.

[27] The name of cathedral school became more common during the time of Chrodegang, bishop of Metz (742-766), who revived and propagated the observance of community life among the diocesan clergy. The schools attached to such communities were called cathedral or canonical schools. They were practically the same as the episcopal schools, and were merely the result of better clerical organization in diocesan centers. Both were designated by the same canonical term *episcopia*. Cf. Hinschius, *System des katholischen Kirchenrechts* (Berlin, 1869-1888), II, 52-56.

[28] Thomassinus, *Vetus et Nova Ecclesiae Disciplina*, pars I, lib. III, c. 8, nn. 1-2.

this type flourished at this time in almost every episcopal city of the Christian world and was especially efficient in the West.[29] Traces of episcopal schools could be found in Italy at the beginning of the sixth century,[30] and the second Council of Tours (567) indicated that the system of episcopal schools was widespread in Gaul during the fifth and sixth centuries.[31] While the principal aim of the bishops in establishing them was the preparation of levites for the sanctuary, other students were not denied admission. From the curriculum followed in the early episcopal schools of Gaul, and from the number of lay teachers engaged (sometimes these were converted rhetoricians), it may be concluded that a considerable portion of students had no intention of entering the clerical state. Converts were instructed there, and under the Merovingian emperors, when the bishops became proprietary lords with the duty of providing education for all, it was but natural that they should first equip their own schools for general educational purposes. The famous schools of Arles, Paris, Poitiers, Bourges, Clermont, Vienne, Chalon-sur-Saône, and Gap were well attended when the State schools fell into decline.[32] The same was true of Spain. The second Council of Toledo (531) took for granted the existence of such institutions at that early date, and prescribed that students on reaching their eighteenth year should be left free to choose publicly—*coram totius cleri plebisque conspectu*—between the married state and the priestly life.[33] Worthy of particular mention here is the school of Barcelona y Vich, which was attended by many illustrious youths,

[29] Cf. Cubberley, *Syllabus of Lectures on the History of Education* (New York, 1902), I, 60.

[30] Manacorda, *Storia della Scuola in Italia* (Palermo, 1913), I, part I, 13-14; Manitius, *Geschichte der lateinischen Literatur des Mittelalters* (München, 1911), pp. 162-164.

[31] Hardouin, III, 355; cf. especially c. 12—Hardouin, III, 359.

[32] Denk, *Geschichte des Gallo-Frankischen Unterrichts und Bildungswesens*, p. 191.

[33] C. 1—Hardouin, II, 1139.

even from France and Italy.[34] A century later, another council at Toledo (633) confirmed the necessity of the episcopal schools, and in addition prescribed the erection of an auxiliary institute, outside the bishop's palace, in which the younger students should be trained under the guidance of an approved senior priest.[35]

The parish also supplied an important educational institution. Since in many cases, as in rural districts, it was not feasible for students to attend either the episcopal or the monastic schools, it became necessary to establish rectory schools in individual parishes. The students were taught by the pastor, who was usually assisted in the various parochial functions by clerics in minor orders.[36] The subjects taught in these schools were of a rather elementary character. Christian doctrine and liturgical chant, together with reading and writing, constituted the chief part of the curriculum. Those pupils who later wanted a more advanced education could receive it in one of the neighboring episcopal or monastic schools, the curriculum of which embraced, besides elementary subjects, the liberal arts, known at that time as the *trivium* and the *quadrivium*.[37]

The origin of the parochial schools can be traced back to the fourth century, when Protogenes taught the children of his parish.[38] A similar school was founded at Rennes in the year 480.[39] However, it was only in the year 529 that the parochial

[34] Blanco Nájera, *Derecho Docente*, p. 26.

[35] C. 24—Hardouin, III, 586.

[36] Cf. Andrieu, "Les Ordres Mineurs dans l'Ancien rit romain," *RSR*, V (1925), 234.

[37] Cf. Allain, *L'Instruction primaire en France avant la Révolution* (Paris, 1881), p. 23; Rajna, "Le denominazioni 'trivium' e 'quadrivium,'" *Studi medioevali*, I (1928), 4; Mabillon, *Praefationes in Acta Sanctorum Ordinis Sancti Benedicti conjunctim editae* (Venetiis, 1740), praef. in saec. IV, p. 286, n. 184.

[38] Theodoret, *Hist. Eccl.*, IV, 15—*MPG*, LXXXII, 1158.

[39] Denk, *Geschichte des Gallo-Frankischen Unterrichts und Bildungswesens*, p. 194.

school system received an official sanction at the Council of Vaison. The first decree of the council urges the foundation of parochial schools in Gaul and makes reference to the custom of parochial instruction obtaining throughout Italy and to its good results in that country. This instruction had been fruitful in fostering vocations to the priestly state, and that undoubtedly was one of the chief aims of the bishops of Gaul in urging its imitation. There is, nevertheless, a warning in the canon, that those who desire to take up the married state be given freedom to do so.[40]

In Spain the Council of Merida (666) attests to the continued growth of the parish school system during the seventh century, and it also makes provision for the material support of students.[41] Not all children attending these schools were to become priests, nor were they obliged to embrace the clerical life. The Council of Vernum in Normandy (755) seemed to restrict the schools to students who had not yet entered the clerical state, for it decreed, that all tonsured clerics should live either in a monastery or under episcopal guidance.[42] The *Regula Canonicorum* of Bishop Chrodegang (762) also makes mention of parochial schools and furthermore calls attention to the obligation of pastors to see that the youth attending them be kept under ecclesiastical discipline, so that their age, so prone to sin, be not an occasion for spiritual ruin.[43]

[40] C. 1: "Hoc enim placuit, ut omnes presbyteri, qui sunt in parochiis constituti, secundum consuetudinem, quam per totam Italiam satis salubriter teneri cognovimus, juniores lectores quantoscumque sine uxore habuerint, secum in domo, ubi ipsi habitare videntur, recipiant: et eos quomodo boni patres spiritualiter nutrientes, psalmos parare, divinis lectionibus insistere, et in lege Domini erudire contendant; . . . Cum vero ad aetatem perfectam pervenerint, si aliquis eorum pro carnis fragilitate uxorem habere maluerit, potestas ei ducendi conjugem non negatur."—Hardouin, II, 1105.

[41] C. 18—Hardouin, III, 1004.

[42] C. 11—Hardouin, III, 1997.

[43] Cap. 48: "Solerter Rectores Ecclesiarum vigilare oportet, ut pueri et adolescentes qui in congregatione sibi commissa nutriuntur, vel *erudiuntur*, ita jugibus Ecclesiasticis disciplinis constringantur; ut eorum lasciva aetas,

The importance of these schools cannot be overestimated, for they served the cause of education even during periods of decadence in general learning.[44]

et ad peccandum valde proclivis, nullum possit reperire locum, quo in peccati facinus proruat." — Hartzheim, *Concilia Germaniae* (Coloniae Augustae Agrippinensium, 1759-1790), I, 110.

[44] Cf. Muratori, *Antiquitates Italicae* (Mediolani, 1740), III, diss., 43, c. 809, C-D, and c. 810, B.

CHAPTER III

1. Carlovingian Legislation and Subsequent Councils

The energetic interest of Charlemagne (745-814) in popular education is a matter of universal knowledge. This Imperial Maecenas, besides founding in his realm the Palace School, called upon the Church to aid him in giving effect to the establishment and reorganization of all educational institutions. For this end he addressed a Capitulary in 787 to the abbots of monasteries and to all Frankish bishops, exhorting them to promote the spirit of study, and the work of teaching in their respective communities. Charlemagne's concern for a more widespread devotion to the study of letters and to the art of teaching, can be seen from the text of the Capitulary: "We exhort you," he wrote, "not only not to neglect the study of letters, but to apply yourselves thereto with perseverance and with that humility which is well pleasing to God . . . (and) let there be chosen for this work men, who are both able and willing to learn, and who are desirous of instructing others, and let them apply themselves to the work with a zeal equalling the earnestness with which we recommend it to them."[1] Other Capitularies were drawn up, as for instance those of 789 and 804, as explanations of the means to be adopted, in order to comply with the imperial demands. They were addressed to the monks and the secular clerics, and concerned discipline, studies, and preparation of candidates for Orders. The Capitulary of March 23, 789, contains an espe-

[1] This Capitulary is known as the *Epistola de Litteris Colendis* and it is preserved in the form of a letter to Baugulf, abbot of Fulda—*MPL*, XCVIII, 896; cf. *MGH, Legum Sectio*, II, *Capitul.*, I, 79. Tr. (with some modifications) by Mullinger, *The Schools of Charles the Great and the Restoration of Education in the Ninth Century* (New York, 1911), pp. 97-98.

cially interesting order in regard to elementary schools. Like the Fathers of the Council of Vaison before him, the Emperor drew his inspiration from the example of the clergy of Rome,[2] and prescribed that a school for the instruction of the young be established in each monastery and episcopal see. The boys were to be taught grammar, arithmetic, singing, music, and the psalter; moreover, the Catholic books placed in their hands were to be of correct composition, and to be kept in good condition.[3] The Capitulary of 802 enjoins that "every one should send his son to study letters, and that the child should remain at school with all diligence until he had become well instructed in learning."[4]

The impulse given by Charlemagne to education was well seconded by the Church, and brought about a real restoration of schools in many dioceses and monasteries. In the diocese of Orléans, for instance, the bishop, Theodulf, a former pupil of the Palace School, and apparently Alcuin's successor as State Minister of Education, endeavored to carry out all the details of the Capitularies affecting education. He made his episcopal school the equal of any in the realm and, in a Capitulary addressed to the clergy of his diocese, embodied a famous decree in behalf of free parish schools:

> Let the priests keep schools in the villages and towns, and if anyone of the faithful shall wish to give his little ones to learning, they ought willingly to accept them and teach them gratuitously remembering what has been written: "They that

[2] Cf. Jaffé, *Monumenta Carolina, Bibliotheca Rerum Germanicarum* (Berolini, 1867-1873), IV, 343.

[3] C. 70: "Ut scholae legentium puerorum fiant. Psalmos, notas, cantus, compotum, grammaticam per singula monasteria vel episcopia discant. Sed et libros catholicos bene emendatos habeant. . . . Et pueros vestros non sinite eos vel legendo vel scribendo corrumpere."—Mansi, XVII b, 237; cf. also *MPL*, XCVII, 517.

[4] "Ut unusquisque filium suum litteras ad discendum mittat, et ibi cum omni solicitudine permaneat usque dum bene instructus perveniat." *Capitula Examinationis Generalis*, 12—*MGH*, *Legum Sectio*, II, *Capitul.*, I, 235.

> are learned shall shine as the brightness of the firmament; and they that instruct many to justice, as stars for all eternity." And let them exact no price from the children for their teaching, nor receive anything from them save what the parents may offer voluntarily and from affection.[5]

The free parish schools, established by Theodulf, encouraged the bishops and the nobility to found and to endow similar institutions. In some of the monasteries it was customary to accept fees from the students of the exterior schools, and gradually such schools became rather distinguished for the number of wealthy pupils they received. The poor, in consequence, were loath to attend them. A strong protest was raised against this practice existing in the monastery of Tours by Amalric, archbishop of the diocese. The prelate wanted to see all possible barriers to the reception of the poor removed, and in 843 gave the monks a generous donation to be used for the maintenance of poor students.[6] William, the abbot of St. Benigne, in the same century opened in his monastery a free school where pupils received board and clothing gratuitously. The general sentiment was that an education could not be bought, nor learning taxed. The Abbey of St. Peter in Salzburg bore this inscription over its portals: "Discere si cupias, gratis, quod quaeris, habebis," — a line from the poem of Alcuin, "*De via duplici ad scholam et cauponam.*"[7]

[5] "Presbyteri per villas et vicos scholas habeant. Et si quilibet fidelium suos parvulos ad discendas litteras eis commendare vult, eos non renuant suscipere et docere; sed cum summa caritate eos doceant, attendentes illud quod scriptum est: 'Qui autem docti fuerint, fulgebunt quasi splendor firmamenti; et qui ad justitiam erudiunt multos fulgebunt quasi stellae in perpetuas aeternitates.' Cum ergo eos docent, nihil ab eis pretii exigant, nec aliquid ab eis accipiant; excepto, quod eis parentes eorum caritatis studio sua voluntate obtulerint." — *MPL*, CV, 196.

[6] Maitre, *Les écoles épiscopales et monastiques de l'Occident* (Paris, 1866), p. 49, 203.

[7] *MPL*, CI, 757; cf. Mullinger, *Schools of Charles the Great*, p. 134; McCormick, *The Education of the Laity in the Early Middle Ages* (Washington, 1912), pp. 36 ff.

Similar solicitude for the erection of schools, where the children of the people could be taught in virtue as well as in letters, was manifested by other bishops. Thus, Hérard, the archbishop of Tours (858), ordered his priests to keep schools. "Ut scholas presbyteri pro posse habeant, et libros emendatos." [8] Vautier, the archbishop of Orléans (860), enacted similar legislation,[9] and Hincmar, the archbishop of Rheims (852), prescribed that qualified parochial visitors investigate whether each priest had a cleric who could teach in the school and assist in the services of the church.[10] Finally, Atto (+964), bishop of Vercelli, gave further impetus to gratuitous education by reproducing verbatim in a Capitulary the decree of Theodulf of the preceding century.[11]

To the carrying on of this work, fostered by Christian rulers and so well supported by the activities of bishops and abbots, the decrees and canons of councils and provincial synods, throughout France and other countries, contributed in no small degree. In France laws on schools were incorporated in the decrees of the Councils of Chalons-sur-Saône (813),[12] Arles (813),[13] Attigny (822),[14] Paris (829),[15] Meaux (845),[16] and

[8] C. 17—Hardouin, V, 451.

[9] C. 6: "Ut unusquisque presbyter suum habeat clericum quem religiose educare procuret. Et si possibilitas illi est, scholam in ecclesia sua habere non negligat: solerterque caveat, ut quos ad erudiendum suscipit, caste sinceriterque nutriet." — Hardouin, V, 461.

[10] C. 11: "Si habeat clericum, qui posset tenere scholam, aut legere epistolam, aut canere valeat, prout necessarium sibi videtur." — Hardouin, V, 396.

[11] C. 61—*MPL*, CXXXIV, 40.

[12] C. 3—Hardouin, IV, 1032.

[13] C. 3—Mansi, XIV, 59.

[14] Cc. 3, 4—Hefele, *Conciliengeschichte* (2nd ed., Freiburg im Breisgau, 1873-1890), IV, 34; *MGH, Legum Sectio*, II, *Concilia*, I, 357; cf. also *MGH, Legum Sectio*, II, *Capitularia*, I, 304 (anno 825).

[15] C. 30—Mansi, XIV, 558.

[16] C. 35—Mansi, XIV, 826.

Savonnières (859).[17] The Council of Paris (846), moreover, urged compulsory attendance at school,[18] and canon nineteen of the Council of Arles (813) reminded parents, as well as sponsors of children, of their duty to bring the young up properly and have them educated.[19] The Council of Valence, in the year 855, decreed the restoration of schools for divine and human letters.[20] In Germany the Council of Mainz (813) commanded parents to send their children to Catholic schools,[21] and the Council of Aachen (816) legislated on the discipline to be maintained.[22] The Council of Rome (826), convened under Eugene II (824-827), took action upon the question of schools for the guidance of the bishops of Italy. Noting that devotion to letters and teaching had fallen into disuse in certain places, the sixty-seven bishops present decreed that in all the dioceses and parishes a sufficient number of teachers should be appointed, who would assiduously promote the study of letters and of the liberal arts, in the spirit of the Church.[23] Another Council of Rome, held in the year 853 under Leo IV (847-855), confirmed the preceding canon and added that the teachers should make an annual report to the bishop concerning school activities.[24]

The progress made in the field of primary and intermediate schools during the ninth century may well be judged by the

[17] C. 10—Mansi, XV, 539.

[18] C. 78—Mansi, XIV, 840.

[19] Mansi, XIV, 62; cf. also Hardouin, V, 452, where it is mentioned that Hérard of Tours required this attention even towards the very young.

[20] C. 18—Mansi, XV, 11.

[21] C. 45: "sive ad monasteria, sive foras presbyteris."—Mansi, XIV, 74.

[22] *MGH, Legum Sectio*, III, *Concilia*, II, 413.

[23] C. 34: "De quibusdam locis ad nos refertur, non magistros, neque curam inveniri pro studio litterarum. Idcirco in universis episcopiis, subjectisque plebibus, et aliis locis in quibus necessitas occurrerit, omnino cura et diligentia habeatur, ut magistri et doctores constituantur; qui studia litterarum, liberaliumque artium ac sancta habentes dogmata, assidue doceant."—Mansi, XIV, 1008; cf. c. 12, D. XXXVII.

[24] *Additio Leonis*, c. 34—Mansi, XIV, 1014.

number and tenor of the foregoing councils. Moreover, in consideration of the great help rendered by the clergy and the encouragement given the movement by the Christian rulers, there is foundation for the statement of Professor Laurie that "after all, the early half of the ninth century perhaps did more for education, as that word was then understood, in proportion to the means and opportunities available, than any period since."[25]

2. Other School Legislation up to the Lateran Councils

There are two documents, dating from the ninth century, that call for the establishment of a State school system in the Empire. The first is the *Capitulare ecclesiasticum primum,* known also as the *Capitulare Olonnense*, which was promulgated in the year 825 by Lothaire, to whom Louis the Pious had entrusted the government of Italy. The Emperor, recognizing the deplorable condition of learning which circumstances had brought about in Northern Italy, endeavored to reorganize education by instituting schools in nine important places—Pavia, Ivrea, Turin, Cremona, Florence, Fermo, Verona, Vicenza, and Friuli. He also ordained the reorganization of the school districts for the greater convenience of the population, and decreed that all those who, by the king's authority, had been constituted teachers in the various districts should apply themselves assiduously to instruction.[26]

[25] *Rise and Early Constitution of Universities* (New York, 1898), p. 77.

[26] "De doctrina vero, quae ob nimiam incuriam atque ignaviam quorundam praepositorum, cunctis in locis est funditus extincta, placuit ut sicut a nobis constitutum est, ita ab omnibus observetur, videlicet ut ab his qui nostra dispositione ad docendos alios per loca denominata sunt constituti, maximum detur studium, qualiter sibi commissi scolastici proficiant, atque doctrinae insistant, sicut praesens exposcit necessitas. Propter opportunitatem tamen omnium apta loca destinata ad hoc exercitium providimus, ut difficultas locorum longe positorum, ac paupertas, nulli foret excusatio . . . "—*MGH, Legum Sectio*, I, 249 (ed. Pertz); cf. Muratori, *Antiq. Italicae*, III, 815.

Much could be said concerning this action of the Emperor. Some have even seen in it a monopoly in school matters, by which the State, and no longer the Church, was to be the custodian of learning.[27] Nothing, however, is said in the Capitulary itself in this regard, nor is there any provision whatsoever for the general management of the schools. On the other hand, mention is made of the bishop of Ivrea, who was to organize the new school system in his diocese (*in Eporegia ipse episcopus hoc per se faciat*), and express mention is made of the name of a teacher in the school at Pavia: Dungall, probably an Irish monk.[28]

No doubt, the decline in learning in this part of the Empire was also due to the inactivity of those in charge of the schools in previous times (*ob . . . incuriam atque ignaviam quorundam praepositorum*). The many occupations of the clergy, especially in parochial institutions, did not always allow them to devote their time to intellectual pursuits and to the cause of letters. To some extent they could well expect support from the Christian civil authority. In the Providence of God Lothaire had simply done what in later years many other noblemen endeavored to do in England, Germany, and Italy, when external circumstances forced the Church's activity to a standstill. That the intention of Lothaire was not to make the school a monopoly of the State, but rather, together with the Church, a means to advance the cause of learning, is clear from the fact that he himself made use of churchmen to carry out his project. Again, four years later, the bishops of France, aware perhaps of the good results that these schools were producing, and certainly anxious to continue the movement so well inaugurated by Charlemagne, suggested to Louis the Pious to found three or more public schools in important centers of the Empire. This suggestion of the bishops is contained in

[27] Manacorda, *Storia della Scuola in Italia*, I, part I, 58.

[28] Sandys, *History of Classical Scholarship* (Cambridge, 1906), I, 462; Monti, *La Libertà della Scuola*, p. 110.

the VI Council of Paris (829) and forms the second of the two documents mentioned above, which call for the establishment of a State school system in the Empire. It reads as follows:

> Similiter obnixe ac simpliciter vestrae celsitudini suggerimus, ut morem paternum sequentes, saltem in tribus congruentissimis imperii vestri locis, scholae publicae ex vestra auctoritate fiant: ut labor patris vestri . . . per incuriam, quod absit, labefactando non depereat. Quoniam ex hoc facto et magna utilitas, et honor sanctae Dei ecclesiae, et vobis magnum mercedis emolumentum, et memoria sempiterna accrescet.[29]

The fact that the reference is to imperial schools is apparent, for the Emperor is asked to found them by his own authority (*ex vestra auctoritate*). Perhaps the term *publica,* applied to these schools, has reference to the fact that they cultivated the *studia publica,* that is, the liberal arts. Because of the dearth of evidence, it is furthermore impossible to know whether the Emperor carried out the suggestions of the bishops of France. It is very likely that he did not, for Louis the Pious, a weak and irresolute character, never really showed an interest equal to his father's for the welfare of letters.[30] The Church, however, continued her work in the establishment and upkeep of her schools, for both boys and girls, and even as late as the year 889 one finds the bishop of Soissons urging his priests to be assiduous in their duty as teachers: " Monemus praeterea, ut presbyteri sic ruralibus, id est, terrestribus, ut ceteris occupationibus inserviant, quatenus divinum officium non negligant, et scholarios suos modeste distringant, caste nutriant, et sic literis imbuant, ut mala conversatione non destruant: et puellas ad discendum cum scholariis suis in schola sua nequaquam recipiant; et ut turpi lucro et negotiationibus non inserviant." [31]

[29] Cap. 12—Mansi, XIV, 599.

[30] Cf. Monti, *La Libertà della Scuola,* pp. 110-111.

[31] *Constitutio Riculfi,* c. 16—Mansi, XVIII a, 87; cf. also *Histoire littéraire de la France* (ed. Palmé, Paris, 1733-1898), VI, 29.

Unfortunately, the impulse given to educational institutions during the ninth century was destined to suffer a temporary setback during the next two centuries, the iron age. The political, social, and religious crisis which followed in the wake of the dissolution of the Empire was bound to retard progress in letters. Political anarchy, the invasion of the barbarians and Mohammedans, the difficulties and dangers of communication, the scarcity of books, the multiplication of dialects, the poverty of the people, — all these factors and more, concurred in discouraging scholastic endeavor.[32]

In spite of these disturbed conditions, however, the lamp of science was kept burning through the efforts of churchmen and leading laymen, whose services to learning were nothing less than heroic. Each century saw its zealous leaders striving for the preservation of ecclesiastical life in the monasteries and the canonicates, eager for the restoration and perfection of the schools, and endeavoring to provide for the moral and spiritual enlightenment of the people. Learning flourished in the great monasteries, such as that of St. Gall (Switzerland), St. Maximin (Trier), and in the more outstanding cathedral schools, such as those at Rheims and Lyons.[33] Montalembert says that, in the tenth and eleventh centuries, the abbatial schools of Fleury and St. Benoit-sur-Loir alone counted five thousand pupils.[34] In the populous centers of Germany, and particularly within the royal household, learning was kept alive. Of Italy, Gerbert of Aurillac, later Sylvester II (999-1003), wrote to the monk Rainauld: "You know how many writers there are everywhere, both in the cities and in the rural districts." [35] Again, it would be quite erroneous to assume that the system

[32] Monti, *La Libertà della Scuola*, p. 112.

[33] Cf. Turner, "Schools," *Cath. Encycl.*, XIII, 557; *Histoire littéraire de la France*, VII, 9-10; Moore, *The Story of Instruction—The Church, the Renaissances, and the Reformations* (New York: Macmillan, 1938), p. 240.

[34] *Monks of the West*, V, 130.

[35] Epistola CXXX—*MPL*, CXXXIX, 233; cf. also Ratherius, *Synodica*, c. 13—*Opera Omnia* (ed. Ballerini, Verona, 1765), p. 419.

of parish school education was entirely neglected.[36] In England, the revival of letters that had been wrought by Alfred the Great (849-900) continued to bear fruit. Towards the end of the tenth century, the ecclesiastical law of that country enjoined on the priests in the villages the duty of learning and teaching the manual arts, and explicitly commanded them to "keep schools . . . and to teach small boys free." The law also stated: "Priests ought always to have schools of schoolmasters in their houses, and if anyone of the faithful wish to give his little ones to learning, they ought willingly to receive them and teach them gratuitously. You ought to think that it is written: 'they that are learned shall shine as the brightness of the firmament; and they that instruct many to justice, as stars for all eternity.' But they ought not to expect anything from their relations except what they wish to do of their own accord."[37] The wording of this decree is indeed almost identical with that of the famous Capitulary of Theodulf of Orléans, in the latter part of the eighth century.

[36] Cf. c. 3, X, *de vita et honestate clericorum*, III, 1; Scarascia, *Le Scuole Parrocchiali e degli Istituti Religiosi e l'Istruzione Elementare in Italia* (Torino: Soc. Ed. Internazionale, 1936), p. 55.

[37] Wilkins, *Concilia Magnae Britanniae et Hiberniae* (Londini, 1737), I, 270. The following are passages concerning the learning and teaching of manual arts by the clergy during King Edgar's reign (958-975): C. 11: "Docemus . . . (etiam), ut sacerdos quilibet ad augendam scientiam opificium discat diligenter." *Canones editi sub Edgaro Rege*—Hardouin, VI a, 660; c. 51: "Docemus etiam, ut sacerdotes sedulo erudiant juventutem, et ad artificia ediscenda eos pertrahant, futuros utpote in rem ecclesiae."—Hardouin, VI a, 663.

Much of the impulse given to learning in England during this century is due to St. Dunstan (924?-988). As abbot of Glastonbury, bishop of Worcester, London, and Canterbury, he looked especially to the condition of the schools. Historians speak of his habit of visiting and teaching the boys in the cathedral school at Canterbury, and of the esteem in which he was held by them. Cf. McCormick, *Education of the Laity in the Early Middle Ages*, pp. 48-50; Anderson, "Industrial Education during the Middle Ages," *Education* XXXII (1912), 6; Moore, *The Story of Instruction—The Church, the Renaissances, and the Reformations*, p. 231.

CHAPTER IV

1. Revival of Schools

Towards the end of the eleventh century, social and political conditions righted themselves throughout Europe to an extent that permitted a scholastic revival. It was Rome that sounded the note which marked the beginning of the new golden era of the medieval schools. A council (1078) under Gregory VII reaffirmed the old obligation: "Ut omnes episcopi artes litterarum in suis ecclesiis doceri faciant. . . ."[1] As only the title of this canon is extant, it is not known whether the council made a more precise disposition of the matter or not. Of capital importance, however, is the III Lateran Council, held in the year 1179 under Alexander III (1159-1181). It provided in canon 18 for the education of the poor in the cathedral schools, and prescribed that no suitable persons were to be prevented from giving instruction. To the last two provisions was attached the legal sanction of deprivation of benefice for any ecclesiastic who disobeyed the requirements of the law.

> The Church of God as a devoted mother is bound to provide for those in need, not only in the things that pertain to the body but also in those that pertain to the good of souls. Wherefore, that the opportunity of acquiring an education may not be denied to the poor who cannot be aided by their parents' means, let some suitable benefice be assigned in every cathedral church to a master who shall teach *gratis* the clerics of that church and the poor students, by means of which benefice the material wants of the master may be relieved, and to the students a way open to knowledge. In other churches also and monasteries, let it be restored if in times past something of this sort has therein existed. For the

[1] Hardouin, VI a, 1580.

> permission to teach, no one shall exact a fee or under pretext of custom ask something from those who teach; nor shall anyone who is qualified and seeks a license be denied the position to teach. Offenders shall be deprived of their ecclesiastical benefice, for it is meet that, in the Church of God, he who hinders the progress of the churches by selling, from cupidity, the permission to teach, should be himself deprived of the fruit of his labor.[2]

As these ordinances were evidently not put into effect immediately in all localities, a later council (the IV Lateran [1215] held under Innocent III) confirmed this legislation and added two important clauses: first, that not only in the cathedral churches, but in others where circumstances permitted, a teacher should be installed to be chosen by the prelate with his chapter; and secondly, at each metropolitan church a school of theology, accessible to the laity as well as to the clergy, was to be opened.[3]

Strict observance of the Lateran legislation was demanded by the decrees of Honorius III,[4] and by the Council of Esthonia (1287),[5] and even in the Councils of Palencia (1322)[6] and of Basle (1438)[7] the echo of the Lateran canons may be recognized. In the year 1300 two other councils encouraged education and training, by prohibitions against conferring ecclesiastical positions and benefices on the illiterate.[8]

The zeal of the Church for learning extended to every field of knowledge, from the primary curriculum to that of more advanced schools. A special interest also developed at this time

[2] Hardouin, VI b, 1680-1681; cf. c. 1, X, *de magistris*, V, 5. Tr. (with some modifications) by Schroeder, *Disciplinary Decrees of the General Councils* (St. Louis: Herder, 1937), p. 229.

[3] C. 11—Hardouin, VII, 30; cf. c. 4, X, *de magistris*, V, 5.

[4] Bulla *Super specula* (1219), c. 5, X, *de magistris*, V, 5.

[5] C. 29—Hardouin, VII, 1102.

[6] C. 20—Hardouin, VII, 1477.

[7] Sessio 31, c. 3—Mansi, XXIX, 163-164.

[8] Council of Cologne, c. 17—Hardouin, VII, 1221; Council of Bayonne, c. 46—Hardouin, VII, 1233.

in the study of languages, and some of the Popes even requested many religious institutes to establish courses in primitive sciences.[9]

In consequence of these enactments, episcopal and parochial schools began to multiply and flourish.[10] The monastic schools also, notwithstanding the partial decline of the Benedictine institutes in the twelfth century, were revived by the vigorous spirit of Cluny and Citeaux,[11] and by the birth of two new orders of religious, the Franciscans in 1209, and the Dominicans in 1216, who undertook the work of education and extended it also to institutions of higher learning.

Side by side with the Church schools there sprang up at this time other schools of a more private nature, sometimes established by an individual, sometimes by the guilds.[12] As a result of donations and grants these schools came under municipal control, and were known as burgher, city or common schools.[13] In Germany, the town councils began to establish the *Stadtschulen, Ratschulen*, and *scholae senatoriae*, which differed

[9] Council of Vienne (1311-1312), c. 11—c. 1, *de magistris: et ne aliquid exigatur pro licentia docendi*, V, 1, in Clem.; cf. also: Benedict XII, const. *Fulgens sicut stella*, 12 iul. 1335, § 42—*Bullarium Romanum* (Editio Taurinensis, 1857-1872), IV, 341; const. *Summi Magistri*, 20 iun. 1336, cap. VI ff.—*Bull. Rom.*, IV, 357; const. *Redemptor noster*, 28 nov. 1336, § 12—*Bull. Rom.*, IV, 397; const. *Ad decorem Ecclesiae*, 15 maii 1339, § 22—*Bull. Rom.*, IV, 434; Langasco, *De Institutione Clericorum in disciplinis inferioribus*, p. 116.

[10] Cf. Allain, *L'Instruction primaire en France avant la Révolution*, pp. 27-30; Ravelet, *Blessed John Baptist de la Salle* (Paris, 1888), pp. 18, 20.

[11] A Benedictine reform originated at Cluny in 910 under St. Berno (+ 924); another Benedictine reform under the Cistercians originated at Citeaux in 1098 under St. Robert (+ 1117).

[12] The chantry schools, numerous particularly in England, were taught by a priest who had received a benefice, to the holding of which was attached the obligation of teaching. Of similar nature were the schools so called of *Cappella*, in Italy. Cf. Scarascia, *Le Scuole Parrocchiali e degli Istituti Religiosi*, pp. 61, 62.

[13] Cf. Monti, *La Libertà della Scuola*, pp. 116, 118; Hinschius, *Kirchenrecht*, IV, 575-577; Scherer, *Handbuch des Kirchenrechtes* (Graz und Leipzig, 1886-1898), II, 50.

from the cathedral schools only in their curriculum and method of support. All these institutions were, however, under the care and supervision of the Church,[14] and it was undoubtedly the freedom of just such establishments as these that was guaranteed by the III Lateran Council (1179)—"nec docere quempiam, petita licentia, qui sit idoneus, interdicat." [15]

Although a great part of this encouragement was given to higher centers of learning during these centuries, it must not be supposed that the lower schools were neglected. According to Delisle, "rural schools were multiplied throughout Normandy during the thirteenth century and those following it." [16] The famous monastery of la Sauve-Majeure, near Bordeaux, was open to the children of the neighborhood. There they could receive a free and adequate education.[17] Gerson in his treatise on episcopal visitation, written towards the beginning of the fourteenth century, gives still further testimony to the zeal of the Church in the establishment of schools. In it the bishops are strongly urged to inquire "if every parish has a school, and how the children are taught, and to open a school there if there be not one already." [18] Similar regulations were inserted in the decrees of the Council of Rheims of the year 1408,[19]

[14] Kandel, *History of Secondary Education* (Boston: Houghton Mifflin, 1930), p. 49; cf. Schmid, *Geschichte der Erziehung* (Stuttgart, 1884-1892), II, pt. 1, 328.

[15] C. 18—Hardouin, VI b, 1680; c. 1, X, *de magistris*, V, 5.

[16] *Études sur la condition de la classe agricole, et l'état de l'agriculture en Normandie au moyen-âge* (Paris, 1903), p. 175; cf. Luce, *Histoire de Duguesclin* (Paris, 1876), pp. 13-16; de Beaurepaire, *Recherches sur l'Instruction publique, dans le diocèse de Rouen, avant 1789* (Evreux, 1872), I, 26-78.

[17] Ville, *Histoire de l'abbaye de la Sauve* (Bordeaux, 1844), I, 317.

[18] *Tractatus de visitatione praelatorum et curatorum. Gersonii Opera* (ed. du Pin, Antuerpiae, 1706), II, 650-651.

[19] "Item (investigetur) qualiter instruuntur pueri in parochia et si sint scholae ibidem vel prope. Similiter quaeratur hoc in omni loco visitando, sive sit in religione vel alibi, quia a pueris debet inchoare reformatio ecclesiae." *Ad Remense Concilium Additio*—Mansi, XXVI, 1072.

and the Council of Rouen (1445) demanded that the care of schools be assigned only to persons of mature judgment, commendable at the same time for intelligence and good morals. Moreover, the conferring of such a position was to be free of charge.[20]

Canon Allain, who made a rather exhaustive study of the whole subject, summarizes the situation up to the Council of Trent in the following words: "I repeat, if there is any fact which must strike as incontestable all who have studied, even superficially, the history of popular education in France, it is the devotion with which (the Church) has always labored for the spread of instruction among the masses. It was the councils which proclaimed the necessity of primary instruction; it was the diocesan synods which, having inflamed the clergy with zeal and enjoined upon them the use of all their resources in the establishment of schools, also gave them rules for guidance; it was the bishops and the priests who founded, endowed and inspected these schools; and the religious congregations trained untold multitudes of children of the common people." [21]

The history of the great universities, the crown of the scholastic system of the Middle Ages, is beyond the scope and purpose of this study. It is important to note, however, that in their origin they were secondary schools, "vast high schools," as Laurie calls them,[22] and in many cases, as at Paris, they had grown out of the cathedral schools.[23]

[20] C. 13—Hardouin, IX, 1297.

[21] *L'Église et l'enseignement populaire sous l'ancien Régime* (Paris, 1901), p. 38.

[22] *Rise and Early Constitution of Universities*, p. 195.

[23] Joly, *Traité Historique des Écoles Épiscopales et Ecclésiastiques* (Paris, 1678), part 2; cf. also Wernz, *Ius Decretalium*, III, pars I, n. 85; Pius XI, const. ap. *Deus scientiarum Dominus*, 24 maii 1931—*AAS*, XXIII (1931), 243.

2. Supervision of Schools During the Middle Ages

During the Middle Ages, the control of secular as well as clerical education in the diocese appears to have been vested in the archdeacon, who, with regard to episcopal and parochial schools, held powers of visitation and administration similar, in many respects, to the supervision exercised by modern diocesan superintendents of schools in the United States of America. The Decretals of Gregory IX describe his office as follows:

> Ut archidiaconus post episcopum sciat se vicarium esse eius in omnibus, . . . sive (de) doctrina ecclesiasticorum, vel caeterarum rerum studio; et delinquentium rationem coram Deo redditurus est.[24]

These duties of supervision were shared at least, and sometimes entirely fulfilled, by the *primicerius,* who had charge of and taught in the diocesan episcopal schools.[25]

It is interesting to note how the duties and privileges associated with these offices became more clearly and positively defined. Already in the year 666, the Council of Merida in Spain prescribed certain moral qualifications for the incumbents of these offices.[26] In the following century the rule of Chrodegang, while outlining the duties and moral prerequisites of the archdeacon and the *primicerius,* also insisted that they be endowed with a comprehensive knowledge of the Scriptures and of the sacred canons.[27] Moreover, it is significant to observe that, in the supervision of cathedral and parish schools, the power of the archdeacon was unquestioned, while

[24] C. 1, X, *de officio Archidiaconi,* I, 23.

[25] C. un., *de officio Primicerii,* I, 25; St. Isidore of Seville treats of the obligations of the *primicerius* in his epistle to Ludefredus—*MPL,* LXXXIII, 896.

[26] C. 10—Mansi, XI, 81.

[27] *De Archidiacono, vel primicerio,* c. 25—Mansi, XIV, 325.

his right of visitation in the monastic schools extended only so far as established custom permitted.[28]

Towards the end of the eleventh century, the duty of school supervision devolved upon the canon who was deemed to possess the best qualifications for it, and he was given the title of *scholasticus*. At first he was a mere official. His jurisdiction was limited to the cathedral and monastic schools, which he himself directed. Later, however, his jurisdiction extended over the whole diocese, and the office of *scholasticus* became a benefice, and even a canonical dignity.[29] How far his powers extended is not exactly known. Much depended on the various diocesan statutes. Generally speaking, one may say that he was exercising the power of supervision over the schools attached to the churches of the diocese, and had the right to select the teaching personnel. He was consequently known as the official who granted the license to teach to each individual teacher.[30] The right to teach [31] should have been accorded gratuitously, but in both England and France there arose the abuse of exacting a fee before the granting of the license. The Council of London (1138) severely denounced this practice,[32] and in 1170 Alexander III, in a letter to the bishops of France, decreed deposition from office and deprivation of benefice for

[28] C. 10, X, *de officio Archidiaconi*, I, 23.

[29] This dignity is still conserved nowadays in the cathedral chapters of Spain. Blanco Nájera, *Derecho Docente*, p. 24.

[30] Cf. Monti, *La Libertà della Scuola*, pp. 124-126; Hinschius, *Kirchenrecht*, II, 100 ff.

[31] From the wording of the Council of Amiens in France (1464) it seems that the license to teach was not required for teachers in the elementary schools: "ne quis in civitate vel dioecesi nostra docere vel scholas tenere in quacumque facultate praesumat, absque nostra licentia speciali; alphabetum tamen, psalterium tantum . . . unusquisque et ubique libere docere possit."—Martène et Durand, *Veterum Scriptorum et Monumentorum Historicorum Dogmaticorum Amplissima Collectio* (2nd ed., Paris, 1724-1733), III, 1268; Manacorda, *Storia della Scuola in Italia*, I, part I, 91-92.

[32] C. 17—Hardouin, VI b, 1206.

those guilty of it.[33] The III Ecumenical Lateran Council (1179) reaffirmed the condemnation of this abuse.[34]

[33] *MPL*, CC, 741; cf. c. 3, X, *de magistris*, V, 5. There are also three other letters of this Pontiff which bear witness to the zeal of the Papacy in fostering a diffusion of free schools: a letter to the Chapter of Chalon-sur-Saône (1167)—*MPL*, CC, 440; to the archbishop of Rheims (1171)—*MPL*, CC, 840; to Card. Peter, his legate (1174)—*MPL*, CC, 998.

[34] C. 18—Hardouin, VI b, 1680.

CHAPTER V

1. Religious Revolution in Europe and Catholic Counter-Reformation

At the beginning of the sixteenth century the condition of the Church reflected a great change. The long period of the Avignon captivity and the Western Schism, the great cultural awakening stimulated by the splendors of the pagan Renaissance and the invention of printing, the discovery of a new continent and the development of commerce and industry, the gradual rise and development of independent national unities and the keenly sensed need of greater liberty for the people together with the decline of the influence and prestige of the Church which was then absorbed in vast political and religious conflicts—all these factors constituted the forerunners of grave changes which were soon to take place. These changes were first manifested in Germany by a determination to reform the abuses extant in the Church, the necessity of which, indeed, had been felt and admitted by the Church herself long before the time of the Schism.[1]

The Protestant Reformation, brought about by Martin Luther in 1517, had an immediate and serious effect on education, not only in Germany, but also in other countries. A sudden revolt against the Church and ecclesiastical authority, it struck a severe blow at the educational institutions then flourishing everywhere, with the result that schools were confiscated, disorganized and in many places closed.[2] Furthermore, when the

[1] Scarascia, *Le Scuole Parrocchiali e degli Istituti Religiosi*, p. 71; Marique, *History of Christian Education* (New York: Fordham University Press, 1924-1932), II, 82, 86.

[2] Paulsen, *German Education, Past and Present* (tr. by Lorenz, New York, 1908), p. 54; de Beaurepaire, *Recherches sur l'Instruction publique, dans le diocèse de Rouen, avant 1789*, I, 77-78.

authority of the Church had been denied, it became necessary to find another power to insure the acceptance of the particular doctrine favored by each reformer. No other authority of sufficient force was at hand, except that of the civil rulers, and to them was given, according to the Reformation theory, the supreme control over religious matters in their respective realms. In this way the monarchs came to take a hand in the schools.[3] This entry of the State into the field of education has frequently been misconstrued by historians as the beginning of the public elementary school system,[4] while, as a matter of fact, there were more free schools and better provision was made for primary education before the Reformation than for a century afterward.[5]

The complaint of the bishop of Evreux in the diocesan statutes of the year 1576, sums up the situation, at least with regard to France: "We admire in our diocese the solicitude of our Fathers; for there was scarcely a parish of any importance where there was not a schoolhouse, and a foundation for the endowment of the school. But at the same time we must condemn the negligence, or rather the sacrilegious conduct of our age, in which we have seen gentlemen, parishioners, usurp or alienate the schoolhouses and the property settled upon them; so that now we seldom find a school or a master, we

[3] Monti, *La Libertà della Scuola*, pp. 412-416; Wernz, *Ius Decretalium*, III, pars I, n. 75. The gradual process of State monopolization, however, received its full actuality only towards the end of the 18th century and the beginning of the 19th. Meanwhile the Protestant princes intervened in the management of schools as organs of the ecclesiastical authority, and in the quality of temporal administrators of the evangelical church.

[4] "L'insegnamento primario nei suoi principii è cosa protestante e la Riforma ne è stata la culla." Compayré, *Storia della Pedagogia* (tr. by Valdarini, Torino, 1919), p. 87.

[5] Cf. Leach, *English Schools at the Reformation* (Westminster, 1896), pp. 5, 100; Gasquet, *Henry VIII and the English Monasteries* (London, 1906), II, 520; Janssen, *L'Allemagne et la Réforme* (Paris, 1887-1907), VII, 20; Rendu, *De l'Instruction populaire dans l'Allemagne du Nord* (Paris, 1855), pp. 5-6.

will not say in the country-places, but even in the towns, nay, even in the largest cities." [6]

Already during the early part of the sixteenth century two main councils attempted to stamp out abuses and stem the tide of the oncoming Protestant Reformation. In the V Lateran Council Leo X (1513-1521) in the Constitution "*Supernae dispositionis*" of May 5, 1514, insisted "that masters and teachers instruct their pupils not only in grammar, rhetoric, and other subjects of this kind, but impart to them also religious instruction, dealing especially with the commandments, the articles of faith, hymns, psalms, and the lives of the saints." [7] In 1536 the Council of Cologne urged a process of purging the primary schools and moreover demanded, in view of the many heresies current throughout Germany, that the teachers of such schools be men of sound doctrine and of good moral character.[8]

But the Reformation within the Church received its greatest impulse with the appointment of the Commission of Reform by Paul III in 1538. First among the measures proposed by the nine Cardinals forming the Commission was the restoration of the cathedral schools.[9] It was at this period that Reginald Cardinal Pole, a member of the Commission, promulgated in England on February 9, 1556, the legislation which was later amplified and incorporated into the decrees of the Council of Trent. No doubt, his predominant purpose was to prepare boys for the clerical state, so that they might continue the work of promoting education, but at the same time he made express provision for the admission of other youths who did not intend

[6] de Beaurepaire, *Recherches sur l'Instruction publique, dans le diocèse de Rouen, avant 1789*, II, 5 (Appendix). This remark of Bishop de Sainctes at the Synod of Evreux is not found in any of the general collections.

[7] Hardouin, IX, 1754. Tr. by Schroeder, *Disciplinary Decrees of the General Councils*, p. 495.

[8] Pars 12, c. 1—Hardouin, IX, 2022-2023.

[9] "De l'éducation cléricale et des Séminaires Provinciaux, IV Etat de la discipline au seizième siècle; . . ." *AJP*, I (1855), 664.

to study for the priesthood.[10] The Council of Trent (1545-1563), reading the signs of the times, renewed the decrees of the Lateran Councils (1179-1215),[11] and demanded that chairs of Theology and of Holy Scripture be established in each important collegiate church and monastery, in order that a love for the revealed truths might be fostered and, it may be surmised, upheld against all heretical attacks. It ordered, besides, that at least a teacher of grammar be maintained in all other churches, where clerics and indigent scholars could receive a gratuitous education. Provision was also made for the upkeep of this teacher, in order that the work be not inhibited under any pretext whatsoever.[12]

Thoroughly stirred by the dangers of the Reformation and led on by the Tridentine legislation, the whole Church in its councils and provincial synods attended to the welfare of the schools with the greatest solicitude.[13] The Council of Augsburg (1548) threatened with penalties those who attended schools suspected of heretical teaching, and enacted further legislation

[10] "Ad scholam grammaticae et alia commoda, discendi causa, admittantur alii etiam civitatis et dioecesis pueri: qui tamen sint honeste educati, bonis moribus praediti. . . . Ex his autem qui maxime idoneus erit, et ecclesiae inserviendi voluntatem praesefert, in eius locum sufficietur, qui ex clericorum numero desiderabitur."—Hardouin, X, 409.

[11] C. 1, 4, X, *de magistris*, V, 5.

[12] "Ecclesiae vero quarum annui proventus tenues fuerint, et ubi tam exigua est cleri et populi multitudo, . . . saltem magistrum habeant, ab episcopo cum consilio capituli eligendum, qui clericos aliosque scholares pauperes grammaticam gratis doceat, . . . Ideoque illi magistro grammatices vel alicujus simplicis beneficii fructus, quos tamdiu percipiat quamdiu in docendo perstiterit, assignentur; dum tamen beneficium ipsum suo debito non fraudetur obsequio: vel ex capitulari, vel episcopali mensa condigna aliqua merces persolvatur: . . . ne pia haec, utilis atque fructuosa provisio quovis quaesito colore negligatur."—Sess. V, *de reform.*, c. 1.

[13] Maggiolo wrote in this regard: "L'examen de nombreuses pièces d'archives, m'a laissé la conviction que partout, de bon gré ou par nécessité, les 526 chapitres qui existaient en France . . . remplissaient l'obligation qui leur était imposée par les Conciles de fonder et d'entretenir des écoles pour le peuple."—"Chapitre," *Dictionnaire de Pédagogie et d'Instruction Primaire* (ed. Buison, Paris, 1882), Appendix, p. 364.

concerning the establishment of Catholic institutions.[14] The second Council of Cologne (1549), reserved the judgment of the fitness of teachers to the diocesan ordinary and demanded the use of approved textbooks.[15] At Milan, a council urged the magistrates to employ only those teachers who were highly commended for faith and knowledge. Those in charge of schools were also asked to make use of books that were not only not forbidden by the Index, but morally safe and sound.[16] In a council at Mechlin (1570), the parochial nature of elementary schools was stressed, and a profession of faith was henceforth to be required of the teachers.[17] At Rouen (1581), a council enjoined upon the bishops to pass censures against those who, by unlawfully holding Church property, made the reopening of the schools impossible.[18] The Council of Tours (1583), restated the Tridentine legislation, and urged the bishops to exhort the pastors by synodal law to be insistent in recommending to the people the support of schoolteachers. It further admonished the local ordinaries to prevent heretics from taking the office of teachers in the schools.[19] The Council of Toulouse (1590), laid special stress on the education of youth, especially concerning the truths of faith and morals.[20]

[14] C. 26—Mansi, XXXII, 1319.

[15] Cc. 1, 3—Mansi, XXXII, 1363-1364.

[16] First Council of Milan (1565), c. 3—Hardouin, X, 639; cf. also c. 30—Hardouin, X, 675.

[17] *De Scholis*, cap. 1, 2—Hardouin, X, 1196-1197.

[18] Hardouin, X, 1256, n. 1.

[19] C. 21—Hardouin, X, 1440-1441.

[20] Pars 3, c. 3: "Cum (enim) omnis ignorantia perniciosa sit, tum ea potissimum, quae de divinis rebus est, perniciosissima semper existere consuevit."—Hardouin, X, 1809; cf. also c. 4, n. 6—Hardouin, X, 1810.

Similar scholastic legislation is to be found in the following provincial councils: Council of Narbonne (1551), c. 56—Hardouin, X, 462; Council of Ravenna (1568), cc. 1-5—Mansi, XXXV a, 592; I Council of Lima (1582), cap. 43, in which it was also provided that the Indians be well instructed in the Spanish language — Mansi, XXXVI bis, 209; Council of Urbino (1569), c. 3—Mansi, XXXV a, 701; Council of Bourges (1684), titl. 28, c. 6

Of paramount importance is the legislation of the Council of Cambrais (1565), which in an entire title devoted to the school question summarizes all the new elements of sixteenth-century scholastic legislation. The bishops were to restore the schools in their dioceses and to ensure therein the teaching of the rudiments of faith. In so far as possible the boys were to be separated from the girls. The teachers were to make use of only such textbooks as were approved by the bishop or his representative. An annual profession of faith was required of the teachers. On the pastors was placed the duty of inquiring monthly into the progress of the pupils, and of watching over religion and morals. Finally, the rural deans were to visit the *scholae minores* during each semester, or at least annually, and make a careful report to the ordinary of the diocese.[21] The regulations of the Council of Salzburg (1569), are noteworthy in their detailed outline concerning the schools in Austria. Each metropolitan, collegiate, and monastic church had to have a school, and all the other churches to which schools were not attached were to make provision for their establishment within six months.[22]

—Hardouin, X, 1490; Council of Aix (1585)—Hardouin, X, 1552 D; Council of Avignon (1594), cc. 6, 8, 10—Mansi, XXXIV b. 1333-1337; Council of Aquileia in Illyria (1596), titl. 1—Mansi, XXXIV b, 1369; Council of Tarragona (1685), const. 2—*Coll. Lac.*, I, 743; Council of Naples (1699), c. 2, which stressed particularly the importance of religious instruction—*Coll. Lac.*, I, 159; Council of Avignon (1725), titl. 4, c. 1, titl. 5, cc. 2, 3—*Coll. Lac.*, I, 482-483.

[21] Title III—Hardouin, X, 577-578. A later council (1586) confirmed this legislation. Moreover it gave minute regulations concerning the visitation of the schools and emphasized the necessity of having good moral books.—Title 21—Hardouin, IX, 2176. For the decrees of the last Council of Cambrais (1631) concerning the schools, cf. de Resbecq, *Histoire de l'Instruction primaire dans les Communes qui ont formé le département du Nord* (Paris, 1878), pp. 327-328. De Resbecq's work is rich with unedited documents and statistical material.

[22] C. 2: "Ideo mandamus nostrae metropoliticae, caeterisque cathedralium et collegiatarum ecclesiarum et monasteriorum praepositis . . . ut qui penes suas ecclesias et monasteria scholas habent, easdem sustentare non desistant,

The solicitude of the Church for the instruction of youth is furthermore unequivocally expressed by the words of the Council of Bordeaux, held in the year 1583: "It was well said . . . ," the council insists, "that there is nothing one could do more divine or more agreeable in the sight of God than to instruct children. For youth is the hope and the seed of the realm, and if while yet tender in years and tractable in spirit it be diligently taught, it will in abundance bring forth fruit of a wonderful savour, whereas contrariwise, if it be neglected and disdained, it will either not bring forth any fruit at all, or it will produce only a very bitter fruit. . . . Christians must, therefore, provide with all means in their power that in every parish, or at least in every well-known and well-populated borough, there be a school-master, who, besides grammar, will teach the children whatever is of concern to their religion." [23]

During the sixteenth century and the succeeding one, the cause of Catholic education was further advanced by the founding of several religious communities, not only of men, but also of women, who were devoted to the education of the young. Chief among these was the Society of Jesus, which was founded by St. Ignatius in 1534, and which at its suppression in 1773 was imparting instruction to two hundred and ten thousand students.[24] Upon the suppression of the Society of Jesus, many of its schools were taken over by the Society of the Oratory, founded in 1613 by Cardinal de Bérulle. A large part of the burden of the education of youth was likewise assumed by the

sed omni diligentia conservent et augeant. Non habentes autem, sub poena diminutionis fructuum et proventuum, pro arbitrio Ordinariorum taxandae, in spatio sex mensium, scholas pro loci commoditate atque necessitate instituant, magistros idoneos honesto stipendio adsciscant, et puerorum ingenia, ad reipublicae christianae usum, pie informari curent."—Mansi, XXXVI a, 291*; cf. constitutio 59—Mansi, XXXVI a, 291*-296*.

[23] Title 27 — Mansi, XXXIV a, 781. *Decreta Concilii Provincialis Burdigalae habiti, sub RR.DD. Ant. P. Sansaco* (Bordeaux, 1623), pp. 169-172.

[24] Schwickerath, *Jesuit Education: its History and Principles in the Light of Modern Educational Problems* (St. Louis, 1903), p. 145.

followers of St. John B. de la Salle (1651-1719), commonly known as the Brothers of the Christian Schools. At the same time many congregations of religious women took up the task of instructing Catholic girls. Perhaps the most outstanding among these were the Ursulines, who were founded by Angela Merici (1474-1540), for the express purpose of serving the cause of Catholic education by training adolescent girls.[25]

2. Remaining School Legislation up to the Code

During the period immediately following the Reformation, religious instruction, although heretical in its character, was maintained in the schools of those countries which had turned away from Catholicism. The Treaty of Westphalia (1648), which regulated this condition in Germany, proclaimed the famous principle: "*cuius regio eius religio*", and declared furthermore that the school was to be an institute annexed to the Church. Church and school were to remain in the control of that particular religion which flourished in a given locality or state in the year 1624, for this year was designated as the normative determinant for the application of the accepted rule.[26] In England, Catholic education met with even more drastic civil legislation. There, all the teachers were obliged to abjure *papism,* to adhere to Anglicanism and to attend the state-church publicly. In the higher schools, moreover, religious tests were demanded from both pupils and teachers.[27]

The Church, in her legislation concerning the schools which resulted from such civil laws, followed the precedent which she had established in her attitude towards the pagan schools

[25] Cf. McCormick, *History of Education,* pp. 244, 297; Allain, *L'Instruction primaire en France avant la Révolution,* pp. 47, 176; Marique, *History of Christian Education,* II, 127-157.

[26] Art. 5, 32—Monti, *La Libertà della Scuola,* p. 418; Hinschius, *Kirchenrecht,* IV, 578.

[27] Cf. Lischka, *Public Education and Catholic Education in England and Wales* (Washington: National Catholic Welfare Conference, 1937), p. 12; Monti, *La Libertà della Scuola,* pp. 531, 555.

of missionary countries. In 1659, an instruction of the Sacred Congregation for the Propagation of the Faith urged that no Catholic youth be entrusted to infidels for instruction and, as an efficacious remedy for this, insisted on the establishment of strictly Catholic schools.[28] About two hundred years later, this instruction was repeated in substance, though it was couched in stronger terms: "Omnino prohibeantur christiani adolescentes paganorum scholas frequentare, attento periculo perversionis et idolatriae."[29] Attendance at heretical schools was likewise prohibited. In 1699, the Holy Office explicitly declared that a prominent English convert who, owing to peculiar circumstances, was unable to manifest his conversion publicly, could not have his children instructed by heretical teachers.[30] In the same manner the bishops of Ireland were strongly advised to prevent Catholic youth from attending the schools established by the Protestant Biblical Society.[31]

A similar problem arose in the Oriental countries, when the Protestant denominations there began their missionary work. The Holy See simply reiterated its former stand, and warned all the bishops of the East of the grave danger to which Catholic youth is exposed in attending the schools directed by schismatics and Protestants.[32] At about the same time the Vicars Apostolic of the East Indies were advised to make every possible effort to establish schools in order to remove from Catholic youth the danger of attending non-Catholic institutions.[33] The solicitude on the part of the Church to preserve

[28] S. C. de Prop. Fide, instr. (ad Vic. Ap. Societ. Mission. ad Exteros), a. 1659—*Fontes*, n. 4463.

[29] S. C. de Prop. Fide (C. P. pro Sin.), 19 iul. 1838—*Fontes*, n. 4773.

[30] S. C. S. Off., 29 iul. 1699—*Fontes*, n. 762.

[31] S. C. de Prop. Fide, litt. encycl. (ad Ep. Hiberniae), 18 sept. 1819—*Fontes*, n. 4714.

[32] S. C. de Prop. Fide, litt. encycl. (ad Ep. Orient.), 20 mart. 1865—*Fontes*, n. 4863; cf. also, instr. 25 apr. 1868—*Fontes*, n. 4873.

[33] "Cum vero ex relationibus Visitationis Ap. manifestum sit unum ex praecipuis mediis a protestantibus adhibitum ad populos suorum errorum

the spiritual welfare of her children against the virus of heretical teachings is further manifested in the manifold regulations of the Roman Pontiffs, particularly Innocent XIII (1721-1724),[34] Benedict XIII (1724-1730),[35] Benedict XIV (1740-1758),[36] and Clement XIII (1758-1769).[37]

With the French Revolution another force antagonistic to Christian principles of education lifted its head over Europe, namely, a nationalism of a new and modern type. As a doctrine it asserted "the primacy of the nation and the State over personality," [38] a tenet from which State monopoly of the control of education was but a logical and necessary deduction. However, the French Revolution was not wholly the cause of the modern system of schools under the control and direction of the State. The movement had been in progress at least since the Treaty of Westphalia, and it had roots extending as far back as the Reformation. It had been working itself into definite form, here under one influence, there under another, at one place rapidly and elsewhere more slowly, usually in connection with religion. One by one the nations followed suit in claiming exclusive jurisdiction over the schools. In Germany the principle of State control was finally recognized by the beginning of the nineteenth century.[39] In Italy, a series of

veneno inficiendos positum esse in scholis quas ad instituendos pro suo lubitu pueros ac puellas per omnes Indiarum civitates aperiunt, EE.PP. hortandos esse iusserunt universos VV.AA. ut omnes vires ac studia sua in hoc conferre satagant ut per catholicarum scholarum institutionem sacrae puerorum puellarumque educationi ubicumque possunt provideant."—S. C. de Prop. Fide, instr. (ad Vic. Ap. Indiar. Orient.), 8 sept. 1869, n. 35—*Fontes*, n. 4876.

[34] Const. *Apostolici ministerii*, 23 maii 1723, n. 11—*Fontes*, n. 280.

[35] Const. *In Supremo*, 23 sept. 1724, n. 3—*Fontes*, n. 283.

[36] Litt. encycl. *Cum Religiosi*, 26 iun. 1754, § 4—*Fontes*, n. 429.

[37] Const. *In Dominico agro*, 14 iun. 1761—*Bullarii Romani Continuatio* (Prati, 1845-1854), V, n. CCXXIX, 522-525.

[38] De Hovre, *Philosophy and Education* (tr. by Jordan, New York: Benziger, 1931), p. 268.

[39] Cf. Maas, "Der Schulconflict im Grossherzogthum Baden," *AKKR*,

Napoleonic decrees (1802-1811) aimed at making the State supreme in that realm especially in the intermediate and secondary schools.[40] In France, the schools became subservient to the Emperor in 1808.[41] In Austria, the government passed a law in 1868, withdrawing the schools from the jurisdiction of the Church.[42]

Early in his reign (December 8, 1849) the Sovereign Pontiff, Pius IX, addressed the archbishops and bishops of Italy on the dangers to which Catholic youth was then exposed. Relative to their duty as chief pastors in this regard he said:

> It is incumbent upon you, and upon Ourselves, to labor with all diligence and energy, and with great firmness of purpose, and to be vigilant in everything that regards schools and the instruction and education of children and youth of both sexes. For you well know that the modern enemies of religion and of human society with a most diabolical spirit direct all their artifices to pervert the minds and hearts of youth from their earliest years. Wherefore, they leave nothing untried and shrink from no attempt to withdraw all schools and institutions destined for the education of youth from the authority of the Church and the vigilance of her holy pastors.[43]

XXXVIII (1877), 176-208. Willmann properly gives a place to the motives which led to consider education a national affair in his *Didaktik*, and he concludes with the following words: "... als der Deutsche zu Anfang unseres Jahrhunderts 'seines Volkstums Hehrheit ahnte,' drängte es alle, sich und andere mit dem neuen Geistesinhalt zu erfüllen, die Jugend verstand, dass sie für das Vaterland lernte, die Volksschule wurde so gut wie die Hochschule zur Pflege der wiedergefundenen nationalen Güter herangezogen und diese erschienen nicht als Bildungsmittel, sondern als vollwichtige Bildungszwecke."—*Didaktik als Bildungslehre nach ihren Beziehungen zur Sozialforschung und zur Geschichte der Bildung* (2nd ed., Braunschweig, 1894-1895), II, 25-26.

40 Monti, *La Libertà della Scuola*, pp. 142-144.

41 Monti, *op. cit.*, p. 356.

42 Cf. Pius IX, allocut. *Numquam certe*, 22 iun. 1868—*Fontes*, n. 550. This action of the Austrian government took place despite the Concordat between Austria and the Holy See which was signed only thirteen years before.

43 Ep. encycl. *Nostis et Nobiscum*, 8 dec. 1849, n. 30—*Fontes*, n. 508.

Again, the same Pontiff, in two separate allocutions of 1850 and 1851,[44] formally condemned the assumption of power by which the State arrogated to itself the right to the *whole* direction and management of the common schools in Christian nations. The condemnation is contained in the forty-fifth of the propositions which make up the famous *Syllabus* or collection of modern errors.[45]

In various localities diverse types of State schools came into existence: the schools of mixed attendance *(scholae mixtae)* and, in particular, the *Simultanschulen* of Germany, where each denomination had " in theory the right to care for the religious instruction of its own members," [46] and the lay or neutral schools of France, in which religious instruction was suppressed by a decree of 1882.[47] Pius IX in a letter "*Quum non sine* ", which contains a sweeping condemnation of all such schools, simply stated in general terms that such institutions, being hostile to the Catholic Church, cannot in conscience be frequented.[48]

In view of the universality of the State school system, and the impossibility of providing Catholic schools in many localities, such a prohibition, if it were enforced in its strictest sense, could not but withdraw from many Catholic youth the opportunity of all scholastic training. Two years after the promulgation of the "*Quum non sine* ", therefore, the Holy See was asked whether parents were permitted to send their

[44] *In consistoriali*, 1 nov. 1850—*Fontes*, n. 509; *Quibus luctuosissimis*, 5 sept. 1851—*Fontes*, n. 512.

[45] Denzinger-Umberg, *Enchiridion Symbolorum* (18.-20. ed., Friburgi Brisgoviae: Herder, 1932), n. 1745.

[46] Turner, " Schools," *Cath. Encycl.*, XIII, 558.

[47] Monti, *La Libertà della Scuola*, p. 389.

[48] "... cogeretur [Ecclesia] omnes fideles monere, eisque declarare, eiusmodi scholas Catholicae Ecclesiae adversas haud posse in conscientia frequentari."—14 iul. 1864, n. 4—*Fontes*, n. 539. The importance of this Apostolic letter to the archbishop of Freiburg im Breisgau is shown in the fact that from it no less than seven of the eighty condemnations as pronounced in the Syllabus were drawn.

children to mixed or neutral schools for instruction. The Holy Office replied: "In general it is not lawful; but in particular cases the matter is to be left to the judgment and conscience of the ordinary, whose duty it shall be to see that opportune precautions be used, not only by himself and his priests, but also by each individual parent, . . . and who shall never cease exhorting parents, especially those who have the means, to send their children to other countries where they may be educated in a Catholic manner." [49]

In 1875, the same Sacred Congregation made a clearer exposition of the matter in an instruction addressed to the American bishops. It "considers" the public school system "to be fraught with dangers and to be very hostile to Catholicity," and if the proximate dangers of perversion are not made remote, such schools cannot be frequented with a safe conscience.[50] Similarly, Leo XIII advised the bishops of Belgium that neutral schools could not be patronized by Catholic youth.[51] Finally, the Third Plenary Council of Baltimore (1884) stated that Catholic parents might not send their children to the public schools unless a sufficient reason were present, sufficient, that is, in the judgment of the ordinary; and were such attendance

[49] S. C. S. Off., instr. 21 mart. 1866—*Fontes*, n. 992; cf. also *Concilii Plenarii Baltimorensis II* (1866) *Acta et Decreta*, nn. 424-426; Council of Smyrna (1869), sect. IV, c. 1, n. 1—*Coll. Lac.*, VI, 576 (a).

[50] S. C. S. Off., instr. (ad Ep. Stat. Foeder. Americae Septentrion.), 24 nov. 1875—*Fontes*, n. 1046.

[51] Leo XIII, after condemning the law of Belgium of July 1, 1880, concerning neutral schools said: "Quam rem more agimus institutisque Apostolicae Sedis, quae semper iudicii atque auctoritatis suae pondere scholas perculit cuiuslibet religionis expertes, quas medias seu *neutras* appellant, quaeque suapte natura illuc tandem evadunt, ut Deum prorsus non agnoscant: neque usquam passa est, eiusmodi scholas a iuventute catholica celebrari, nisi certis casibus, cum eam tempus et necessitas cogeret, cautoque prius ne praesens esset pravae contagionis periculum."—Allocut. *Summi Pontificatus*, 20 aug. 1880, n. 6—*Fontes*, n. 581. Cf. also ep. encycl. *Quod multum*, 22 aug. 1886, n. 7—*Fontes*, n. 594; *Caritatis providentiaeque*, 19 mart. 1894, n. 3—*Fontes*, n. 623; S. C. de Prop. Fide, litt. encycl. (ad Ep. Canad.), 14 mart. 1895—*Fontes*, n. 4932.

allowed, then steps must be taken to make remote the danger of perversion.[52]

While formulating legislation to preserve her children from the insidious dangers of godless schools, it was likewise necessary for the Church to maintain pure and intact within the Catholic schools the standard of Catholic education. "Ut tota in illis studiorum ratio ad Catholicae doctrinae normam exigatur," was the demand of Pius IX.[53] The letters of the Pontiffs during this period show that there was a growing tendency on the part of some educators to relegate instruction in Catholic doctrine to a position of secondary importance in the curriculum. To counteract this, they required that religion must so dominate the course, that it may be in very truth the foundation and crown of the youth's entire training. To use the words of Leo XIII, " it is necessary that religious instruction be given to the young, not only at certain fixed times, but also that every other subject taught be permeated with Christian piety." [54] And again, the more recent pronouncement of Pius XI [55] is but a repetition of the fundamental principle that Catholic education must primarily and essentially be religious and moral in character.

Conclusion

The nature and extent of the provision made by the Church, throughout the centuries, for the education of her people in the elementary and intermediate schools, is evident from the historical outline in the foregoing pages.

It is believed that no undue importance is given to the enactment of ecclesiastical law dealing with the subject. Regarded as evidences of law and precept, and not merely as points of

[52] *Acta et Decreta Concilii Plenarii Baltimorensis Tertii*, n. 198.

[53] Ep. encycl. *Nostis et Nobiscum*, 8 dec. 1849, n. 28—*Fontes*, n. 508.

[54] Ep. encycl. *Militantis Ecclesiae*, 1 aug. 1897, n. 6—*Fontes*, n. 635; cf. also ep. *Officio sanctissimo*, 22 dec. 1887, n. 9—*Fontes*, n. 596.

[55] Cf. litt. encycl. *Divini illius Magistri*, 31 dec. 1929—*AAS*, XXII (1930), 49-86.

recommendation, these enactments are held to be remarkable for their number and variety. They cannot be regarded as seriously defective, because they are wanting in that detail which so many consider as necessary for the inauguration of any new measures of administration or reform. When one realizes how little is said of education or the means of promoting the same in the constitutions of modern States, one appreciates more fully the endeavors made by the Church.

Some of the historical data have been allocated to a more precise place in history, and by the careful study of documents an opportunity has been afforded for the refutation of historians and educators who would deny the Church one of her most cherished and ancient prerogatives, namely, her sponsorship of schools.

PART TWO

POSITION OF THE FAMILY, CHURCH, AND STATE, IN REGARD TO THE CONTROL OF SCHOOLS. COMMENTARY ON THE LEGISLATION OF THE CODE

CHAPTER VI

Position of the Family, Church, and State, in Regard to the Control of Schools

For the Catholic, the question of the respective places of the family, the Church, and the State in education, is fundamentally a question of morality and justice. The ultimate norm of morality for him is God, the proximate norm is the nature of man as a rational and social being.[1] The nature of man is today, in all essential respects, the same as that of the first man. He is a creature made up of body and soul, possessed of the right to live and to enjoy all things necessary to life, under obligations to respect the rights of others and to cooperate with them, and to submit himself to the supreme dominion of Almighty God.

Man, however, does not live segregated from others. He is a social being. Corresponding to his nature as it was created there are two natural societies of which he is a member, the family and the State, each of which has its own proper structure, duties, rights, and powers. It does not rest with the will of man to decide whether the family or the State shall exist or not. By the very fact that men are such beings as they are, there must be families and there must be States. Likewise the rights and the duties of these two institutions exist independently of the choice of man.[2] It is, of course, implied in this doctrine that the neglect of these rights and duties necessarily results in ultimate harm to both States and families, on the one hand, and to individual men, on the other. The primary criterion, furthermore, for defining the limits of the liberty of

[1] Costa-Rossetti, *Philosophia Moralis* (Oeniponte, 1886), p. 67.

[2] Cf. Cathrein, *Moralphilosophie* (2nd ed., Freiburg im Breisgau, 1893), II, 341, 445.

the individual and of the authority of natural society, whether domestic or civil, is to be sought not in the adaptation to particular conditions, nor in the shifting wants of the age, but rather in the nature of man and in the nature of these necessary social institutions.

Besides these two necessary natural institutions there is a third, the Church, which corresponds to the spiritually elevated nature of man and which, in its relation to the individual, occupies a position analogous to that held by the other two, but at the same time unique. Like them, it is a necessary society, independent of the will of men in its functions and its prerogatives, not subject to the development of culture or progress in its essential rights and duties. Unlike them, it is not a derivative of nature and primarily does not serve any merely natural purpose. It was instituted immediately by Christ for the supernatural end of saving men's souls, by teaching them the revealed truths of faith, and by ruling them according to divine law. Its sphere of action is the supernatural, and it has in that sphere rights that may not be destroyed or abridged. For that very reason it does not encroach upon the domain of either the family or the State, both of which exist for natural purposes and have the natural for their province.[3]

The question at issue involves the following queries: who has the right to determine what shall be chosen in the field of knowledge for the instruction of youth? Who has the right to determine what moral standards, ideals of conduct, attitudes towards the world and society shall be impressed upon it, either by direct indoctrination or by the more subtle means of suggestion? The most apparent answer to these questions is that the school is the proper medium for forming the minds and habits of the coming generation. The school, however, is not an auton-

[3] Cf. Pius IX, "*Syllabus*" *seu collectio errorum modernorum*, prop. 19—Denzinger-Umberg, *Enchir. Symbol.*, n. 1719; Vatican Council, sess. IV, *Constitutio dogmatica de Ecclesia Christi*—Denzinger-Umberg, *Enchir. Symbol.*, n. 1821.

omous society. It is merely an agency erected to assist other institutions in carrying on the work of formal education. It has no right to teach except such as is delegated to it by others. To say that this function of deciding the manner of education belongs to the school is merely to throw the question back, and ask: who should control the school?

The problem reduces itself to a choice among the three necessary societies: the family, the Church, and the State. Which of these should control the school? Or, if all should have a hand in such a control, in what should the controlling power of each consist? The Catholic teaching is that there are definite boundaries separating the rights of the individual, the family, the State, and the Church. Authors lay down definite rules to govern the relations among them in the work of education. They may differ from one another about questions of expediency within those limits, but they all agree that there are limits which cannot be arbitrarily transgressed.[4]

First of all to be considered is the place of the family. The function of education is to be deduced from the doctrine that man possesses an unalterable nature, which determines the general outline of his rights and duties regardless of the changing circumstances of time and place. According to this nature of man, the original and immediate right to educate any child belongs to that child's parents. St. Thomas expresses this doctrine in the following words:

> The father is the principle of generation, of education and discipline, and of everything that bears upon the perfecting of human life.[5] The child, indeed, shares in the nature of the father, and at first he is not separated from the parents

[4] Cf. Marion, *Le Problème Scolaire étudié dans ses principes* (Ottawa: *Ottawa Printing Co.*, 1920), pp. 21-42; Hilling, "Naturrecht, Kirchenrecht, Staatsrecht und Privatschule," *AKKR*, CVIII (1928), 3-23.

[5] "Pater est principium et generationis, et educationis, et disciplinae, et omnium quae ad perfectionem humanae vitae pertinent."—*Summa Theologica,* IIa IIae, Q. CII, a. I.

> as to the body, as long as he is contained in the mother's womb. Later, when he has come forth from the womb, he remains . . . under the direction of his parents in a kind of spiritual womb; . . . and so by natural right the child, before reaching the use of reason, is under the father's care. Hence it would be against natural justice, if the child . . . were removed from the care of the parents, or disposed of against their will.[6]

The same argument is appealed to by Pius XI, who furthermore concludes:

> The family, therefore, holds directly from the Creator the mission and hence the right to educate its offspring, a right inalienable because inseparably joined to the strict obligation, a right anterior to any right whatever of civil society and of the State, and therefore inviolable on the part of any power on earth.[7]

Indeed, these words are but the statement of the constant teaching of the Church and authoritatively confirm the writings of Catholic authors who discuss the subject.[8]

This right is not a mere figment of the mind, without a basis in the actual conditions of life. It exists by reason of the needs of man as a rational and social being. The family is

[6] "Filius enim naturaliter est aliquid patris; et primo quidem a parentibus non distinguitur secundum corpus, quamdiu in matris utero continetur; postmodum vero, postquam ab utero egreditur, . . . continetur sub parentum cura, sicut sub quodam spirituali utero; . . . ita de iure naturali est quod filius, antequam habeat usum rationis, sit sub cura patris. Unde contra iustitiam naturalem esset, si puer . . . a cura parentum subtrahatur, vel de eo aliquid ordinetur invitis parentibus."—IIa IIae, Q. X, a. XII.

[7] Litt. encycl. *Divini illius Magistri*, 31 dec. 1929—*AAS*, XXII (1930), 59.

[8] Leo XIII, litt. encycl. *Rerum novarum*, 15 maii 1891, n. 10—*Fontes*, n. 611; Pius XI, litt. encycl. *Casti connubii*, 31 dec. 1930—*AAS*, XXII (1930), 545; Jansen, *De Facultate Docendi seu De Scholis Institutiones Juridicae* (Parisiis et Buscoduci, 1885), p. 104; Cappello, *Summa Iuris Publici Ecclesiastici*, p. 503; Ottaviani, *Institutiones Iuris Publici Ecclesiastici*, II, 233; Michel, *La Question Scolaire et les Principes Théologiques* (Paris: Desclée, 1921), p. 17.

the natural means, provided by God, when He created man such a being as he is, not only for the procreation but also for the education of children.[9] It is not merely an organization of the group, which came into being because it was suited to the needs of men at some particular period of their development. The family is a society necessary for the well-being and even for the continuance of human life, not to be tampered with by social experimentation.[10] The very helplessness of the child, which makes education necessary points to the parents as the natural teachers of their children. The gift of life that they confer would be a useless one, were it not completed by the care and nurture necessary to bring the child from helpless infancy to the health and strength of manhood, and by the constant training of body and mind without which he could hardly take his place in society and do his work in the world.[11] The natural love of parents for their children, and their pride and interest in them, are also an indication that they are teachers intended by nature, commissioned with the responsibility of bringing up their children.[12] So absolutely helpless is the child, so constant and importunate are the demands upon the patience, watchfulness, and self-sacrifice of any one who would educate him rightly, so long-continued is the period of his dependence, that there must be some such compelling force as this parental love and pride to induce one to cooperate in his creation and,

[9] "Societas stabilis matrimonii est immediate naturalis, cuius finis proximus est generatio et educatio liberorum."—Costa-Rossetti, *Philosophia Moralis*, p. 431.

[10] Cf. Taparelli, *Saggio Teoretico di Diritto Naturale* (2nd ed., Prato, 1883), II, n. 1529.

[11] "Non enim intendit natura solum generationem prolis, sed etiam traductionem et promotionem usque ad perfectum statum hominis, in quantum homo est; qui est virtutis status."—St. Thomas, *Supplementum*, Q. XLI, a. I; cf. also Pius XI, litt. encycl. *Casti connubii*, 31 dec. 1930—*AAS*, XXII (1930), 545-546.

[12] St. Thomas, *De Eruditione Principum*, lib. V, cap. II; *Summa Theologica*, Ia IIae, Q. C, a. V ad 4um.

as a necessary consequence, undertake his upbringing and continue faithful to the task.[13]

Corresponding to these duties, parents possess authority over their children and the right to control their education. So far as the mere natural order of things is concerned, this right of the parents is primary and direct. It implies the right of parents to prevent all others from taking a hand in the child's training, except with their consent.[14] So long as parents fulfill their duty in the religious, moral, intellectual, and physical education of their children, no one may interfere with them, either to curtail the training they give, or to increase it, or to substitute for it instruction of another sort. Any measure that destroys or in any essential matter weakens parental authority or responsibility is wrong, because it contravenes the nature of man.

The authority of parents is, however, not an absolute nor a despotic one to be exercised arbitrarily, or merely for the benefit of the parents. It is conditioned by God's plan, by His law, and the divinely established order. The right of parents over their children is the correlative of their duty towards them. It is derived from that duty and finds its limits in the limits of that duty. Thus, for instance, parents may not command their children to do anything morally wrong, nor may they command what is opposed to proper education or defective in this regard.[15]

[13] "Endlich ist auch eine innige Liebe des Wohlwollens die notwendige Voraussetzung und Grundlage zur Lösung der langwierigen und beschwerlichen Aufgabe der Kindererziehung."—Cathrein, *Moralphilosophie*, II, 386. Cf. also Canestri, "De iure educandi liberos, parentibus reservato, in ordinem ad universum systema Ethices catholicae," *Apollinaris*, IV (1931), 287-291.

[14] Taparelli, *Saggio Teoretico di Diritto Naturale*, II, n. 1570.

[15] Cf. Cathrein, *Moralphilosophie*, II, 391; Coronata, *Institutiones Iuris Canonici* (Taurini, Italia: Marietti, 1928-1936), II, 302. For historical proofs dealing with the development of Catholic doctrine concerning the rights of parents over their children together with their limitations and duties, cf. Schröteler, *Das Elternrecht in der katholisch-theologischen Auseinandersetzung* (München: Neuer Filser-Verlag, 1936). The author

It has just been said that, so long as parents fulfill their duties in the education of their children, no one may interfere with them in that work. But, what should be said of the case in which parents manifestly fail in their obligations? This neglect may be considered in two different ways. In the first place, the effects upon the child himself might be considered: his ability to earn his living may not be developed, his health may not be properly cared for, due opportunity may not be afforded for the proper unfolding of his personality and his talents. On the other hand, such neglect may affect society at large: the child, because of the lack of adequate training, may become a burden to the community, or he may become a menace to the rights of others by falling into a life of crime, against which he has not been sufficiently safeguarded by proper religious and moral training.

In the latter case there can be no doubt that public authority has the right to protect itself and its subjects from the danger of dependency and crime, by insisting that parents give their children adequate education. If the parents are proved to be grossly negligent, the authorities may compel them to perform their duty, and, if no other means is effective, they may even take the children from the charge of their parents and themselves send them to school. Such cases, however, are the exception, and real proof of neglect must be forthcoming to justify interference in each individual instance.[16]

The other case, in which there is not question of danger or burden to society, but rather of present or future discontent or unhappiness of the child, requires further distinction. The neglect of the parents may be such as would really affect the life or health of the child; or it may only be a relative neglect, such

treats this question particularly under three headings: the children *oblati*, p. 35; validity of marriage without the consent of parents, p. 137; baptism of infant infidels or Jews, p. 143.

[16] Cathrein, *Moralphilosophie*, II, 513-514; cf. also Wernz, *Ius Decretalium*, III, pars I, n. 69, *d*; Cavagnis, *Institutiones Iuris Publici Ecclesiastici*, I, 48-56.

as a failure to provide for the training of the child to the full extent of his ability, a failure to offer him all the educational opportunities that circumstances might permit. In the second supposition, the public authority has no right to interfere. It is for the parents and not for the children or for any one else to determine what under each one's peculiar circumstances is the best education for a particular child.[17] If, however, the failure of the parents to care for and instruct their children would result in the children's illness or beggary, then there would be a violation of the child's strict right as a human being, and the public authority, as the protector of the rights of its members, would be justified in taking a hand, on the legitimate supposition that parental neglect is a danger to society.

It would be wrong to deny the civil power any natural right in the regulation of the education of its citizens. Pius XI, in fact, speaks of " true and just rights of the State in the education of its citizens," and affirms that " these rights have been conferred upon civil society by the Author of nature Himself . . . in virtue of the authority which it possesses to promote the common temporal welfare, which is precisely the purpose of its existence." [18] The most obvious example showing that the State has an interest in education is the training of public servants. It is a matter of the greatest moment that military and naval officers, as well as diplomatic and other officials, be properly trained for their duties.[19] The control of such training, in naval and military academies and other institutions designed for preparing for public service, belongs to the State,

[17] " Liberi ius strictum non habent a parentibus exigendi, ut determinato modo educentur . . . parentes ius strictum liberorum non laedunt, nisi quatenus hi spectati non ut liberi, sed ut homines, damna in bonis utilibus vere propriis illata patiuntur."—Costa-Rossetti, *Philosophia Moralis*, p. 737.

[18] Litt. encycl. *Divini illius Magistri*, 31 dec. 1929—*AAS*, XXII (1930), 62; cf. also litt. encycl. *Non abbiamo bisogno*, 29 iun. 1931—*AAS*, XXIII (1931), 303.

[19] Wernz, *Ius Decretalium*, III, pars I, n. 69, *c*.

just as the training of the clergy belongs to the Church.[20] It is also within the province of the State to promote the diffusion of knowledge by the encouragement, and even by the endowment and support of libraries, museums, and similar institutions, which are necessary for the cultural welfare of society, but generally beyond the means of individuals to provide.[21]

It belongs to the State also to lay down some requirements necessary for the instruction and training of all those seeking government employment. This principle seems to extend to all those who would engage in public service, as in law, medicine, and the like. The teaching profession, at least in the State schools, would probably be also included, but in regard to it caution should be observed that such requirements be reasonable, rather confined to professional training and not extended to matters of social theory, so nearly related to the sphere of morals. One must note here, however, that in all these questions the power of the State will primarily concern itself with the fitness of the candidates aspiring to such positions. No government, therefore, could compel one to attend only schools of its own, or deprive candidates of civil positions because they, although otherwise fit, did not attend State institutions.[22]

One part of the duty of the State is to prevent the teaching of any doctrines disruptive of public order or harmful to the morals of the citizens.[23] The acceptance of the theory, that the State has an unlimited right to interfere with schools on the ground of morality, would be equivalent to making the State a teacher of morals. No State monopoly of schools, or enforcement of a unique program of instruction will ever be

[20] Pius XI, litt. encycl. *Divini illius Magistri,* 31 dec. 1929—*AAS,* XXII (1930), 64.

[21] Cf. Cathrein, *Moralphilosophie,* II, 526; Steffes, *Religion und Politik* (Freiburg im Breisgau: Herder, 1929), p. 18.

[22] Cf. Cavagnis, *Institutiones Iuris Publici Ecclesiastici,* III, 54-70, 79-80; Taparelli, *Saggio Teoretico di Diritto Naturale,* II, note al capo III, nota CXL, 3, p. 330.

[23] Cathrein, *Moralphilosophie,* II, 525.

justified on the sole ground that it is protecting the State against a teaching which might be harmful to it or its citizens. The principle of the State's right to prevent harmful or immoral teaching can be fully applied only when the State is guided by the Church who is the divinely appointed teacher of morals. In cases of separation of Church and State (apart from the canonical and divine positive illegality of such a condition), this power should not be entirely abandoned nor should everyone be allowed untrammeled liberty for any sort of teaching. But based on natural law and justice, it must be accepted and practiced always with the greatest caution, lest it be made an instrument of tyranny and of State absolutism in the realm of thought.[24]

Another right and duty of the State is to render aid to schools of general education, maintained by the collective activity of its citizens, whenever these schools cannot be properly supported without public assistance. If no other means seems adequate for providing a complete system of public education for the people (as is today generally the case), the State is justified in setting up its own system in addition to the schools maintained by private resources, or by the Church.[25] In the management of such State schools, the rights of the Church and of the parents of the children attending them should always receive first consideration, for they have the prior place in the work of education. For this reason, too, the chief control of these schools should remain within the local community—as far as this is possible without detriment to the schools—and with a minimum of central control.[26]

The place of the State in education is, then, according to Catholic teaching, real but entirely secondary.[27] Parents are

[24] Cf. Leo XIII, litt. encycl. *Libertas*, 20 iun. 1888, nn. 19, 20, 30—*Fontes*, n. 600.

[25] Pius XI, litt. encycl. *Divini illius Magistri*, 31 dec. 1929—*AAS*, XXII (1930), 63.

[26] Cathrein, *Moralphilosophie*, II, 525.

[27] Cf. also Coronata, *Institutiones Iuris Canonici*, II, 303.

the educators designated by the law of nature, and they may be superseded only in those exceptional cases in which their incapacity or neglect would constitute a violation of the rights of the child as a human being, or occasion a menace to society. It is not for the State to put itself between the parent and the child, but rather to protect the parent's rights, to second them, and to encourage their exercise in every way. It may not reserve to itself the sole right to teach, nor may it intrude into the management of schools to the exclusion of the Church, or the parents, but it must respect the rights of both. Present conditions, which render a large measure of government activity necessary, do not change the natural law, which decrees that the father and the mother should control the children's rearing; nor the divine positive law, which makes the Church the teacher of all men in whatever concerns faith and morals.

The fact that the Church's divine mission is not admitted by many modern States, does not destroy her right to control the religious and moral teaching and supervise the whole education of her children. If that control and supervision are denied to the Church, they do not pass to the State, but to the parents, whom the natural law designates as the proper educators of their children. If they choose to commit this function to the Church, no government has the right to hinder them in their choice.

There is one way in which practically all modern States restrict the parents' control of the education of their children, and that is by compulsory instruction laws.[28] Here it may be asked: is such legislation an unjust infringement upon the right of parents to control the bringing up of their children?

In the discussion concerning the place of the family in education it was pointed out that the public authority may inter-

[28] For compulsory school laws in the United States, cf. Carrigan, *The Child and the American Law* [a reprint from the *Pedagogical Seminary,* XVIII (1911), 121-183], p. 141; also Lischka, *Private Schools and State Laws* (Washington: National Catholic Welfare Conference, 1926), under "Compulsory attendance."

vene and compel parents to educate their children, and even take children from their parents, in cases of gross neglect. What constitutes this neglect is, however, not easy to decide, and there is much dispute among Catholic authors as to whether the meaning of such neglect should be left to determination by judicial decision in each particular case, or whether the law should define the minimum of parental obligation. Formerly, many Catholic writers contended that no general rule could be made by law, but that the circumstances of each individual instance must be considered in deciding whether or not a parent had been neglectful of his duty. In the opinion of many it would have been wrong even to prescribe the learning of reading and writing for all children.[29]

This, however, is a matter subject to the changes of social conditions. Pius XI seems to have settled this question. "The State," he says, "can exact and take measures to secure that all its citizens have the necessary knowledge of their civic and national duties, and a certain degree of physical, intellectual, and moral culture, which, considering the conditions of our times, is really necessary for the common good."[30] While not actually mentioning compulsory education, the Pope, by speaking of a certain standard of knowledge and culture as "really necessary for the common good," seems to indicate that legal coercion is proper, if no other means of obtaining such a standard is sufficient. He insists, however, that the State, in promoting education and instruction, must "respect the rights of the Church and the family concerning Christian education, and moreover must have regard for distributive justice." He condemns as unjust any coercion of families in the use of schools "contrary to the dictates of their Christian conscience, or contrary to their legitimate preferences."[31]

[29] Cf. Michel, *La Question Scolaire et les Principes Théologiques*, pp. 47-56, especially p. 52, note 1.

[30] Litt. encycl. *Divini illius Magistri*, 31 dec. 1929—*AAS*, XXII (1930), 63-64.

[31] *Loc. cit.*

Unquestionably, this matter of compulsory schooling is intimately connected with the question of the State's providing the kind of schools that parents may wish for their children. This question cannot be satisfactorily settled on purely political grounds, nor can any Catholic approve of a system that commands all parents to send their children to school, and provides, at the public expense, only that kind of school which the majority of parents happen to want, with no regard for the wishes of those who would have another sort. Only when there is agreement between the Church and the State, can the Catholic give unconditional assent to the principle of compulsion.[32] Since parents are, by natural law, the proper educators of their children, the State is obliged, if it enters into the field of education by establishing its own schools, to have regard for the wishes of all parents, and not merely for the wishes of a majority of parents or of citizens. If the schools are supported by general taxation, it must maintain schools that meet the desires of any considerable minority, or, failing that, it must give assistance to the schools conducted by such a minority, in proportion to the support it gives to its own schools.[33]

The right of the Church must now be considered. The position of the Church as the divinely appointed custodian of truth gives her a unique place in the work of education and, as a consequence, in the control of schools. This place of the Church was first called into question by the Emperor Julian who, in his attempt to reestablish the pagan religion, deprived the Church of any influence in the institutions of learning, and even forbade Christians to hold the position of instructors, unless they first subscribed to the worship of the gods.[34] Besides this form of State interference in education, there could

[32] Cappello, *Summa Iuris Publici Ecclesiastici*, p. 508, note 15.

[33] Ottaviani, *Institutiones Iuris Publici Ecclesiastici*, II, 245.

[34] *Juliani Imperatoris opera quae supersunt, graece et latine* (Lipsiae, 1875-1876), Epistola 42; C. Th. (13.3) 5.

be mentioned the monopoly of State claimed by the French government, at the time of the Revolution of 1789, when the Church was entirely excluded from taking part in the control of education. Such arrogant claims by civil governments are still maintained today in many nations, such as Mexico,[35] Russia,[36] and to a certain extent, Germany.[37] In many others, although the function of the Church in the work of education is recognized, still the exercise of that function is greatly limited and her position jeopardized.

The Church has, nevertheless, rights as well as duties in regard to the work of education and the institutions engaged in it. She was appointed by Christ to teach all men.[38] The content of her teaching is different from that of any other teaching agency. It transcends, partly at least, the natural powers of the human mind, and can be received from no other teacher except the Church.[39] Furthermore, education being concerned with man as a whole, individually and socially, in the order of nature and in the order of grace, it belongs also to the Church in accordance with the dispositions of Divine Providence. Though the primary object of the Church is to teach supernatural truths, her jurisdiction must extend also to whatever is connected with these truths and has relation to the achievement of her end, which is the salvation of men. Thus, in regard to every other kind of human learning and instruction, which is the common heritage of individuals and society, the Church has an independent right to make use of it, and above

[35] Cf. "Responsum publicum Secretarii Educationis publicae ad Instructionem Delegati Apostolici," *Periodica*, XXIV (1935), 58-62.

[36] Cf. Pius XI, chirogr. (ad Em. Card. Pompilj), 2 febr. 1930—*AAS*, XXII (1930), 89-93.

[37] Cf. Allocution of Card. Faulhaber, *Osservatore Romano*, LXXV (1935), febr. 18-19; Schröteler, *Das Elternrecht*, pp. 19, 21-34.

[38] Matthew, XXVIII, 19-20.

[39] Cf. Vatican Council, *Constitutio dogmatica de fide catholica*, sess. III, cap. IV, *de fide et ratione*—Denzinger-Umberg, *Enchir. Symbol.*, n. 1795.

all to decide what may help or harm education. "This must be so," writes Pius XI, "because the Church, as a perfect society, has an independent right to the means conducive to her end, and because every form of instruction, no less than every human action, has a necessary connection with man's last end, and, therefore, cannot be withdrawn from the dictates of the divine law, of which the Church is guardian, interpreter and infallible mistress." [40]

In keeping with these principles of divine positive law and of reason, the Church asserts the following rights in reference to the control of schools: first, she claims the right to demand that religious instruction be given to all her children, and the right to determine how it shall be given, and finally, since religious and moral training cannot be separated, how moral education shall be given.[41] Contained in these rights is the right of the Church to establish and maintain schools of her own, for instruction, not only in religion, but in every branch of learning.[42] This right, which every individual and moral person may claim, belongs to the Church by a special title; for, by the establishment of her own schools, for profane as well as religious instruction, she can more effectually execute her special task, for the accomplishment of which there is, in many cases, no other means available.

Parents are bound to educate their children for the correct performance of their duties, for the enjoyment of happiness in this world, and for the attainment of their destiny in the world to come. Included in the prerogatives of the Church, however, is the right to determine the duties of parents regarding the religious and moral training of their children. The Church does not intrude in any matter of a strictly profane nature.

[40] Litt. encycl. *Divini illius Magistri*, 31 dec. 1929—*AAS*, XXII (1930), 54. Cf. Wernz, *Ius Decretalium*, III, pars I, n. 72.

[41] Cappello, *Summa Iuris Publici Ecclesiastici*, pp. 501-503.

[42] Canon 1375.

She has, however, indirect authority over such matters in so far as they relate to spiritual issues and involve a moral content. Consequently, in all that relates to the supernatural order or pertains to it she has a right, and parents, in such matters, may well be said to be her delegates and instruments in the performance of her work for the salvation of souls.[43] She, therefore, forbids parents to send their children to any school but one that is Catholic, except in cases in which the bishop of the diocese judges that attendance at another school may be allowed without danger to the children's faith.[44] Consistently with her conviction that intellectual, moral, and religious training cannot be separated from one another without harm to the pupils, she makes it her law that every Catholic school must include religious training.[45]

It is not the desire of the Church that all schools must be under her sole control. While she claims the right of erecting schools, she recognizes that right in others also. In every school, however, that is attended by Catholic pupils, whether public or private, she affirms that she ought to be permitted to safeguard the faith and morals of those pupils even by supervising the secular training as far as is necessary.[46] Religious training is, furthermore, by right subject to her sole authority and supervision; to the latter, bishops are bound in virtue of their office, and consequently have an inalienable right to see to it that nothing contrary to faith or morals be taught in any school within their dioceses. They must approve of teachers and textbooks of religion, and, for the purpose of safeguarding religion and morals, they have also the power to demand the

[43] Cappello, *Summa Iuris Publici Ecclesiastici*, p. 505. Cf. also Godts, *Les droits en matière d'éducation* (Bruxelles, 1900-1901), IV, 858.

[44] Canon 1374.

[45] Canon 1373.

[46] Litt. encycl. *Divini illius Magistri*, 31 dec. 1929—*AAS*, XXII (1930), 56; Wernz, *Ius Decretalium*, III, pars I, n. 69, *c*.

removal of any teacher from the school, or to forbid the use of any book.[47] Finally, the Church makes it the duty of all, especially of the bishops, to see to the provision of Catholic schools where they are lacking, and she stresses the obligation of all the faithful to contribute to their support according to their means.[48]

The full extent of the claims made by the Church will not be admitted by those who do not believe in her divine mission and juridic necessity. Nevertheless, some of these claims are based on the natural law, altogether apart from Revelation. Prescinding from her supernatural prerogative, the Church is a moral person and possesses all the natural rights of any moral person.[49] It is, therefore, within her competence to maintain schools of her own, so long as they observe the just regulations of the State and do not disturb the public order. Her laws obliging Catholics to patronize Catholic schools only cannot look for recognition from those not of the faith. On the other hand, Catholics may not, in justice, be prevented from establishing and patronizing such schools, since they have, by the natural law, the primary power to determine the education of their children. The right of the Church to control religious training and to supervise the other branches of learning, nay, the whole curriculum of instruction, in schools other than her own, will not be admitted by those who do not recognize in the Church a society founded by Christ for the purpose of saving souls; but there is nothing in the natural law to prevent the recognition of the rights of the Church, especially in schools controlled by Catholics.[50]

[47] Canon 1381. Cf. also canon 1382.

[48] Canon 1379.

[49] Ottaviani, *Institutiones Iuris Publici Ecclesiastici*, II, 186.

[50] Cf. "Staat und Erziehung und Schule," *Lexikon der Pädagogik der Gegenwart* (hrg. vom Deutschen Institut für wissenschaftliche Pädogogik, Münster i. W., Freiburg i. Br., 1930-1932), II, 1018-1019.

The position of the Church has been thus far exposed, though without particular details. A more thorough explanation and application of the different prerogatives of the Church in reference to education and to the institutions of learning is given in the commentary to each individual canon, according to the order followed by the Code of Canon Law.

CHAPTER VII

Obligation of Religious and Moral Training

Canon 1372, § 1: Fideles omnes ita sunt a pueritia instituendi ut non solum nihil eis tradatur quod catholicae religioni morumque honestati adversetur, sed praecipuum institutio religiosa ac moralis locum obtineat.

The Code starts the treatise on schools with a fundamental rule, doctrinal in character and extensive in scope. In beginning thus, the legislator follows the method employed in other parts of the Code,[1] since positive law by its very nature rests upon the natural and divine law.[2] The first paragraph of canon 1372 establishes the principle on which all school legislation is based and which is, as it were, the fundamental norm of all Christian education. An analysis of the enactment under consideration will explain more in detail the nature as well as the import of the above assertion.

I. Those for whom Religious and Moral Training is Prescribed

" Fideles omnes ita sunt a pueritia instituendi . . . "

By the " faithful " are meant those baptized Christians who are in communion with the Church and who, as persons, are the subjects of rights and duties in the Church.[3] In law a juridical person must be distinguished from a metaphysical person. Here consideration is given to juridical persons and

[1] Cf. v. g. cc. 87, 218, 1012.

[2] Cf. Schultes-Prantner, *De Ecclesia Catholica—Praelectiones Apologeticae* (2nd ed., Parisiis: Lethielleux, 1931), pp. 317, 645.

[3] Cf. canon 87.

there is question of the rights and duties of the faithful only.[4] For those outside the body of the Church it is the natural law that at all times will be their general norm. Therefore, pagan parents are gravely obliged to impart to their children a religious and moral education which is in conformity, both negatively and positively, with the natural law.

Canon 87, in declaring that the baptized are the subjects of duties, states an article of faith. The Church of Christ is a visible society with a supernatural end, endowed with social power to command its members. Duties and rights are correlative. If a society confers rights on its members it can exact corresponding duties. These rights and duties condition the very existence of a society which, in fact, is defined as a moral union of individuals subject to the same authority and united for the attainment of a common end, by common means.[5] Each individual, therefore, as part of the social unity is bound by some obligations towards the common good and, correlatively, each individual enjoys corresponding rights.

As the society of the baptized, the Church has been instituted by Christ, and endowed with divine power for the sanctification of men.[6] In the Church, therefore, as in every other society, there exist rights and duties: of member towards member,[7] of members towards the whole,[8] of the whole towards the members.[9] Among the rights of the members of the Church one finds the right to a Christian education. This right, of its

[4] Cf. Ojetti, *Commentarium in Codicem Iuris Canonici* (Romae: apud Aedes Universitatis Gregorianae, 1927), II, can. 87; Vermeersch-Creusen, *Epitome*, I, n. 177.

[5] Gredt, *Elementa Philosophiae Aristotelico-Thomisticae* (7th ed., Friburgi Brisgoviae: Herder, 1937), II, n. 1007.

[6] "Ecclesia est societas christifidelium baptizatorum, a Christo Domino instituta, ad sanctificandos homines, potestate sacra a Christo Domino instructa."—Schultes-Prantner, *De Ecclesia Catholica*, p. 140.

[7] v. g., canon 1372.

[8] v. g., canon 1379, § 1.

[9] v. g., canons 1374 and 1381.

nature, belongs to the field of justice, and constitutes for the members of the Church an essential means for the attainment of their end.

It is true that the mission of the Church, by the will of Christ, extends to every creature.[10] But in pursuing its divinely established purpose the Church must have a care, in the first place, for those who are of the "household of the faith."[11] And why? Because even though the Church is a society which intentionally embraces all men, its actual members have a right, before all others, to whatever assistance is necessary for the attainment of their end.[12] The very existence of the Church demands this. Furthermore, just as the common good of temporal society demands a respect for the rights of the individuals composing it, so the common good of the Church requires, before all, that the means of salvation be rendered accessible to each of her members. For this reason the society founded by Christ is justly concerned with her own children before all others. This is demanded, moreover, by a due observance of the order of charity.[13]

In determining the mode of Christian education, and in fixing the time when it must begin, the Code emphatically states that it must start in the early years of childhood: *a pueritia.* This point has never been questioned within the Church, but it is being ever more and more assailed from without. The theory of absolute liberalism demands that the child be given a free

[10] Canon 1322, § 1: "Christus Dominus fidei depositum Ecclesiae concredidit, ut ipsa, Spiritu Sancto iugiter assistente, doctrinam revelatam sancte custodiret et fideliter exponeret. § 2: Ecclesiae, independenter a qualibet civili potestate, ius est et officium gentes omnes evangelicam doctrinam docendi: hanc vero rite ediscere veramque Dei Ecclesiam amplecti omnes divina lege tenentur." This principle is once more repeated here in the treatise dealing with Christian education.

[11] Galatians, VI, 10.

[12] Solieri, *Institutiones Iuris Ecclesiastici* (2nd ed., Romae: Pustet, 1921), pp. 179-180.

[13] Cf. Merkelbach, *Summa Theologiae Moralis ad Mentem D. Thomae et ad Normam Iuris Novi* (Parisiis: Desclée, 1931-1933), I, nn. 911-912.

choice between religion and irreligion. The theory of mitigated liberalism allows its followers to choose among several beliefs. The growing naturalism, which rejects the fact of original sin and the entire supernatural economy, would leave the child to its natural development, endeavoring to segregate youth from all religious influence, or at least to prevent the teaching of religion before the child attains a certain age.[14] Against all this the Church has constantly proclaimed the necessity of an early religious training: *officium gravissimum.* The history of the Church testifies to the constant repetition of the principle that youth, from its earliest years, be educated in the Catholic religion.[15] This attitude of the Church, moreover, is easily justifiable, and proof of its soundness can be furnished from a consideration of several points of view:

a) *From the theological point of view*

By Baptism the child becomes a member of the Church and immediately acquires the right to all the helps necessary for the attainment of his eternal destiny. From the very beginning of his intellectual life he has the duty of directing himself towards his supreme end and, as a consequence, he has the primordial and essential right to a Christian education, since this is an inseparable condition for the achievement of his destiny.[16]

A doctrine which would dare retard Christian education and religious orientation to a later age, under pretext of allowing the youth to choose freely, is erroneous in faith and injurious to God and the Church.[17] This liberalistic doctrine implies that the Catholic faith does not contain truths of absolute cer-

[14] Cf. Blanco Nájera, *Derecho Docente*, pp. 267-271.

[15] "Filii tibi sunt? Erudi illos, et curva illos a pueritia illorum."—Eccl., VII, 25. "Quisquis unum ex huiusmodi pueris receperit, in nomine meo, me recipit."—Mark, IX, 36.

[16] De Meester, *Juris Canonici et Iuris Canonico-Civilis Compendium* (Brugis: Desclée, 1921-1928), III, pars I, 226.

[17] Cf. Taparelli, *Saggio Teoretico di Diritto Naturale*, II, nn. 1564, 1567.

tainty which can be presented to youth at an early age. It assumes that one should adhere to the Catholic faith only in later life. Canon 1372, however, teaches an altogether different doctrine, and the Vatican Council has solemnly declared that the Church has within herself irrefutable evidences of her divine origin.[18] Liberalism, furthermore, in all its degrees has been condemned by the Church,[19] and its theories may well be disregarded when legislating for the education of youth.

b) *From the philosophical point of view*

If one considers the true notion of education, namely, the endeavor to develop integrally all the faculties of man, it is evident that moral development and religious orientation cannot be postponed until after the complete or even partial unfolding of the physical and intellectual faculties of man. Body and soul are so intimately connected in the composition of man, and exercise so great a mutual influence, that any balanced perfection of man's faculties demands that the integral education of either part be concomitant to, and coordinated with that of the other. As the organs of the body must be developed from earliest youth, so the aptitudes of the soul must be bent, so to speak, while they are still tender and manageable.[20]

c) *From the pedagogical point of view*

The same must be said, since pedagogical principles must be deduced from the combination of both theological and philosophical arguments. The subject to be educated is a being made up of body and soul, and it must never be overlooked that the equilibrium of this being has been disturbed by original sin. If the fact that the perverse inclinations of fallen man develop

[18] Sess. III, *Constitutio dogmatica de fide catholica,* cap. 3—Denzinger-Umberg, *Enchir. Symbol.*, n. 1794.

[19] Pius IX, "*Syllabus,*" prop. 77, 80—Denzinger-Umberg, *Enchir. Symbol.*, pp. 1777, 1780.

[20] Cf. Taparelli, *Saggio Teoretico di Diritto Naturale*, n. 1569.

from his earliest years be kept in mind,[21] it becomes obvious that, unless the power of intelligent choice is developed early by his moral training, the adolescent will follow the easier path of self-indulgence. The Catholic faith is not only a body of truths; it is a way of life. Therefore, unless the child is trained from the very beginning, the youth will never put forth the effort that is demanded by the rigorous character of Christian doctrine.[22] Any other view contradicts daily experience, and supposes that man is guided in his free choice by the cold light of principle and is entirely uninfluenced by the passions, which are so strong in adolescence. In a word, it is to adopt the *a priori* principle that youth is naturally good, thus denying both the fact and the effects of original sin.

It is not out of place, meanwhile, to refer to the open contradiction in the theories of those who would deny any religious training to youth or arbitrarily establish an age limit in religious and moral education, for they do their utmost to seize youth at the earliest age in order to imbue it with their politico-social theories and hypotheses.[23]

2. THE MEANING OF RELIGIOUS AND MORAL TRAINING

> "... ut non solum nihil eis tradatur quod catholicae religioni morumque honestati adversetur, sed praecipuum institutio religiosa ac moralis locum obtineat."

The latter part of the canonical enactment under consideration sets down a negative and a positive precept concerning Christian education. A negative religious and moral training

[21] Cf. Fiessinger, "Les médecins et l'école—L'éducation laïque fait fausse route—Elle ravit à l'enfant la maîtrise de soi-même," *Documentation catholique*, XIV (1925), 737.

[22] Matthew, XVI, 24. Cf. also Fiessinger, "Les médecins et l'école...," *Documentation catholique*, XIV (1925), 740.

[23] Cf. Pius XI, litt. encycl. *Non abbiamo bisogno*, 29 iun. 1931—*AAS*, XXIII (1931), 281 ff.; litt. encycl. *Mit brennender Sorge*, 14 mart. 1937—*AAS*, XXIX (1937), 145 ff.; litt. encycl. *Firmissimam constantiam*, 28 mart. 1937—*AAS*, XXIX (1937), 189-199.

is not enough, that is, it is not sufficient that youth be taught nothing against Catholic faith and good morals, but it is imperative that youth be formed in a positively Christian manner.

NEGATIVE RELIGIOUS AND MORAL TRAINING. Negative religious and moral training is an impossible goal; a silence in matters so important as religion and morality is tantamount to an implicit negation of the same. Not to speak of God to children is to deny God, and not to educate them in a Christian manner is to educate them atheistically. To disregard religion is to persuade them that religion does not mean anything, serves no purpose, and has no place either among the syntheses of knowledge or in the scheme of human behaviour. Moreover, to teach youth to disregard God or the moral law, or, what is even worse, to instill in them a denial of either God or morality, is to pervert the natural norm of life and to start youth on the path of sin and crime.[24]

POSITIVE RELIGIOUS AND MORAL TRAINING. On the contrary, there must be a positive religious and moral element throughout the entire training of Christian youth. This training is canonically called *institutio,* a word which the Code constantly uses, both in the treatise on schools and in that on catechetics.[25] The term literally signifies a building up or formation. A religious and moral formation, therefore, is the object, purpose, end, and aim of the obligation on which the legislator insists in this canon. This formation of the faithful, especially during youth, entails a twofold procedure, each part of which is distinct but at the same time inseparable from the other. This process of formation involves both doctrinal instruction and disciplinary education. The first of these concerns the training of the mind, the second, the training of the will. Mental instruction, while it effects what *in itself* is a

[24] Cf. Spalding, *Means and Ends of Education* (3rd ed., Chicago, 1901), pp. 168-173.

[25] Canons 1329-1336.

speculative rather than a practical condition, nevertheless includes not only the presentation of those principles which relate to the perfection of the intellect, but also those which pertain to the perfection of the will. It comprises, therefore, not only the principles of faith and reason but also those of morality. The second of these institutive elements is the training of the will in the practical application of those doctrines to which the mind adheres, whether this external behaviour is demanded by the tenets of faith, reason, or morality, since the truths of these categories have a practical content and import. Thus, although the two elements, the instructive and the educative, are distinct in themselves, because they have different objects as their direct and immediate aim, they are inevitably joined in the complete formation of men, for mental convictions exercise an inescapable influence on practical conduct, because conduct is dictated by convictions. Hence, it is evident that while the quality of mental training is the cause of a similar quality in voluntary conduct, the latter is the necessary complement of the former.

This, therefore, is the significance of the word *institutio* used in the canon, and in this sense it must be applied throughout the following discussion.[26]

With this in mind, one can readily see both the difference and the relation between the religious and the moral formation which the Code distinguishes. It seems that the former refers primarily to the doctrinal content. Moral formation, on the other hand, refers to the disciplinary content which, though not separable from the religious formation, extends farther than the latter. As morality is based on religion, religious formation, complemented by the moral, imbues the souls of children with a practical inclination which will constantly direct them towards good, thus causing the doctrine imparted by the teacher to take a real part in the lives of the pupils taught. This is the meaning of education in the highest sense, and, when properly used, the word denotes both these concepts.

[26] Cf. Leo XIII, ep. *Officio sanctissimo*, 22 dec. 1887, n. 9—*Fontes*, n. 596.

This religious and moral formation, according to the Code, must take the first place. The word *praecipuum* at the beginning of the proposition clearly indicates the purpose of the legislator to place above all else a religious and moral formation. The imperative text of the canon under consideration is a precise résumé of the prescriptions often given by the Holy See. It is at the same time a juridical echo of the divine precept: "Seek ye therefore first the kingdom of God, and His justice, and all these things shall be added unto you." [27]

3. SPECIAL OBLIGATION RESTING ON PARENTS AND OTHERS WHO HOLD THE PLACE OF PARENTS

> Canon 1372, § 2: Non modo parentibus ad normam can. 1113, sed etiam omnibus qui eorum locum tenent, ius et gravissimum officium est curandi christianam liberorum educationem.

The precise purpose of this section of the canon is to specify those on whom the obligation of providing this integrally religious and moral education rests. Because, as the preceding paragraph of the canon demands, this training must be begun and at least essentially completed during youth, the necessity of providing it must be primarily a parental duty, since it is to the care of their parents that children are first of all confided. Consequently, the canon begins by referring to canon 1113, in which the concern which parents must have for their children is amply delineated:

> Parentes gravissima obligatione tenentur prolis educationem tum religiosam et moralem, tum physicam et civilem pro viribus curandi, et etiam temporali eorum bono providendi.

By parents is meant here, according to the Latin terminology of the canon, fathers and mothers. To them belongs in the first place, by divine will, the education of their offspring. It is in fact the primary purpose of marriage to educate as

[27] Matthew, VI, 33.

well as to procreate children.[28] By parents, moreover, is meant all those who beget children by physical generation, whether legitimately in marriage or illicitly outside of wedlock. Hence parents of illegitimate children, natural or spurious, are also obliged to provide for the religious and moral instruction of their offspring. If parents are legitimately separated by a sentence of the ecclesiastical judge, or by a decree of the local ordinary, or by their own authority according to canons 1129 and 1131, the education of the children will rest with the innocent party, or with the Catholic party, if the other is a non-Catholic. If the good of the children demands it, the local ordinary, keeping in mind the safeguarding of the Catholic education of the children, can make an exception in either case.[29]

There are other persons, furthermore, on whom, even though they are not natural forbears, the same obligation rests, and who may be called secondary or subsidiary agents. Concerning their status with reference to the influence they exercise in Christian education and their obligation concerning the same, two categories can be distinguished: necessary agents—who assume this obligation in defect of parents, and agents freely chosen—whom the parents substitute freely.[30]

a) *Necessary agents*

When parents are dead or when they lack the capacity for imparting an education to their children, this duty and right devolves *per se* on persons designated either by nature itself, as brothers and sisters, and the ascendents, that is, grandfather and grandmother, or on persons designated by law as, for instance, guardians,[31] and sponsors. As to sponsors, canon 769 simply says that in virtue of the office which they

[28] Canon 1013, § 1. Cf. also Gredt, *Elementa Philosophiae*, II, n. 1017.

[29] Canon 1132.

[30] De Meester, *Compendium*, III, pars I, 228.

[31] Canon 89.

have accepted, it is their duty to have a lasting interest in their spiritual child, and to take good care that he lead a truly Christian life, as in the solemn ceremony they have pledged that he would do.

By this law, the Church has enlarged the family circle to include also godparents, in order that the child may be given greater security against misfortunes that might result either from the loss or neglect of the parents. The importance of this office is indicated by the canonical effects which arise by reason of ecclesiastical law from the spiritual relationship contracted by sponsor and child.[32] This obligation is truly a moral duty and obliges the sponsors to act, as the Holy Office declared,[33] in case the parents are negligent in the spiritual education of the child.

b) *Agents freely chosen*

Here there is question of those whom parents call to their aid in order to provide their children with an education. In this category is included the school, the ordinary and most stable agent to which parents entrust the education of their children, and which as such is the subject of this treatise. A school is often called the annex of the family. " Since on the one hand, the young generation," writes Pius XI, " must be trained in the arts and sciences for the advantage and prosperity of civil society, and, since, on the other hand, the family itself is unequal to this task, it was necessary to create that social institution, the school. . . . Hence, considered in its origin, the school is by its very nature an institution subsidiary and complementary to the family and to the Church." [34] Thus it is clear that parents, while conserving their proper rights, are supplanted, at least to a great extent, in the exercise of their

[32] Canons 768 and 797.

[33] Dec. 9, 1745—*Collect. S. C. de P. F.*, n. 355; cf. also the response of the Commission for the Interpretation of the Code, June 3, 1918, n. 8—*AAS*, X (1918), 346.

[34] Litt. encycl. *Divini illius Magistri*, 31 dec. 1929—*AAS*, XXII (1930), 76.

educative rights by teachers and instructors of their own choice. Their obligation, however, remains *in solidum,* that is, it is their duty to look after the education which others in their place undertake to give their children.[35]

Similarly, and in virtue of the same principle, these substitutes will have to submit themselves to the parents' reasonable prescriptions and abide by them. Indeed, it is just this collaboration and right understanding between teachers and parents which guarantees efficacious results in the training of Christian youth.[36]

As already remarked, canon 1113 indicates the characteristics of the education which parents must be solicitous to procure for the child, not only by their personal influence, but also by making use of the means which the Church and the State have provided. Proper care must be taken of the child's physical education, his life, his food, and his material status. Moreover, an effort must be made to see to it that the child becomes a worthy member of the political society in which he has to live. Finally, parents must procure for their offspring the proper religious and moral education, on which depends the eternal welfare of the child.[37] Since this eternal welfare is the immediate purpose of the Church, it is therefore, primarily with this religious and moral education that she is concerned in her legislation respecting the duties of parents and others who hold the place of parents, although she takes occasion to emphasize also the duty of parents to provide for the physical and material needs of their children. She does so, not only because it is her right and duty to supervise her subjects as to the fulfillment of all their moral duties, but also because some temporal security is required. As St. Thomas

[35] Cf. *Acta et Decreta Concilii Provincialis Mechliniensis Quarti* (1922), n. 90; Dupanloup, *L'Éducation* (Paris, 1861), II, 163, 183.

[36] Michel, *La Question Scolaire et les Principes Théologiques,* p. 70; Sertillanges, *La Famille et l'État dans l'éducation* (Paris, 1907), p. 23.

[37] Aertnys-Damen, *Theologia Moralis secundum Doctrinam S. Alphonsi de Ligorio* (11th ed., Taurinorum Augustae: Marietti, 1928), II, 366-371.

says: "A certain minimum of well-being is necessary for the practice of virtue." [38] This is also the demand of Pius XI in the midst of the present crisis.[39]

Canon 1113, then, enumerates explicitly the divers elements which enter into the notion of a veritable Christian education: a religious and moral training,[40] together with a civic and physical one, all of which must be imparted to the greatest extent possible (*pro viribus curandi*).

In reference to the rôle that parents and others who take the place of parents have in imparting to children a Christian education, the Code speaks of *ius* and *officium:* a right and a duty.[41] These two terms are correlatives. They denote things which are related as means and ends. Although they originate and exist concomitantly, the obligation logically precedes and postulates the right, for whenever a duty exists, the one obliged by it must have the power to fulfill it. Moreover, the gravity of the obligation determines the extent of the right.

The Code speaks emphatically of the gravity of this duty in two instances, in canons 1113 and 1372, and calls it an *officium gravissimum* for parents as well as for those who take the place of parents.

The gravity of an obligation is measured by the importance of the purpose to be attained and also from the disorders which its non-observance would entail. Here there is question of a primary goal, which touches the very end of human society—to allow the members of society to attain supreme happiness. To achieve this end a thorough Christian education is essential

[38] *De Regimine Principum*, I, 15.

[39] Litt. encycl. *Quadragesimo anno*, 15 maii 1931—*AAS*, XXIII (1931), 177-228.

[40] This training must have the principal place: *praecipuum locum obtineat* (canon 1372, § 1).

[41] "Est officium", remarks Cavagnis, "quia tenetur filios in vera religione instituere; est ius, quia cura filiorum cum nascuntur et sibi consulere nequeunt, est a natura auctore, ipsis patribus directe et immediate concredita."—*Institutiones Iuris Publici Ecclesiastici*, III, 14-15.

and indispensable.[42] It is, therefore, an obligation resting primarily on parents and those who take their place, nay, it devolves on every authority on earth to use the maximum of resources in order that this duty be fully accomplished.

The importance of the duty of families in regard to the Christian education of their children cannot be overestimated. This, in fact, constitutes their primary social duty both as Christians and as citizens. All those in care of souls should, therefore, constantly remind the faithful of this obligation, which is vitally important not only to themselves, but also to the Church and to temporal society. At the same time, the Catholics as citizens should be united in defending the interests and rights of family education. If, on the other hand, a conformity with Christian principles is hindered because of contrary civil legislation, it is the wish of the Church that Catholics continue to pursue their aim in as far as circumstances will allow, and later on, by legitimate means and methodical procedure, obtain greater freedom and cooperation.[43]

As to the right which parents and those who take their place have of fulfilling this very grave duty, the legislator merely mentions it, without further explaining its nature. It seems that by mentioning it first, he desires to show that the unjustifiable pretences of certain States which, far from promoting the rights of the family and the Church in the matter of education, assume the sole control of schooling, are without juridical foundation. The injustice of such a demand has already been shown in the previous chapter. It will be sufficient to recall here just a few points concerning the nature of the right itself:

1) The right of parents in matters of education is natural, inalienable, and direct.

[42] Pius XI, litt. encycl. *Divini illius Magistri*, 31 dec. 1929—*AAS*, XXII (1930), 51.

[43] Cf. Leo XIII, ep. encycl. *Affari vos*, 8 dec. 1897, nn. 6, 9—*Fontes*, n. 636; Pius XI, litt. encycl. *Non abbiamo bisogno*, 29 iun. 1931—*AAS*, XXIII (1931), 303-305.

2) The State has a mere right of protection, of encouragement, and of exigence, but as to this latter its right is rather limited, since it is not an original right, but merely one of a devolved character.[44]

3) Every agent of education must be directly subordinated to the Church in whatever concerns religion and morals.[45] A pontificial document defines well the position of families in this regard: " Hisce in officiis, simul cum procreatione liberorum susceptis, noverint patresfamilias, totidem iura inesse secundum naturam et aequitatem, atque esse eiusmodi, de quibus nihil liceat sibi remittere, nihil cuivis hominum potestati liceat detrahere, quum, officiis solvi quibus homo teneatur ad Deum, sit per hominem nefas." [46]

4. THE PRINCIPLE OF RELIGIOUS TRAINING WITH REFERENCE TO THE SCHOOL

> Canon 1373, § 1: In qualibet elementaria schola, pueris pro eorum aetate tradenda est institutio religiosa.
>
> § 2. Iuventus, quae medias . . . scholas frequentat, pleniore religionis doctrina excolatur, et locorum Ordinarii curent ut id fiat per sacerdotes zelo et doctrina praestantes.

This canon sets forth a double norm for religious training in the school. It states first of all the kind of religious training which the school must provide, and secondly, the manner in which it is to be given.

In substance the obligation imposed by the canon concerning the religious element in the schools is double. It comprehends, according to the meaning of the word *institutio,* as explained above, religion as an instructive element or the knowledge of the fundamental principles of religion, and also religion as an educative element or the practice of these principles.[47]

[44] Cf. Gredt, *Elementa Philosophiae*, II, n. 1044, 6.

[45] Canons 1381 and 1382.

[46] Leo XIII, ep. *Officio sanctissimo*, 22 dec. 1887, n. 9—*Fontes*, n. 596.

[47] Blanco Nájera, *Derecho Docente*, p. 317.

This is but a logical consequence of the principles considered in the preceding canon: the obligation resting on all the faithful to be trained in a positive Christian manner from the earliest years, and the duty of parents and of those who take their place to impart a Christian education to their children.

As was mentioned above, the school is an institution derived from the family and conducted for the family. It forms a second family for the children. Over it there must necessarily be extended that guardianship which God has granted to parents in reference to their children. It is, therefore, indispensable that school, teachers, and parents be of common accord, and that there be no antagonism or spiritual incompatibility among them. The very obligation which rests on parents extends therefore also to the school.

In the pedagogical theories, however, which have appeared frequently since the French Revolution, there is a general tendency to delete the religious element entirely from the school curricula.[48] At present, too, many modern writers on education regard the work of education as something entirely separated from religion. The school, according to their theories, should be a place where mere citizens are formed, where the development of youth's faculties should aim no longer at the attainment of Heaven and supernatural things, but where they should be directed to mundane problems so as to train youth exclusively as members of human society.[49]

The Christian point of view is quite the opposite. To separate religion from the school is to go against a precedent established centuries ago by the Church, which cannot conceive

[48] Cavagnis, *Institutiones Iuris Publici Ecclesiastici*, III, 16-17; Spalding, *Means and Ends of Education*, pp. 156-159.

[49] "Nicht für die Zwecke des Himmels und für übernatürliche Dinge, sondern für ihre irdischen Aufgaben und als Mitglieder der menschlichen Gesellschaft sollen die Kinder erzogen werden."—Schulz, *Die Schulreform der Sozialdemokratie* (2nd ed., Berlin, 1919), p. 89. Cf. Scharnagl, *Religionsunterricht und Schule nach dem neuen kirchlichen Gesetzbuch* (2nd ed., Gladbach, 1923), p. 16.

of a non-religious training.[50] The Church, in fact, has constantly demanded that religion be a vital part of the school program, and that it be taught with the other branches of learning.[51] She has also condemned the assertion of those who would uphold a method of education separated from Catholic faith and concerned only, or primarily, with knowledge of natural things, and the ends of earthly social life.[52]

As to the manner in which religious training is to be provided by the school, the canon states that it must be proportioned to the capacity of the students, so that it will be more complete in the higher institutions and given by priests of outstanding zeal and learning. These two distinct aspects of the canon will be considered separately.

A. *The Kind of Religious Training to be Provided in the School*

To prove adequately the precepts contained in canon 1373, three postulates are to be set down. These postulates are so intimately connected with the question at issue, that they are constantly used by canonists[53] in defending the necessity of religious training in the schools:—the instruction of youth cannot be separated from education; both must be moral and religious; this latter among Catholics must be Catholic.

1) Instruction of youth cannot be separated from education.

The purpose and aim of schools, particularly the lower schools, is not merely the intellectual development of the pupils, but also their practical formation, namely, a training of the will towards good. The reason why there must be a

[50] Cf. cc. 10, 12, 13, D. XXXVII; Cassiodorus, *De instit. divin. litter.—MPL*, LXX, 1105, praef.

[51] Leo X, const. *Supernae dispositionis*, 5 maii 1514, § 32—*Fontes*, n. 65; Leo XII, const. *Quod divina sapientia*, rubrica—*Bull. Rom. Continuatio*, VIII, 95.

[52] Pius IX, "*Syllabus*," prop. 48—Denzinger-Umberg, *Enchir. Symbol.*, n. 1748.

[53] Cavagnis, *Institutiones Iuris Publici Ecclesiastici*, III, 18; Cappello, *Summa Iuris Publici Ecclesiastici*, pp. 501-503.

union between instruction and education lies in the fact, proved by experience and prudent judgment, that whenever a teaching that disregards education is imparted, little or no profit is obtained and the very work of education is rendered more difficult. For though instruction itself or the teaching of principles, as distinct from education which concerns the practice of these principles, is necessarily primary in point of time, it is not primary in the order of importance. Instruction is related to education as the means are related to the end. The mind must be trained, but precisely in order that the will may be inclined to act; otherwise mental training is barren and sterile, and is frustrated in its natural function. The intrinsic reason, then, for such an inseparability consists in the very unity of the human person. All the faculties must be developed harmoniously and concomitantly, if their natural unity is to be practically duplicated and the natural balance of the faculties preserved. If, on the contrary, children at school are taught only what is conducive to the formation of the intellect, they will fail to grasp the real importance of what they have learned, and recognizing no necessary connection between principles and practice, they will be governed in their conduct rather by caprice and passion than by fundamental truths. Leo XIII well proved this point in his letter to the Cardinal Vicar of Rome when he said that the judgment of Solomon cannot be reproduced without fatal consequences. That is to say, the separation of mental instruction from the education of the will is a disastrous division of the child's naturally united faculties.[54]

[54] "E questo esige altresì la natura del fanciullo . . . Non si può a nessun patto rinnovare sopra il fanciullo il giudizio di Salomone e dimezzarlo con un taglio irragionevole e crudele tra la sua intelligenza e la sua volontà: mentre si prende a coltivare la prima, fa d'uopo avviare la seconda al conseguimento degli abiti virtuosi e dell'ultimo fine. Chi nell'educazione trascura la volontà, concentrando tutti gli sforzi alla cultura della mente, giunge a fare dell'istruzione un'arma pericolosa in mano dei malvagi."—Ep. *In mezzo*, 26 iun. 1878, n. 4—*Fontes*, n. 574.

The same doctrine is but the repetition of the constant teaching of sound pedagogy whether old or new.[55]

2) Not only must there be no separation between instruction and education, but both must be of a moral and religious character.

Education must be moral, that is, children and youth must be taught according to those moral principles which are based on the natural law, and which will lead them on the right path by directing them to do good and avoid evil. The same education must furthermore be religious.

It is deplorable that today education has in many schools departed from this general norm of divine positive law. Even Catholic teaching has been often impaired to a great extent in the effort to attain its end by being forced to follow the State program, from the elementary to the higher grades.[56] The Catholic view of this question is clearly defined. It rests upon the general ground that man is created for a supernatural end, and that the Church is the divinely appointed agency to help him to attain his supreme destiny. If education is a training for completeness of life, its primary element is religious, for complete life is life in God. Hence, one may not assume an attitude toward the child which might imply that life apart from God could be anything else than broken and fragmentary. A complete man is not one whose mind alone is active and enlightened; the complete man is he who is alive in all his faculties. The truly human is found not only in knowledge alone, but also in faith, in hope, in love. Religion is the vital element in character, and to treat it as though it were but an incidental phase of man's life is to blunder in a matter of the highest and most serious import.

[55] Cf. Dupanloup, *L'Éducation*, I, 18; Paquet, *Droit Public de l'Église—L'Église et l'éducation à la lumière de l'histoire et des principes chrétiens* (Québec, 1909), p. 265.

[56] Guay, "Le canon fondamental du traité 'De Scholis,'" *Revue de l'Université d'Ottawa*, VII (1937), 204*.

Religion cannot be left optional nor may it be excluded from the curriculum. If the chief end of education is virtue, if conduct is three-fourths of life, if character is indispensable, while knowledge is only useful, then it follows that religion—which, more than any other vital influence has power to create virtue, to inspire conduct, and to mould character—must enter into all the processes of education and find its place in all schools. To leave religion out or to make it optional is to misunderstand the nature of youth and to exclude or make possible the exclusion of a vital element in life as well as in knowledge.[57]

Religion is a necessary part of training because moral principles that are not based on religion lose their authority and strength. Education implies a direct training of the will; and the ideal held up must be a moral system, which presupposes religion as its requisite and adequate foundation. Religion, in fact, teaches what are the obligations which bind man to God, how he is destined for God as his ultimate end, how in God man finds the only lasting sanction for the keeping of the moral order, so that, once the concept of God is taken away or the tie of religion broken, there can be no concept of morality.[58]

Religious and moral training is indeed necessary in order that the child may reach its supernatural end, and it is indispensable even for good citizenship. It is, as Leo XIII stresses in his letter to the bishops of Canada,[59] a dangerous error to believe that a child may be trained without religion to a morally strong character, for one cannot train to virtue, if its foundation has not first been laid by a firm belief in God. This principle should be applied not only to private but also to public life, for if civil order is to have permanence, it should

[57] Leo XIII, ep. *In mezzo*, 26 iun. 1878, n. 7—*Fontes*, n. 574; Cavagnis, *Institutiones Iuris Publici Ecclesiastici*, III, 26.

[58] Cf. Leo XIII, ep. encycl. *Nobilissima*, 8 febr. 1884, n. 4—*Fontes*, n. 590; litt. encycl. *Sapientiae*, 10 ian. 1890, nn. 16, 20—*Fontes*, n. 605; Cappello, *Summa Iuris Publici Ecclesiastici*, pp. 502-503.

[59] Ep. encycl. *Affari vos*, 8 dec. 1897, n. 3—*Fontes*, n. 636.

be founded upon religion, morality, and the law of God. Hence, Leo XIII adds: " Whoever conducts teaching in such a fashion that it has nothing in common with religion, exposes what is good and noble to perdition, and does not afford any support to his country; but rather will lead the human race to destruction and perdition." [60]

3) Religious training for Catholic youths must be Catholic.

Since religion is necessary in education and consequently in the school, it cannot be of a general nature, for such does not exist, but it must be of the nature of the denomination to which the child belongs. Furthermore, since Jesus Christ founded only one Church, and Catholics recognize this Church as the Catholic Church,[61] for Catholic children there must be only one Catholic education which, at the same time, is the only authentically Christian education.

It is well to recall here the conditions for Christian education, as set forth by Pius XI, in his encyclical letter on this very subject.

a) As to the instructive element:—the teachers and the curriculum must be Christian.

" Perfect schools are the result not so much of good methods as of good teachers, teachers who are thoroughly prepared and well-grounded in the matter they have to teach; who possess the intellectual and moral qualifications required by their important office; who cherish a pure and holy love for the youth confided to them, because they love Jesus Christ and His Church, of which these are the children of predilection; and who have, therefore, sincerely at heart the true good of family and country." [62]

[60] Ep. encycl. *Militantis Ecclesiae*, 1 aug. 1897, n. 5—*Fontes*, n. 635; cf. also Scharnagl, *Religionsunterricht und Schule*, p. 17.

[61] Vatican Council, *Constitutio dogmatica de Ecclesia Christi*, sess. IV—Denzinger-Umberg, *Enchir. Symbol.*, n. 1821.

[62] Litt. encycl. *Divini illius Magistri*, 31 dec. 1929—*AAS*, XXII (1930), 80-81.

" In such schools, in harmony with the Church and the Christian family, the various branches of secular learning will not enter into conflict with a religion to the manifest detriment of education. And if, when occasion arises, it be deemed necessary to have the students read authors, propounding false doctrine, for the purpose of refuting it, this will be done after due preparation and with such an antidote of sound doctrine, that it will not only do no harm, but will be an aid to the Christian formation of youth." [63] The teaching of the Catholic religion must be an integral part of the curriculum, where it must hold the most important place, thus forming the crown of the youth's entire training.

b) As to the educative element:—the atmosphere must be Christian.

" In order to obtain perfect education, it is of the utmost importance to see that all those conditions which surround the child during the period of his formation, in other words, that the combination of circumstances which are called environment, correspond exactly to the end proposed." [64] How is this possible in the pagan atmosphere which characterizes the present-day world? Will it be necessary to practice a sort of isolation? Certainly not, even though the conditions of modern life require more than ordinary vigilance of those who are responsible for the formation of the child. " This necessary vigilance does not demand that young people be removed from the society in which they must live and save their souls; but that today more than ever they should be forewarned and forearmed as Christians against the seductions and the errors of the world. . . . Let them be what Tertullian wrote of the first Christians, and what Christians of all times ought to be, ' sharers in the possession of the world, not of its errors.' " [65]

[63] Pius XI, *loc. cit.*, p. 79.

[64] Pius XI, *loc. cit.*, p. 73.

[65] Pius XI, *loc. cit.*, p. 82.

Although these two elements in the formation of youth must be the concern of both parents and school, the instructive element is predominantly supplied by the latter, and the educative element by the former of these agencies. It may even happen that the instructive element is almost entirely beyond the capacity of the parents, immersed as they are in temporal cares. On the other hand, while the school is perhaps the only suitable agency for instruction as such, it cannot exclude the educative element from its purpose, but must share the responsibility for this with the parents. To quote Leo XIII: "It is necessary that the young be instructed in religion not only at certain fixed times, but also that every other subject taught be permeated with Christian piety. If this is wanting, if this sacred atmosphere does not pervade and warm the hearts of masters and scholars alike, little good can be expected from any kind of learning, and considerable harm will often be the consequence."[66]

The principle laid down in canon 1373, therefore, is the principle on which is founded a school that complies with the demands of the Church and at the same time endeavors to bring about among Catholic youths the fulfillment of their obligations. For it is this Catholic religious spirit, actuating teachers and pupils, manifesting itself in the entire educational system, and bearing the burden of the work of education, that constitutes the essence of the Catholic school. In a true sense of the word, this spirit makes it an *Einheitschule,* because it creates inherent unity: unity of curriculum, union between teacher and pupil, between school and Christian family. It is this very unity which alone can endow education with abiding success.[67]

The Church, realizing the importance of religion in the education of children, both as Christians and as worthy members of human society, sets down the principles to be followed.

[66] Ep. encycl. *Militantis Ecclesiae,* 1 aug. 1897, n. 6—*Fontes,* n. 635.

[67] Scharnagl, *Religionsunterricht und Schule,* p. 20.

Whenever these principles are not heeded, she demands the erection of her own schools, making it obligatory upon parents to send their children to these schools, where they may receive an education in conformity with and founded upon Christian religion and morality. It is well to remark here that the Church, in obliging her faithful to attend such Catholic schools, does not infringe on the rights of parents which, as described in the preceding chapter, is absolute and inalienable concerning matters of a strictly profane nature, but subordinate to the regulations of the Church in those which are of a spiritual import. True, apart from religion, purely profane subjects are also taught in the Catholic schools. The Church, however, in her command does not touch these subjects directly, but only by reason of the religious element which is essential in the school and which the pupil could not receive otherwise, much less in the public common institutions. This is especially true of the United States, where the public schools are generally considered as a real danger to Catholic youth.[68]

B. *The Manner in which Religious Training is to be Given in the School*

As to the manner in which religious training must be provided in the school, canon 1373 establishes two principles. The first concerns the degree of this training, with specific reference to the instructive element; the second considers the teachers themselves by whom this training is to be given, and has particular reference to the educative element. In all cases, the degree of religious instruction must be sufficient for the needs of the students.

In the elementary schools it must be accommodated to immature minds, and relatively submissive wills. The principles must be presented as simply as possible, and their application must be adapted to the comparatively sheltered life of the

[68] S. C. S. Off., instr. (ad Ep. Stat. Foeder. Americae Septentrion.), 24 nov. 1875—*Fontes*, n. 1046; *Acta et Decreta Concilii Plen. Baltim. Tertii*, n. 199, IV.

students. The child's training, however, even in the elementary grades, while remaining as simple as possible, must be progressive.

In the higher grades, it will be not only possible but even necessary that a more profound training be given, since the students are mentally more developed and have gained wider experience. They are more alive to the world and to its dangers, and unless proportionately equipped for life, they will succumb to those dangers. When a youth reaches the stage of secondary schooling, he faces problems which are entirely new to him and which influence his conduct at a time when he is beginning to think for himself. His mind develops and reaches out towards new horizons; he begins to reason upon facts which before he took for granted. The very subject matter of his curriculum may distract him somewhat from the religious atmosphere in which he has been living; the development of his body and of his inquisitive mind together with the many dangers facing adolescence, render him more prone to deviate from the path of virtue.[69] It is for these reasons that the Holy See in its manifold instructions issued in this regard, and in the Code of Canon Law embodying them, demands that a more thorough religious training be given to youth in the intermediate and higher schools.[70]

Naturally, the teaching of religion, like any other teaching, if it is to be at all efficacious, will have to be imparted according to rules and pedagogical procedure. Children in the elementary grades will have to be treated differently than youths in the more advanced classes. It will be the concern of the local ordinary to establish the norms which are to regulate the

[69] Cf. Lebacqz, "L'enseignement religieux dans les collèges," *NRT*, LII (1925), 137-138; Delcuve, "Où l'enseignement de la Religion rencontrera-t-il la jeunesse moderne?," *NRT*, LXV (1938), 1177.

[70] Cf. Lavallée, "Réflexions sur l'instruction religieuse dans les collèges catholiques," *Revue Apologétique*, XXXIII (1921), 5, 20; Creusen, "L'enseignement de la Religion—Documents pontificaux," *NRT*, LII (1925), 163-175.

teaching of religion in the schools of his diocese.[71] This may be done either in the diocesan synod or independently thereof. In both instances, however, the ordinary cannot prohibit anything that is certainly and expressly commanded by the Code; for instance, no law could be enacted whereby those who have already received some instruction at home or in the parish classes would be exempt from further instruction in the school. Neither can he permit anything which is forbidden by the common law.[72] Rather, it may be said that the legislative efforts of the bishop will be directed to determining more specifically the prescriptions of the common law, according to conditions as they exist in each particular diocese.

Nothing is said in paragraph 1 of canon 1373 as to who is to teach religion in the primary schools. It is, indeed, important that mentally well-trained and morally exemplary persons be entrusted with this work. However, because the very young child will believe and behave, more because of his awe of authority than from reasoned conviction, it is relatively not so important in the lower grades as it is in the higher that the teachers of religion be capable not only of convincing the students of the truth, but also of influencing their moral inclinations and tendencies in the face of more conscious and serious temptations.

The teaching of religion, being part of the magisterium of the Church, belongs *ex officio* to the bishops. Because it is practically impossible for them to discharge this duty personally, they must associate others with themselves in the work. Those best equipped to substitute for the bishops in this regard are obviously the priests, and these should always be first considered. Although the text of the canon does not expressly demand that they be employed in the elementary schools, they

[71] Canon 1336; cf. S. C. C., decret. *Provido sane*, 12 ian. 1935—*AAS*, XXVII (1935), 148.

[72] Vermeersch-Creusen, *Epitome*, I, 271; Wernz-Vidal, *Ius Canonicum* (Romae: apud Aedes Universitatis Gregorianae, 1923-1938), II, 631.

should no doubt be appointed to this work wherever possible. However, in consideration of other canons,[73] it is also permitted to make use of other persons, for instance, religious or laymen, for the teaching of religion. In the primary schools the entire class work is often conducted by one teacher only. It is fitting, therefore, that this teacher also take care of the religious instruction. Thus he may be better enabled to impart it in keeping with the ability of the students. In this way the very work of the teacher and school program will be organically attached to religion, responding more effectively to the demands of the Holy See that the entire curriculum of the primary schools be primarily and essentially a religious work.[74] The practice of having one teacher for all subjects is generally followed in the Catholic primary schools of this country. In many countries of Europe, particularly in Alsace-Lorraine and Luxemburg, this had been found to have great advantages also in the common schools, so that in 1912 when the civil law of the latter country did away with this practice of one teacher great complaint was made on the part of Catholics, especially voiced by the hierarchy.[75]

As to the teaching of religion in the intermediate schools, paragraph 2 of canon 1373 specifically mentions that priests be selected by the local ordinary for this work. These priests must, moreover, be conspicuous for their zeal and learning.

Although the canon suggests that the teaching of religion in such schools be done by a priest, it does not seem to exclude the cooperation or even the employment of others. Undoubtedly a priest, being so familiar with the truths of religion, is more qualified for this office. With his knowledge of profane sciences, too, he will be able to explain to students the relation-

[73] Canons 1333, 1334.

[74] Pius IX, ep. *Quum non sine*, 14 iul. 1864, n. 4—*Fontes*, n. 539; Leo XIII, const. *Romanos Pontifices*, 8 maii 1881, §§ 18-19—*Fontes*, n. 582.

[75] Michel, *La Question Scolaire et les Principes Théologiques*, pp. 87-90; Rogmann, "La question scolaire dans le Grand Duché de Luxembourg," *Questions Ecclésiastiques*, II (1913), 145.

ship between faith and reason, and, if the need arises, he may apply a Christian antidote for possible attacks or misrepresentations on the part of other teachers. From his store of experience and knowledge of human nature, he will be able efficiently and effectively to direct the students in their personal problems, and because he will usually enjoy their confidence, he will have the opportunity to guide them in the practical application of the truths they have learned and so strengthen their character. If however, some exemplary and well-instructed layman is at hand, he may be used by the ordinary for this teaching without violating the spirit of the canon. This appears clearer when considered in the light of the provisions made in Concordats between the Holy See and various nations,[76] when viewed according to the mind of the Roman Pontiffs as expressed in their encyclical letters, and when understood in the pronouncements of Roman documents, dealing with the teaching of religion.[77] The decree *Provido sane* [78] asks especially for the cooperation of those members of Catholic Action groups that are specifically prepared for this work, since it is the purpose of Catholic Action to collaborate with the Church in her teaching mission.

In the schools of the Church this work is better carried on by priests. Indeed, the real purpose for which so many priests and religious undertake the teaching of science and letters is practically no other than that they may have an opportunity of teaching the truths of religion and thus reaching the very souls of the students.[79]

[76] Cf. for instance: art. 36 of the Concordat with Italy—*AAS*, XXI (1929), 291; art. 20, § 2 of the Conc. with Rumania—*AAS*, XXI (1929), 449; art. 6, § 1 of the Conc. with Austria—*AAS*, XXVI (1934), 255.

[77] Cf. Leo XIII, ep. encycl. *Constanti Hungarorum*, 2 sept. 1893, n. 7—*Fontes*, n. 620, where it is explicitly mentioned that *viri probati et docti* be used in the teaching of religion in the intermediate and higher schools.

[78] S. C. C., 12 ian. 1935, n. 4—*AAS*, XXVII (1935), 152.

[79] Lebacqz, "L'enseignement religieux dans les collèges," *NRT*, LII (1925), 141.

It may be permitted to remark here that the principle of canon 1373 is concerned with those schools in which a general education is imparted. Would this include also professional schools where, for instance, merely technical subjects are taught? There is no doubt that religious instruction is useful even in these institutions, though they do not seem to be included among the schools, as this term is understood by the canon. The subjects taught in professional schools have no proximate connection with a moral formation or with the truths of religion. Therefore, if the students attending these schools receive a religious instruction elsewhere, such as is generally given in the church or in the parish classes, it seems that this would suffice for them.[80]

[80] Cavagnis, *Institutiones Iuris Publici Ecclesiastici*, III, 39.

Important in the question of education and the school, because touching religion and morality, is the matter of sex-education. Much has been written on this subject of late, but canonically two documents are of importance:—the letter of Pius XI, *Divini illius Magistri*, of December 31, 1929 (*AAS*, XXII [1930], 71), and the decree of the Holy Office of March 21, 1931 (*AAS*, XXIII [1931], 118), the latter referring for its practical application to the former. Since the matter does not belong to the school, no further consideration will be given to the problem in this study. It may be remarked, however, that neither Pius XI nor the decree of the Holy Office condemns teaching of sex knowledge; the prohibition obtains only when this is done publicly, indiscriminately, and with exposure to danger, not when it is given privately, by the proper persons, and when deemed necessary. The persons best suited for this work are the parents who, more than others, are intimate with and enjoy the confidence of their children.

For a further study, cf. Creusen, "Actes du Saint Siège—Décret sur *l'éducation sexuelle* et sur *l'eugénique*," *NRT*, LVIII (1931), 525-529; Beecher, "The Holy Office Decree on the Angelic Virtue," *IER*, V ser., LII (1938), 561-569. The latter says that the action of the Holy Office was taken after the ecclesiastical authority of the archdiocese of New York had reported to Rome the fact that in the State schools there had begun a campaign of teaching youth about sex-organs. The mind of the Church is that in schools youth be taught a love for virtue and modesty. The Church then depends upon parents and other proper persons to instruct children about the facts of life at the proper place and time. Cf. also S. C. de Relig., litt. 23 aug. 1924, *d—Monitore Ecclesiastico*, IV ser., X (1928), 298.

CHAPTER VIII

Attendance at Non-Catholic Institutions

1. Prohibition and Tolerance

Canon 1374: Pueri catholici scholas acatholicas, neutras, mixtas, quae nempe etiam acatholicis patent, ne frequentent. Solius autem Ordinarii loci est decernere, ad normam instructionum Sedis Apostolicae, in quibus rerum adiunctis et quibus adhibitis cautelis, ut periculum perversionis vitetur, tolerari possit ut eae scholae celebrentur.

So far the Code of Canon Law has established the positive principles and the rules to follow in the important subject of Christian education. With the present canon a negative principle is laid down, namely, a prohibition which is to be drawn from the established principles.

The problem dealing with the attendance at other than Catholic schools is partly old and partly new. Already at the beginning of the Christian era the Christians were confronted with the problem of attending the pagan schools of the time. Although no specific legislation was then formulated, the Fathers of the Church warned parents against placing their children under pagan tutelage, and the bishops, whenever possible, assigned the office of teaching to priests and other Christians, in order that the youth of that time could receive a Christian education.[1] During the Middle Ages the instruction as well as the whole education of youth was confined to the Church.[2] With the sixteenth century, however, the prob-

[1] Cf. Part one—Historical synopsis, pp. 13, 15 ff.

[2] For the status of heretics and schismatics during this period, cf. Choupin, "Hérésie," *Dictionnaire Apologétique de la Foi Catholique* (ed. D'Alès, Paris: Beauchesne, 1911-1922), II, 453-457.

lem appeared anew, and ever since then there can be distinguished two successive phases in the organization of non-Catholic schools: the denominational Protestant institutions, and the public State schools whether lay, neutral, or mixed. Provision relative to such and similar schools is to be found in the canon here considered.

Two parts can be distinguished in canon 1374: the first declares a general prohibition, the second establishes with certain restrictions and measures a possible exception to this prohibition.

A) *Prohibition*

> "Pueri catholici scholas acatholicas, neutras, mixtas . . . ne frequentent."

Literally the present canon mentions only children—*pueri,* and would thereby seem to refer only to the more elementary schools.[3] Canonists do not all agree on the extent of the actual precept, but all are unanimous in admitting some kind of prohibition. Some, like De Meester,[4] include under the term "school", institutions of every rank and grade, and consequently apply the ecclesiastical precept to every school age. Blat[5] and Nájera,[6] on the contrary, restrict the same ecclesiastical precept to children of elementary school age (canon 1373, § 1), and allow youth more advanced in studies (canon 1373, § 2) to regulate their conduct by principles of natural and divine law (which forbid one to expose himself to the occasion of sin and the loss of faith), and by particular regulations as set forth by the ecclesiastical authority. While practically there will be no difficulty, canonically the view of

[3] Cf. Vermeersch, "Quinam sunt pueri de quibus in can. 1373, § 1, et 1374," *Periodica,* XVII (1928), 145*-148*.

[4] *Compendium,* III, pars I, 231.

[5] *Commentarium Textus Codicis Iuris Canonici* (Romae: Collegio "Angelico," 1921-1927), III, pars III, n. 257.

[6] *Derecho Docente,* p. 330.

De Meester seems to be preferred, because the term *pueri* in this canon is used generically, and thus includes youth of any school age. It would, indeed, be a fallacy to understand *pueri* in the sole light of canon 88, § 3. Besides, according to canon 6, n. 2, those canons which are in consonance with the old law must be given the same interpretation as the old. Now, the former law speaks of *pueri* in a general sense and applies the prohibition to any grade of school.[7]

The Church, meanwhile, takes care to determine specifically which schools are forbidden. This she does in order to avoid any misinterpretation of her law designed to protect souls. Such misinterpretation might arise, for instance, if one, while not daring to attend schools hostile to Catholicism, would, nevertheless, attend a neutral school. It is conceivable that this practice might be rather common, had not the Church made definite provision to the contrary.

The term non-Catholic school (*schola acatholica*) can be understood either in a general or a specific sense. Generally speaking, one would consider as non-Catholic, any school the distinct purpose of which is not the imparting of Catholic education or training. In this sense it will comprehend neutral, mixed, and lay institutions. More specifically, it may mean either an anti-Catholic school, namely, an institution the principles of which are directly opposed to Catholic principles, or a non-Catholic school, whether it propounds a heretical, a schismatic or a pagan religion. It is in this more restricted rather than in the wider sense that the Code uses the term *acatholica*, since it distinguishes non-Catholic from neutral, and mixed schools; therefore, the two latter classes must not be understood as being mentioned in the canon merely by way of example.[8]

[7] Cf. particularly S. C. de Prop. Fide, litt. encycl. (ad Ep. Canad.), 14 mart. 1895 — *Fontes*, n. 4932; S. C. Ep. et Reg., instr. 21 iul. 1896. — *Fontes*, n. 2031.

[8] Cf. Schmid, "De vi verborum 'acatholicus, secta acatholica, minister acatholicus' in Iure Canonico," *Apollinaris*, IV (1931), 559.

Neutral schools are those which in many localities are commonly called "public." Their type is at present increasing in almost every country and they have as their general goal the temporal end of man to the exclusion of any specific religious tenet.[9] A neutral school is also frequently called lay. This expression, of French origin, when applied to schools, designates an institution independent of ecclesiastical authority, in regard both to its teaching and to its personnel. Many,[10] however, do not agree that "lay" and "neutral" are interchangeable. According to them, a lay school is not agnostic and silent in the face of spiritual problems. On the contrary, it opens the way to a free discussion of any religious, moral, or philosophical question; and, without teaching one religion rather than another, puts them all before the eyes of the student, cultivates in the pupil a critical sense, so as to help him to think for himself in a way supposedly more fitting to his individual mind and conscience. The Sovereign Pontiffs have frequently spoken of these schools as being in reality centers of religious indifferentism and dangerous to Catholic youth.[11]

A mixed school, finally, can be one to which youth of both sexes are admitted, and then the school is termed a coeducational institution. Again it may be one which receives children of any religious denomination. Religious instruction is here imparted as a unit of the school curriculum, but is taught separately according to the different beliefs of the pupils. Often, too, tenets common to all religions are taught indiscriminately to the students. The present canon speaks of mixed schools

[9] For further knowledge concerning school neutrality and its different divisions, cf. Monti. *La Libertà della Scuola*, p. 44.

[10] Cf. Blanco Nájera, *Derecho Docente*, p. 325.

[11] Leo XIII, ep. encycl. *Nobilissima*, 8 febr. 1884, n. 4—*Fontes*, n. 590; Pius XI, litt. encycl. *Divini illius Magistri*, 31 dec. 1929—*AAS*, XXII (1930), 76-77.

only in the latter meaning: *quae nempe etiam acatholicis patent.*[12]

The Church forbids attendance at any of these various schools, for she finds in them a danger to the faith of her children. These dangers may exist by reason of the teachers themselves, of the subjects taught (*curriculum*), or of the promiscuous association with students of so many different beliefs.

The teachers, in fact, because of the very close association existing between them and the pupils whom they teach, inevitably exercise an influence over them.[13] Now, if the teacher is a non-Catholic, he will easily influence his pupils according to his way of thinking, and he will imbue their minds with error or, to say the least, with indifferentism. "One must be a novice in human affairs," wrote the Holy Office, "who does not see the dangers which teachers not of the fold bring into

[12] Although no canon is found in the Code of Canon Law referring to coeducation, the mind of the Church is against this practice and urges that, whenever possible, boys be separated from girls. Pius XI wrote in this regard: ". . . fallax atque christianae institutioni infensa illa adolescentes instruendi ratio habenda est, quam vulgo coeducationem appellant; eorum enim qui ipsam tuentur, bene multi idcirco tuentur quia aut non considerant aut negant, protoparentum labe vitiatum nasci hominem, plerique vero omnes, quia tali notionum perturbatione laborant ut legitimum hominum convictum habeant quasi quendam virorum ac feminarum omnibus plane rationibus parium inconditum acervum. . . . Alter autem et alter sexus a Dei sapientia ad hoc sunt constituti ut in familia et societate mutuo se compleant et in unum quid apte coalescant, ob illud ipsum corporis animique discrimen quo inter se differunt, quod idcirco in educatione atque institutione tenendum, immo fovendum est per aptam distinctionem ac separationem, aetatibus ac conditionibus congruentem. Eiusmodi vero praecepta, ad christianae prudentiae praescriptum, *tempestive atque opportune servanda sunt . . . in scholis omnibus, praesertim per trepidos adolescentiae annos,* unde totius ferme futurae vitae ratio omnino pendet."—Litt. encycl. *Divini illius Magistri,* 31 dec. 1929—*AAS,* XXII (1930), 72-73. Italics are the author's. Cf. also S. C. de Prop. Fide, litt. (ad Archiep. Ultraiecten.), 16 nov. 1870—*Collect. S. C. de P. F.,* n. 1359; *Acta et Decreta Concilii Plenarii Americae Latinae* (1899), n. 690.

[13] Cf. Casotti, *Maestro e Scolaro — Saggio di Filosofia dell'Educazione* (Milano: Soc. Ed. "Vita e Pensiero," 1930), p. 17.

the class-room. In season and out of season they take every possible occasion to circumvent the simplicity of youth and to bend it, so to speak, into conformity with their tenets; their schemes becoming even more efficacious as they are secret." [14]

The curriculum of these schools also presents a constant peril to the faith of Catholic youth. If the curriculum is devoid of all religious instruction, the pupil is deprived of knowledge most necessary for life, without which one cannot live as a Christian.[15] If all religious doctrines are presented indiscriminately, the result for the student will most frequently be an attitude of indifferentism, which allows him to regard one faith as of equal worth with another. If religious doctrine is taught but divorced from the rest of the curriculum, the pupil is not likely to set a just value on its practical significance in life, but will consider it as a rather speculative problem.

Finally, the daily intimate companionship of Catholic youth with those of other faiths or of no faith whatever, militates against the security of the Catholics' faith in much the same way and for the same reasons as the influence of the teacher is detrimental thereto. Moreover, Catholics in such schools are generally a numerical minority, of inferior social station, possessed of much less wealth than their non-Catholic companions, and as a result develop an inferiority complex which they may ultimately attribute to their being Catholics. The outcome of this is all too frequently the abandonment of their faith.[16]

It is in the light of these manifold dangers that one must gauge the force of the prohibitive precepts of the divine, the natural, and the ecclesiastical law.

[14] S. C. S. Off., instr. 21 mart. 1866—*Fontes*, n. 992.

[15] S. C. S. Off., instr. (ad Ep. Stat. Foeder. Americae Septentrion.), 24 nov. 1875—*Fontes*, n. 1046.

[16] Cf. S. C. de Prop. Fide, litt. encycl. (ad Ep. Angliae), 6 aug. 1867—*Fontes*, n. 4868; instr. 25 apr. 1868—*Fontes*, n. 4873; *Acta et Decreta Concilii Plenarii Quebecensis* (1909), n. 277.

Faith, together with sanctifying grace, is the greatest gift of God to the soul. To run the avoidable risk of losing it is to offend the Author of this gift and, at the same time, implies putting oneself in the occasion of danger to the soul. Now there can be no doubt that attendance at any other than Catholic schools constitutes a more or less proximate occasion of losing the faith. It is for this reason that the natural and the divine positive law forbid Catholic youth to attend these institutions *proportionately to the danger which one may find therein.* In view of such a peril the Church corroborated the precepts of the natural and the divine positive law by an ecclesiastical precept which expressly forbids each and everyone of her subjects to patronize non-Catholic schools.

It is, therefore, not a matter for the faithful to decide for themselves. In other words, it is no longer in their discretion to evaluate or determine the gravity of the danger which attendance at non-Catholic schools entails. There is question here of an ecclesiastical law which can neither be infringed nor suspended arbitrarily, even if the danger in a particular case does not exist. The law in question is given in view of a general danger, for the common good, and canon 21 expressly states that laws made for the purpose of safeguarding the public against a common danger bind, even though in a particular case there is no danger.[17]

On the other hand, the ecclesiastical prohibition, though absolute in its tenor, admits the possibilities of an exception. What are these possibilities?

B. *Tolerance*

> " Solius autem Ordinarii loci est decernere, ad normam instructionum Sedis Apostolicae, in quibus rerum adiunctis et quibus adhibitis cautelis, ut periculum perversionis vitetur, tolerari possit ut eae scholae celebrentur."

[17] " Leges latae ad praecavendum periculum generale, urgent, etiamsi in casu peculiari periculum non adsit."

It belongs to the local ordinary alone to judge as to the warrant for an exception to the prohibitive precept of canon 1374. The term " local ordinary " embraces here the following officials: the residential bishop, the abbot or prelate *nullius,* and their vicars general, the administrator, the vicar or prefect apostolic, and those who succeed to the government according to the law or approved constitutions, when the offices of the aforesaid become vacant.[18] Outside of the local ordinary, therefore, all others, such as confessors, pastors, spiritual directors, theologians, etc., are excluded. This exclusion is absolute and holds in every instance save, of course, the case in which a special power was received from the local ordinary through delegation. That such delegation, furthermore, can be granted follows from the general rule of delegation as laid down in canon 199.[19]

The local ordinary is to decide under what circumstances and with what safeguards against perversion the attendance at such schools by Catholics may be tolerated. The usual procedure according to which the ordinary exercises this power may consist either in passing judgment in each individual case or simply in laying down general rules applicable to the whole diocese. In his judgment and in his regulations, however, the local ordinary must be guided, as the canon itself indicates, by the instructions of the Holy See which still retain their force even after the promulgation of the Code.

[18] Canon 198. Since the term includes those who succeed to the government of a vacant see, the vicar capitular (in a diocese, or in an abbacy *nullius,* or a prelature *nullius, cf.* canons 327, § 1; 431, § 1; 432) and the pro-vicar or pro-prefect (in an apostolic vicariate, or a prefecture, *cf.* canon 309, § 1) are local ordinaries during the interregnum. It is worthy of mention here that while canon 198 does not speak of vicars general in reference to the vicars and prefects apostolic, these have, nevertheless, the power to appoint a vicar delegate with practically the same authority as the vicar general of a diocese. S. C. de Prop. Fide, 8 dec. 1919, II—*AAS,* XII (1920), 120.

[19] Cf. Schaaf, " Our bishops' prohibition against sending Catholic children to non-Catholic schools," *Acolyte,* V (1929), 4-5.

Since the attendance at non-Catholic schools has always been a major question of grave and great importance, it is easy to understand why the Holy See has often reserved to itself the supreme judgment in such a matter; determining, whether for the whole Church, or for a country, or again, for a particular diocese, under what conditions and within what limits attendance at such institutions could be tolerated. On the other hand, since the conditions of localities and likewise the attitudes towards the Church differ, the Holy See has appointed the local ordinaries as the immediate judges in the application of her directions in this matter.

What are these directions? One can find them in the following sources: general documents, encyclical letters sent to the whole Church—for example, the recent encyclical on Christian education of youth [20]—and particular documents sent to certain dioceses or countries.[21] These instructions generally begin by calling to mind the manifold dangers which attendance at non-Catholic schools presents to Catholic youth. To this question, there is joined that concerning the proximate and remote occasion of sin. Finally, these directions determine the circumstances which would permit attendance at such institutions, and the precautions to be taken to neutralize the occasion of sin.

These circumstances, as resumed from pontifical documents, are usually considered to exist:

a) when Catholics are confronted with the alternative either

[20] Pius XI, litt. encycl. *Divini illius Magistri*, 31 dec. 1929—*AAS*, XXII (1930), 49-86.

[21] v. g., besides those cited in the following footnotes, cf. S. C. Ep. et Reg., instr. 21 iul. 1896—*Fontes*, n. 2031; S. C. de Prop. Fide, instr. (ad Vic. Ap. Societ. Mission. ad Exteros), a. 1659—*Fontes*, n. 4463; litt. encycl. (ad Ep. Hiberniae), 18 sept. 1819—*Fontes*, n. 4714; litt. (ad Archiep. Hiberniae), 16 ian. 1841—*Fontes*, n. 4787; litt. encycl. (ad Ep. Orient.), 20 mart. 1865—*Fontes*, n. 4863; instr. (ad Vic. Ap. Indiar. Orient.), 8 sept. 1869, n. 37—*Fontes*, n. 4876; litt. encycl. (ad Ep. Canad.), 14 mart. 1895—*Fontes*, n. 4932.

of leaving the whole education to heretics or of being satisfied with a neutral school; [22]

b) when there is a true necessity, and not merely an imaginary or fictitious one.[23] In judging this necessity there should be considered primarily the principles of faith and Christian morality, and not personal tastes, fashions, or pretended social conveniences.[24]

There is no true necessity if nearby there be a Catholic school which, at the same time, is suited to the conditions of the student, or if, without grave inconvenience Catholic children can be sent elsewhere to be educated.[25]

The greater and more immediate the danger is, the more cogent must be the circumstances to justify Catholics attending non-Catholic schools. This is a mere application of a principle of moral theology. Therefore, attendance at a sectarian non-Catholic school cannot be tolerated unless it be in a case of extreme necessity. Regarding the species most alien to the Catholic, that is, pagan schools, the Sacred Congregation for the Propagation of the Faith explicitly states in an instruction: "Omnino prohibeantur christiani adolescentes paganorum scholas frequentare, attento periculo perversionis et idolatriae." [26] Similarly, in 1867, the same Sacred Congregation forbade Catholic youth to attend the schools of Oxford and Cambridge. In its encyclical letter to the English bishops the Congregation observed that the whole atmosphere of these institutions, along with their courses of studies, was imbued with errors. Moreover, the total absence in the curriculum of

[22] Cf. S. C. S. Off., instr. 21 mart. 1866—*Fontes*, n. 992.

[23] S. C. S. Off., *loc. cit.*

[24] S. C. S. Off., instr. (ad Ep. Stat. Foeder. Americae Septentrion.), 24 nov. 1874—*Fontes*, n. 1046.

[25] S. C. S. Off., instr. 21 mart. 1866—*Fontes*, n. 992; instr. (ad Ep. Stat. Foed. Americae Septentrion.), 24 nov. 1875—*Fontes*, n. 1046; cf. also *Acta et Decreta Concilii Plenarii Baltimorensis Tertii*, n. 198.

[26] (C. P. pro Sin.), 19 iul. 1838—*Fontes*, n. 4773. Cf. also Historical synopsis pp. 48-50.

any solid Christian doctrine as an antidote, constituted a proximate danger to the faith of adolescents, who are naturally unstable and easily impressionable. Because of these conditions, it was noted that, as a rule, a reason could hardly be advanced which would justify the enrollment of Catholic youth in either of these institutions.[27]

Finally, of singular importance in the present discussion is the instruction sent by the Congregation for the Propagation of the Faith to the bishops of Ireland.[28] This instruction, which embraces a series of other pontifical responses, deals with the school organization of that country, which was, at the time, that of the interdenominational schools, that is, for Catholics and non-Catholics alike. It includes, therefore, the *scholae mixtae* as understood by canon 1374.

Having been asked to pass judgment, the Sacred Congregation, after a careful consideration of the peculiar circumstances in Ireland, did not deem it advisable to render a definite decision. The matter was left in the hands of the bishops, who were recommended, at the same time, to await the result of a longer experience obtained by the *l'essai forcé du système*. In order, however, to guide the action of the local ordinaries,

[27] Litt. encycl. (ad Ep. Angliae), 6 aug. 1867—*Fontes*, n. 4868. These conditions are changed at present. Cf. Monti, *La Libertà della Scuola*, p. 557. In the United States of America the conditions of the colleges vary in each locality. Some are no longer sectarian, while others retain their allegiance to some particular religion and even demand of the students attendance at their chapel exercises. Each bishop, therefore, before allowing any of his subjects to attend them, must consider the nature as well as the statutes of these colleges within his jurisdiction. Today, however, there seems to be a general tendency to depart from the sectarian element in practically all of these colleges. Their chapel exercises, too, seem to take the form of civic and social functions rather than of a religious service. In particular instances, therefore, the bishop may allow some of his subjects to study a profane topic in these colleges, provided there is a sufficient reason and the danger of perversion is made remote. Cf. *Acta et Decreta Conc. Plen. Baltim. Tertii*, n. 210; also canon 1258, § 2.

[28] S. C. de Prop. Fide, instr. (ad Archiep. Hiberniae), 7 apr. 1860—*Collect. S. C. de P. F.*, n. 1190.

the Congregation submitted to them the following rules of conduct: 1) all books which are in any way against Scripture or dangerous to faith and morals must be banished from the school. 2) The teaching of religion, morals, and the history of religion, are to be entrusted to Catholics who are prepared for this office exclusively by Catholic instructors. 3) In the class-rooms common to all students only profane subjects will be taught, and, instead of imparting to all indiscriminately what are called the fundamentals of religion, namely, truths common to every denomination, the pupils will be separately instructed in religion according to their beliefs. 4) All these points must come under the immediate supervision of the bishops, and both, bishops and pastors, are to do all in their power to safeguard Catholic youth from any danger which may come to them from this system of national education as long as it continues, and for the time that it must be accepted. Their interest and concern should, however, not be limited to adapting themselves merely to existing conditions. It should be directed as far as possible toward the betterment of the Church's position and towards the recognition of her right to educate her children, and to possess and conduct her own schools. 5) The tolerance which, in accordance with the judgment of the bishop under existing circumstances, may possibly be granted in regard to primary schools, should not be extended to other more advanced institutions of learning. To this effect the bishops of Ireland were finally urged to organize schools of their own which would fulfill the needs of adolescents seeking higher education.

Some of the precautions to be taken by those who have the duty of watching over the education of youth, have already been enunciated above. In addition the following, likewise taken from pontificial documents, may be mentioned.

Parents are to make constant inquiries concerning the teaching imparted to their children while examining them on the lessons received in class.

They shall watch their children so as to shield them from any dangerous contacts with heretical and schismatical companions.

Bishops shall redouble their vigilance especially through visits and pastoral letters.

Children and youth are to receive catechetical instruction from a Catholic teacher after school hours, either in the class room or in other places, according to the local circumstances.[29]

This instruction will deal in a special manner with the truths attacked, whether directly or indirectly, by neutral or hostile teaching in vogue in the place. The Holy See, furthermore, urges that on this point the cooperation of good laymen be sought.

Finally, an effort should be made to organize, whenever possible, centers of catechetics everywhere throughout the dioceses.[30]

The reason inspiring the Church to make such legislation in reference to attendance at non-Catholic schools is given by the Code itself: *ut periculum perversionis vitetur.* The Church is the mother of souls and has responsibilities before God. She prefers to see her children less learned perhaps in profane science here below than to expose them to a loss of eternal happiness. This, indeed, is an example of the absolute logic of the ecclesiastical magisterium which judges on the basis of man's ultimate end; and an example also of the logic of Christian education in conformity with the principle established in canon 1372. It should not be inferred, however, that the Church disregards the temporal welfare of her children.

[29] Cf. particularly, S. C. S. Off., instr. (ad Ep. Stat. Foeder. Americae Septentrion.), 24 nov. 1875—*Fontes*, n. 1046; *Conc. Plen. Baltim. II*, n. 435; *Acta et Decreta Concilii Provincialis Portlandensis in Oregon Quarti* (1932), decr. 33, p. 42; *Statuta Archidioecesis Sancti Francisci* (1936), n. 328.

[30] Pius X, litt. encycl. *Acerbo nimis*, 15 apr. 1905, n. 16—*Fontes*, n. 666; S. C. C., decr. *Provido sane*, 12 ian. 1935—*AAS*, XXVII (1935), 145-154. Cf. also Jansen, *Canonical Provisions for Catechetical Instruction*, The Catholic University of America, Canon Law Studies, n. 107 (Washington: The Catholic University of America, 1937), pp. 53-59.

She establishes schools the object of which is to combine a thorough Christian training with the greatest possible measure of secular knowledge. Moreover, as regards the latter it is her desire that Catholic schools should be in no way inferior to other institutions of learning.[31]

By tolerating, on the other hand, attendance at non-Catholic schools, the Code indicates the very last limit to which the Church goes in this regard. It is not a question here either of approving or encouraging attendance at other than Catholic schools. It is a question of simple tolerance in certain cases and with the observance of necessary precautionary measures, which, nevertheless, are not always sufficient to obviate entirely the dangers involved.

Meanwhile the Church must keep in mind human frailty. It is better, at times, for the legislator to tolerate a lesser evil in order to avoid a greater one. Here, then, the imperfection comes not from the legislator, but from the subjects themselves. Should the legislator forbid altogether attendance at non-Catholic schools, the result would be that a good number of students might be deprived of that profane knowledge which is necessary for their temporal welfare, or, even worse, there would be the great probability of numerous transgressions of the particular law. This would result in a contempt for others, and involve graver dangers than the enforcement of the prudent regulations laid down in the present canon.

The Church has occasionally granted this tolerance in consideration of the common good; for example, in the case of the interdenominational schools of Ireland of the past century. When it is a question, therefore, of safeguarding some general

[31] "Est autem ad hoc omnium consensu nil tam necessarium, quam ut catholici ubique locorum proprias sibi scholas habeant, easque publicis scholis haud inferiores. Scholis ergo catholicis sive condendis, ubi defuerint, sive amplificandi, et perfectius instruendis parandisque, ut institutione ac disciplina scholas publicas adaequent, omni cura prospiciendum est." — S. C. S. Off., instr. (ad Ep. Stat. Foeder. Americae Septentrion.), 24 nov. 1875—*Fontes*, n. 1046.

good, such as the peace of the Church in a certain country, the Holy See will be more lenient than she would be in some particular instance. Since her very mission is universal and permanent, she must adapt herself to varied circumstances of time and place. It is for this reason that, when unable to exercise the fulness of her liberty and rights, she desires her children to draw from imperfect and faulty civil legislation all the advantages which can be possibly obtained. This manner of action was particularly manifested in the case of the Irish,[32] the French,[33] and the Manitoban schools.[34]

As a conclusion, it may well be remarked that Catholic Action will find in this matter a great field for work in order to bring about, under the leadership of the hierarchy, an amelioration of present conditions and to harmonize them with the principles of Canon Law and Catholic theology.[35] While no punishments are prescribed by the common law for attendance at neutral or mixed schools, it is nevertheless within the ordinary's power [36] to determine suitable penalties for anyone who would be contumacious in this matter. In such instances, however, care must be taken that sufficient warning be given concerning such punishments. In the internal forum parents who are gravely negligent in the proper training of their children would have to be denied sacramental absolution.[37] Moreover, according to the common law, parents who deliberately (that is, with a knowledge of the law and its punishment) send their children to a school to be educated in a non-Catholic religion incur *ipso facto* an excommunication, the absolution

[32] Cf. S. C. de Prop. Fide, instr. (ad Archiep. Hiberniae), 7 apr. 1860—*Collect. S. C. de P. F.*, n. 1190.

[33] At the time of the nunciature of Cardinal Ferrata (1891-96).

[34] Cf. Leo XIII, ep. encycl. *Affari vos*, 8 dec. 1897, n. 7—*Fontes*, n. 636.

[35] Cf. Civardi, *A Manual of Catholic Action* (tr. by Martindale, New York: Sheed and Ward, 1936), pp. 26-28.

[36] Canon 2221.

[37] Cf. Aertnys-Damen, *Theologia Moralis*, II, 357.

from which is reserved to the ordinary.[38] To incur this censure they must know that such a school not only does not attempt to observe neutrality in religious matters, but also *ex professo* teaches heretical doctrines.[39] The common public schools of the United States are not considered sectarian schools.[40]

2. RELATED QUESTIONS—*Attendance at Catholic Institutions by non-Catholics.*

Before the Code several pontifical documents had laid down precise rules concerning the attendance at Catholic schools by non-Catholic pupils. Among these documents the more important ones are the instructions of the Sacred Congregation for the Propagation of the Faith of April 25, 1868,[41] and October 18, 1883,[42] and the instructions of the Holy Office of June 11, 1866,[43] and of August 22, 1900, respectively.[44]

What is the binding force of these and similar legislative documents enacted prior to 1918? According to canon 6 particular laws not in opposition to the Code are still in force.[45] The Roman decrees, therefore, addressed to particular sections of the Christian world have still their binding force, if they are not in opposition to the Code. The same thing also may be said of diocesan laws and regulations.

Moreover, universal disciplinary laws in force up to 1918 retain their binding power, if they are either explicitly or im-

[38] Canon 2319, § 1, 4°; by reason of paragraph two of this same canon, such parents are also suspected of heresy and subject to the penalties of canon 2315.

[39] Cf. Ciprotti, "De consummatione delictorum attento eorum elemento objectivo," *Apollinaris*, VIII (1935), 248.

[40] Augustine, *A Commentary on the New Code of Canon Law* (4th ed., St. Louis: Herder, 1921-1929), VIII, 300.

[41] *Fontes*, n. 4873.

[42] (Ad Vic. Ap. Sin.)—*Fontes*, n. 4903.

[43] (Leopolis)—*Collect. S. C. de P. F.*, n. 1292.

[44] (Ad Ep. Iassien.)—*Collect. S. C. de P. F.*, n. 2093.

[45] Canon 6, 6°; cf. Blat, *Commentarium*, I, n. 55.

plicitly contained in the Code.[46] Canonists are not always in accord on the sense of the words *implicite, explicite, indirecte, directe.*[47] The following, however, can be considered as certain. Roman legislation on this matter which was originally meant for certain countries or dioceses, acquired, by common usage, an application that was universal throughout the Church. There is here a question, therefore, of legislation touching the whole Church. On the other hand, although the situation considered here is the converse of that with which canon 1374 expressly deals, the canon, it may be said, regulates the problem in these words: "*scholas . . . mixtas, quae nempe etiam acatholicis patent,*" since the condition created by the presence of non-Catholics at Catholic schools is somewhat akin to that of Catholics at non-Catholic institutions. That is to say, the reason for the canonical prohibition of Catholics attending non-Catholic schools (*ut periculum perversionis vitetur*) is present at times in the attendance of non-Catholics at Catholic institutions. This is true at least as to the fact, if not as to the degree of danger.[48] Every previous decree has in view especially this very danger of perversion. One must, therefore, still consider the legislation prior to 1918 and interpret this phase of the question also according to the law existing at the time of the promulgation of the Code.

Naturally here one must see, on the part of the Church, less severity than in cases of attendance at non-Catholic schools by Catholic youth. The teachers, subject matter, books, in a word, the general atmosphere of the school is Catholic. This, no doubt, explains also the tolerance often granted by the ecclesiastical authorities especially in mission countries. Moreover, in certain circumstances the Church not only tolerates, but is openly favorable to the receiving of non-Catholic students

[46] Canon 6, 6°.

[47] Cf. Vermeersch-Creusen, *Epitome*, I, n. 56.

[48] Guay, "Fréquentation des écoles non-catholiques," *Revue de l'Université d'Ottawa*, VII (1937), 49*.

within her own institutions. The school thus, finds occasion in an additional way to serve as an instrument in the work of the apostolate.

Nevertheless, there are situations in which attendance at Catholic schools by non-Catholics presents a real danger. For Catholic pupils, this danger would be that of perversion. This again will depend on local circumstances, individual contacts, the more or less aggressive mentality of the non-Catholic pupils, and their religious attitude. For the non-Catholics there is also a danger, consisting primarily in religious indifference and scandal arising from the sometimes questionable conduct of Catholic pupils.[49] Only too often non-Catholics are prone to be sceptical about the superiority of Catholicism.

It is for these reasons, therefore, that whenever danger is involved, the Holy See exhorts the bishops, especially where the non-Catholics are numerous, to organize as far as possible a particular section of the school for the non-Catholics.[50] Such grouping should not result in any particular difficulties. On the contrary, it should present an efficacious means of direct apostolate. There would then be formed a unit in which the Catholic teacher is in immediate contact with his non-Catholic pupils who come to him to acquire that superior training which they could not obtain elsewhere.[51]

A special case in this regard is the admission of non-Catholic youth to Catholic boarding schools. It would be impossible to give here uniform directions applicable to every place and circumstance. One must study each particular instance and examine, for example, the purpose of the institute, the age of the pupils,[52] the degree and quality of the instruction im-

[49] S. C. de Prop. Fide, instr. 25 apr. 1868—*Fontes*, n. 4873.

[50] Cf. S. C. de Prop. Fide, instr. (ad Vic. Ap. Sin.), 18 oct. 1883, n. XI, 4—*Fontes*, n. 4903.

[51] S. C. de Prop. Fide, instr. 25 apr. 1868—*Fontes*, n. 4873.

[52] S. C. de Prop. Fide, litt. (ad Archiep. Ultraiecten.), 16 nov. 1870—*Collect. S. C. de P. F.*, n. 1359.

parted, the regulations governing the internal discipline of the school, and the arrangements which the parents intend to make concerning the religious training of their children.

Here, however, are some general rules deduced from pontifical documents and indicating the practical mind of the Holy See in particular cases submitted to it:

a) Conditions for admission.

1. It is absolutely forbidden to receive, even as externs, children of apostates.[53]

2. The number of non-Catholic students must be limited. The Holy Office seems to permit a third of the general enrollment.[54]

3. The youths admitted must have a good character.[55]

4. The permission of the local ordinary is required in each individual case.[56]

b) Regulations concerning the daily contacts of Catholic and non-Catholic pupils.

1. The Catholic students must not be exposed to perversion, nor the non-Catholic ones to indifferentism.[57]

2. Neither the natural nor the divine law may be exposed to violation. By admitting non-Catholics to the Sacraments,[58] or by conveying the impression to non-Catholic pupils that any general objective religious equality is admitted or admissible, or that their peculiar beliefs are more than tolerated on the principle of freedom of conscience, the school would run the risk of violating either the natural or the divine law.

[53] S. C. S. Off., 6 dec. 1899—*Collect. S. C. de P. F.*, n. 2070.

[54] S. C. de Prop. Fide, instr. 25 apr. 1868—*Fontes*, n. 4873; S. C. S. Off. (Leopolis), 11 iun. 1866—*Collect. S. C. de P. F.*, n. 1292.

[55] S. C. S. Off., *loc. cit.*

[56] S. C. S. Off., 6 dec. 1899—*Collect. S. C. de P. F.*, n. 2070; cf. also *Synodus dioecesana Quebecensis* (1923), p. 87.

[57] S. C. de Prop. Fide, instr. 25 apr. 1868—*Fontes*, n. 4873.

[58] Cf. canon 731, § 2.

3. Discussions on religious matters among the students must be forbidden.[59]

4. Assistance at Mass and religious exercises can be permitted to the non-Catholic pupils, yet it is not to be imposed upon them.[60]

5. It can be tolerated that the non-Catholics take part in the chant during the religious functions and the exposition of the Blessed Sacrament, provided that there is no scandal and that it is difficult to demand the non-Catholic students to keep silence.[61]

6. Non-Catholic pupils are not to be allowed to participate in the religious ceremonies of their non-Catholic sects. Were this, in a particular case, impossible to prevent, then those in charge of the school must take an absolutely passive attitude, much after the fashion of a religious hospital-attendant caring for a non-Catholic who petitions the help of a non-Catholic minister. They, therefore, are not to supply escorts or in any other way actively to facilitate the attendance of non-Catholic students at the rites of their respective sects.[62]

7. Religious instruction may be imparted at the same time to both Catholics and non-Catholics.[63] The teacher, however, must be Catholic and his teaching thoroughly conformable to the Catholic faith. Never should the school engage a non-Catholic teacher for the religious instruction of the non-Catholic pupils, even when he expressly obliges himself to teach only those truths which are common to every religion. In a

[59] S. C. S. Off. (Leopolis), 11 iun. 1866—*Collect. S. C. de P. F.*, n. 1292; cf. also *Acta et Decreta Conc. Plen. Baltim. Tertii*, n. 213.

[60] S. C. S. Off., *loc. cit.*

[61] S. C. S. Off., 24 ian. 1906—*Collect. S. C. de P. F.*, n. 2227.

[62] S. C. S. Off. (Leopolis), 11 iun. 1866—*Collect. S. C. de P. F.*, n. 1292. The directors of these Catholic boarding schools should regulate all these points with the parents of the non-Catholic students before the latter are admitted to the school.

[63] S. C. de Prop. Fide, intr. 25 apr. 1868—*Fontes*, n. 4873; S. C. S. Off., instr. (ad Ep. Iassien.), 22 aug. 1900—*Collect. S. C. de P. F.*, n. 2093.

particular case, and in order to avoid complaints of parents or guardians, the superiors of these Catholic schools could permit their non-Catholic pupils to be instructed in religion by tutors of their own religious denomination. However, this must be done in a place apart from the Catholic school, and such teachers must be paid by the parents, and not by the institute.[64]

8. Finally, as a last precaution, those in charge of Catholic boarding schools should not let the non-Catholic students be visited by relatives and friends, with the exception of parents or guardians, without the permission of the local ordinary.[65]

On these points the legislation of the Holy See is precise. It safeguards the rights of God and of the Church. As is evident, a certain liberty is left in each instance to the local ordinary who will be able to judge in a more immediate manner the particular circumstances which could not be foreseen by the supreme legislator.

In the United States of America there has developed of late quite a general practice of admitting, especially within the higher Catholic schools, adolescents not of the Catholic faith. No doubt, this has served the purpose of eradicating prejudices against the Church in many instances. It has often proved to be a means of a real apostolate also. However, the admonitions of the Third Council of Baltimore,[66] which are but a brief restatement of the Roman documents dealing especially with the dangers of perversion and indifferentism, should not be forgotten. The evils of these dangers are indeed greater than the good promised by the possible eradication of prejudices.[67]

[64] S. C. S. Off., *loc. cit.*

[65] S. C. S. Off. (Leopolis), 11 iun. 1866—*Collect. S. C. de P. F.*, n. 1292.

[66] *Acta et Decreta Conc. Plen. Baltim. Tertii*, n. 312.

[67] Cf. Michel, *La Question Scolaire et les Principes Théologiques*, pp. 102-103.

CHAPTER IX

THE CATHOLIC SCHOOLS PROPERLY SO CALLED

I. RIGHT OF THE CHURCH TO FOUND AND CONDUCT SCHOOLS

Canon 1375: Ecclesiae est ius scholas cuiusvis disciplinae non solum elementarias, sed etiam medias et superiores condendi.

THE general prerogative of the Church in regard to schools was discussed in Chapter VI. At this point, it is the specific nature of the Church's right concerning the establishment of schools which will be considered more in detail. Meanwhile, it must be noted, that for the Church to found schools, here signifies that she not merely establish scholastic institutions according to the demands of civil law, but also that she control the administrative organization, both didactic and disciplinary, that she nominate and approve teachers, and that she direct these schools with full and independent authority.

With this in mind, the right of the Church may be asserted and proved as follows: the Church has the right to found and govern, according to her own laws, schools of any kind and for any purpose. This right is proper and native (although indirect), partial and cumulative, that is, not exclusive, but nevertheless independent. This right is proper, but at the same time may be of a devolved character; hence it may happen that it is wholly and exclusively exercised by the Church.

I. The right of the Church is *proper* and *native*.

1. The Church by her nature and divine institution is the teacher of men,[1] whom, therefore, she not only can but must teach in order to exercise her native office. This office is

[1] Matthew, XXVII, 18-20.

primarily and directly ordained for the religious training of men. It can hardly be fulfilled, however, without the necessary and suitable means, especially training in the humanities, since by the study of these the human faculties are elevated, ennobled, and well-disposed for a more comprehensive attainment of truth.

The right of the Church is sustained by the fact that abnormal conditions of public morality prevail wherever the schools are not imbued with Catholic principles. In such circumstances, the Church with stronger right founds her own schools, wherein the faithful may be safely trained in the studies useful for social life.[2] This becomes evident among nations where confessional schools are founded for Catholics. When the State refuses to recognize these schools, it directly attacks the right of the Church. This is a real injury to the Church, as is evident, since the Church as a juridically perfect society has the right to all the means required for her end, no less than she has the right to attain that end itself.[3]

2. Moreover, the Church is the mother of all the faithful, whom she brings forth in the order of grace by Baptism and nourishes by the Sacraments and the teaching of doctrine. This teaching office cannot but concern the whole man with all his faculties, both natural and supernatural. Man, indeed, must cultivate his natural faculties without, however, neglecting his supernatural end.

These two arguments are most clearly and extensively set forth in the encyclical letter of Pius XI, the explanation of which thus concludes: " Therefore with full right the Church promotes letters, science, art, in so far as necessary or helpful to Christian education, and to her work for the salvation of souls; founding and maintaining schools and institutions adapted to every branch of learning and degree of culture.

[2] Cavagnis, *Institutiones Iuris Publici Ecclesiastici*, III, 74.

[3] Pius XI, litt. encycl. *Divini illius Magistri*, 31 dec. 1929—*AAS*, XXII (1930), 53.

Nor may even physical culture, as it is called, be considered outside the range of her maternal magisterium, for the reason that it also is a means which may help or harm Christian education." [4]

3. Besides these two titles by which the Church's right over schools is clearly proved from the divine positive law, there is a third, based also on this same law, namely, the Church's express commission from God to do works of charity [5]—a commission carried out by apostolic tradition. Since the training of others in any discipline is particularly a charitable work, it therefore follows that by native and proper right the Church undertakes such a work.[6]

4. Finally, there is the title proceeding from the natural law, which is the basis of the Church's right, namely, that the right of founding and directing schools cannot be denied to any one who is competent. This right cannot therefore be denied to the Church which is a juridic person possessed of the most outstandingly advantageous means for establishing and successfully governing schools.[7]

II. Whilst this right of the Church is proper and native to her, it is nevertheless *indirect,* as is evident from what has been said above. It is a right, the exercise of which pertains to the Church, not for the direct attainment of her end and for the direct fulfillment of her teaching office, whose direct object is religious and moral training, but for the more complete and convenient fulfillment thereof.[8]

[4] Litt. encycl. *Divini illius Magistri—op. cit.*, p. 55.

[5] Matthew, X, 8; Luke, IX, 1-2.

[6] Cavagnis, *Institutiones Iuris Publici Ecclesiastici,* III, 70-71.

[7] This is the right based on the natural freedom of teaching which Catholic jurists and philosophers assert and prove with clear arguments. Cf. Cavagnis, *Institutiones Iuris Publici Ecclesiastici,* III, 54; Cappello, *Summa Iuris Publici Ecclesiastici,* p. 505.

[8] It may be asked whether or not the right of the Church to found schools for the teaching of profane knowledge is not direct at least from the standpoint of charity. The temporal welfare of the students and of society is

III. The right of the Church is *partial* and *cumulative,* that is, it is not *exclusive.* The Church is not the only society to which is entrusted the function of training man as a whole. An analogous office, as has been repeatedly stated, pertains to the family, by natural law, and to the State at least by derived right.[9] Thus the one right pertains at the same time to the Church, to the family, and to the State. The rights and duties of these three societies are not basically opposed, nor is there any occasion for any one of them to reserve to itself the training of its subjects. The several rights and duties, therefore, are to be harmoniously related and regulated.

There has practically never been any difficulty in the mutual relations between the family and the Church in regard to their respective rights. Difficulties may arise, and today do arise, not so much on the part of the family which has always been led by a certain instinct to entrust its offspring to the schools of the Church,[10] but rather on the part of the State. Indeed, it often happens that the State claims for itself a monopoly concerning the education and instruction of youth. Against

at once the direct and primary object both of charity and of the school, which is not touched upon as a means but directly as an end, at least intermediary. An affirmative answer would seem clearly to follow from the argumentation which Cavagnis presents — *Institutiones Iuris Publici Ecclesiastici,* III, 70-71. However, because the office of exercising charity is committed to the Church in reference to a supernatural and supratemporal end, the question must be answered negatively.

[9] Pius XI, litt. encycl. *Divini illius Magistri,* 31 dec. 1929—*AAS,* XXII (1930), 58, 62.

[10] Pius XI wrote in this regard: "Historiae testimonium hoc ipso aptius confirmatur, quod familiae peculiarem in modum Ecclesiae scholis confidunt, ut haud multo ante in epistola ad Cardinalem a publicis Ecclesiae negotiis Nostra scribebamus: 'Familia statim intellexit rem ita se habere, atque, inde a prioribus christiani nominis temporibus ad haec usque nostra, parentes, etsi manca nullave religione, suos mittunt et comitantur liberos ad ea educationis instituta quae condiderit ac regat Ecclesia' [*AAS,* XXI (1929), 302]. Paternus enim sensus, qui a Deo est, ad Ecclesiam sese fidenter convertit, in qua familiarium iurium tutelam inventurum se novit eamque demum concordiam, quam Deus in ordine rerum collocavit."—Litt. encycl. *Divini illius Magistri—op. cit.,* p. 61.

this usurpation of the State there stands the doctrine of the Church expressly condemning any monopoly of this kind.[11] That such usurpation of authority on the part of the State is an abuse is obvious. For the right of the State to the training of its subjects is subsequent to that of the Church and the family. Children pertain primarily in the natural order to the family by birth, and to the Church either by reason of her divine mission or through the sacred nature of Christian marriage. This doctrine is clearly explained and proved in the encyclical letter of Pius XI, as may be seen.[12]

The fictitious reason which the proponents of scholastic monopoly by the State adduce is mistrust of the schools of the Church—as though in these a sufficient training, answering to the needs of the times, could not be had.[13] The true reason is either hatred of the Church or an exaggerated opinion as to the nature and end of the State. Whatever it is, it is imaginary. Regarding the insufficiency of training in the Church schools it implies a double attack on the Church. It denies her legitimate right based on so many titles, as was demonstrated; and it does violence to historical truth [14] and evidence.[15]

IV. This right of the Church is *independent* of any human authority. It is a right consequent upon the juridic nature of the Church. It belongs to her as a juridically perfect society, supreme in her order, and is based on the stronger supernatural

[11] Pius IX, "*Syllabus,*" prop. 45, 47, 48 — Denzinger-Umberg, *Enchir. Symbol.*, nn. 1745, 1747, 1748.

[12] Litt. encycl. *Divini illius Magistri—op. cit.*, pp. 62-63.

[13] If one should admit their hypothesis, namely, that principles are not permanent, then indeed they argue logically. Progress in accordance with the times holds to no fixed principles. It abandons one for an apparently better one. Such procedure is impossible for the Church. Her principles are immutable. Cf. Pius IX, "*Syllabus,*" prop. 80 — Denzinger-Umberg, *Enchir. Symbol.*, n. 1780.

[14] Pius XI, const. *Deus scientiarum Dominus*, 24 maii 1931—*AAS*, XXIII (1931), 241-247.

[15] Cf. Pius XI, chirogr. (ad Em. Card. Gasparri), 30 maii 1929—*AAS*, XXI (1929), 302.

title from which this right arises.[16] As a matter of fact, the Church frequently in Concordats [17] subjects her schools to the civil authority to the extent that in these schools the civil laws govern all those matters which regard not only the public welfare, building specifications, etc., but also the general program of studies and the system of lectures which are to be followed. Such matters are subjected to civil legislation only by reason of the good will of the Church toward the State. The Church in this way cultivates mutual friendly relations, provides for the greater good of souls, and thus better attains her end. Moreover, in many cases, where the Church's tradition of centuries has been abandoned and the school is governed according to more modern principles, which do not always agree with true philosophy, the results have proved detrimental to progress. Hence the instability of the scholastic programs, as well as those difficulties under which the scholastic administration labors in certain States.[18] If the administration of schools were more strictly dependent on the Church, it would thereby be characterized by greater and more lasting stability.

The closeness of the relation between schools and civil administration varies in the concordats mentioned above. Sometimes there is a strict dependence. At other times the relation is more free. It is strict in the concordats with Latvia, Roumania, Germany and Austria. It is free or conditioned upon the recognition of the studies and academic degrees in the concordats with Lithuania and Italy. The Church endeavors to procure this recognition in order to make public

[16] Cavagnis, *Institutiones Iuris Publici Ecclesiastici*, III, 61-67.

[17] Cf. art. 10 of Concordat with Latvia—*AAS*, XIV (1922), 578; art. 5, 6 of Conc. with Bavaria—*AAS*, XVII (1925), 44-45; art. 13, n. 5 of Conc. with Lithuania—*AAS*, XIX (1927), 429; art. 35 of Conc. with Italy —*AAS*, XXI (1929), 291; art. 19 of Conc. with Roumania—*AAS*, XXI (1929), 449; art. 25 of Conc. with Germany—*AAS*, XXV (1933), 403; art. 6, § 3 of Conc. with Austria—*AAS*, XXVI (1934), 257. Cf. Restrepo, *Concordata regnante Sanctissimo Domino Pio PP. XI Inita* (Romae: apud Aedes Universitatis Gregorianae, 1934), p. 21, note 10.

[18] Cf. Charlier, "La Réforme des Humanités," *Études classiques*, IV (1935), 209.

offices accessible to Catholics, as well as for the reason stated above.

V. Finally, the Church undertakes profane training not only by her own proper right, but also at times by a right of devolved character—in place of the family or State. This happens, today at least, more frequently because of family circumstances. Parents, impeded by poverty, ignorance, and other necessities of life, and led by their trust in the Church, freely turn over their children to her for training. How frequently this has occurred has already been noted.

The same right of the Church devolved from the State occurs also today, but more rarely.[19] Formerly, scholastic training, or at least elementary education, was almost exclusively conducted by the Church. The civil authority remained aloof, thus tacitly leaving to the Church the fulfilment of this office.

Occasion may be taken here to consider the objection of certain modern historians relative to the scholastic monopoly of the Church in the Middle Ages. Professor Manacorda, upon citing certain documents in his work "*Storia della Scuola in Italia*,"[20] speaks about the scholastic monopoly which the Church claimed for herself, and concludes: "si vede chiaro come la Chiesa concepisse l'insegnamento pubblico, privato, comunale di qualsiasi materia, come una funzione che da essa sola poteva emanare e di che essa poteva investire uno, come poteva privarlo."[21] Elsewhere in his work he makes similar statements.[22]

[19] Cf. *L'Organisation de l'Instruction Publique dans 53 Pays* (Genève: Bureau Internat. d'Éducation, 1933), p. 187.

[20] The documents cited are: a letter of Clement IV to the king of Aragon, May 31, 1268 (cf. *Thesaurus novus anedoctorum seu Collectio munumentorum, complectens regum ac principum aliorumque virorum illustrium epistolas et diplomata bene multa* [ed. Martène, Parisiis, 1717], II, 603; *Regesta Pontificum Romanorum* [ed. Potthast, Berolini, 1874], n. 20366), and a certain decree of Boniface VIII (1296) (cf. *Codice diplomatica della Città di Orvieto* [ed. Fumi, *Documenti di Storia Italiana*, Firenze, 1884], p. 355).

[21] *Storia della Scuola in Italia*, I, pt. I, 219.

[22] *Op. cit.*, pp. 65-94.

The facts from which these statements are derived may be chiefly reduced to these: the Church claimed for herself the exclusive right to give "the permission to teach" (*licentia docendi*) in any subject; the Church often contested any similar right on the part of the State; and, finally, the civil authority ceded the right over schools to the Church and recognized it as an accepted fact.

Such facts are indeed true, but the conclusions deduced therefrom are exaggerated and arbitrary, if not prejudiced. For if the facts themselves are more thoroughly studied, one must necessarily conclude:

1. The Church sometimes reserved to herself the right to grant "the permission to teach" for the same reason that she claims today the right to approve teachers of religion and the textbooks.[23] Then, indeed, in contrast with the present day, and altogether more properly, there was recognized the inseparability of profane training from religious training. In fact, all schools were first of all religious.[24]

2. Hence, with justice did the Church contest at times the right of the civil authority. Moreover, some of the documents cited show nothing more clearly than the fact that in certain peculiar cases, the rights could not be definitely distinguished.[25] Nor do these documents detract from the force of others in which the rights of both powers are more clearly delimited.[26]

[23] Canon 1381, § 3.

[24] For the school program of the time, cf. the work of Manacorda, *op. cit.*, I, pt. II, 111.

[25] This, and no other, seems to be the reason of the controversy between Clement IV and the king of Aragon. It concerned the right which was disputed between the king and the bishop. This right, which the Pontiff attempted to determine, was eventually vindicated in favor of the bishop.

[26] Cf. *Las siete Partidas del Rey D. Alfonso el Sabio, cotejadas con varios códices antiquos por la real Academia de la historia* (Madrid, 1807), lex 1, tit. XXXI, pars 2; Denifle, *Die Enstehung der Universitäten des Mittelalters bis 1400* (Berlin, 1885), p. 345.

3. Finally, it must be said that the civil authority renounced nothing when it recognized the rights of the Church. These rights were either proper and inalienable or legitimately prescribed.[27] Would that the modern State would show itself so just and agreeable.

There cannot be any solid reason to deny the Church the right to found and maintain schools of her own. Those who claim that the Church's institutions of learning are inimical to society are either ignorant of facts, or they maliciously calumniate her. The State is composed of individuals and families. Therefore, any action which tends to disintegrate or demoralize the family will of necessity militate against the welfare of the State. Now, what educational agency other than the Church so insists upon the sanctity of the marriage bond, upon filial and parental love? Today she stands practically alone against divorce and whatever else disrupts the family and undermines the State by weakening the morality of its citizens.

Civil society finds in the Church's school system its strongest friend and advocate. Christianity is the law of universal charity without which human laws are anemic. Constantly the Church admonishes her children to be "subject to princes and powers, to obey at a word, to be ready to every good work." [28] Charity, brotherhood, liberty are the watchwords of our day; but "it was the religion of Christ that first whispered into the ears of the world these sacred words. It was the religion of Christ that took to its bosom bleeding, agonizing humanity, warmed it with divine love, healed its sores and breathed into it health and vigor ".[29]

27 Cf. the letter of Clement IV to the king of Aragon—*Thesaurus novus*, II, 603.

28 Titus, III, 1.

29 Ireland, *The Church and Modern Society—Lectures and Addresses* (Chicago, 1897), p. 60.

2. OBLIGATION TO ESTABLISH CATHOLIC SCHOOLS

> Canon 1379, § 1: Si scholae catholicae ad normam can. 1373 sive elementariae sive mediae desint, curandum, praesertim a locorum Ordinariis, ut condantur.

The ecclesiastical legislator in the present canon, which is a practical application of the canon just considered, makes it a point of law that there be established Catholic schools where children and youths may receive an education under ecclesiastical supervision in the light of the principles of the Catholic religion. The obligation imposed by the law, however, is conditional. It exists and is mandatory whenever Catholic schools do not exist, or when the existing schools do not respond to the prescriptions of canon 1373, thus presenting a danger to the faith of Catholic pupils attending them.[30]

The Church respects the rights of both parents and of the State in the establishment of schools. She does not claim a monopoly in education, nor undertake the foundation of educational institutions so long as those already existing have due regard for the place that the Church must have by divine and ecclesiastical law in the schools and in the formation of Catholic youth.[31] At present, however, prevailing conditions very seldom permit the Church to receive the recognition which she merits in regard to her influence and active participation in the school curricula. In such and similar circumstances, therefore, the law of establishing Catholic schools under the direct control of the Church becomes mandatory.[32]

The establishment of Catholic schools has ever been recommended, particularly by Leo XIII, as the most proper means of neutralizing the dangers of non-denominational schools for

[30] Canon 1374.

[31] Creusen, "L'École catholique," *NRT*, LIII (1926), 193; Blanco Nájera, *Derecho Docente*, p. 408; cf. also c. 1, X, *de magistris*, V, 5.

[32] Scharnagl, *Religionsunterricht und Schule*, pp. 21-22; De Luca, *Institutiones Iuris Publici Ecclesiastici* (Romae, 1904), II, 229.

Catholic youth. In a letter of November 27, 1885, he expressed full appreciation to the English bishops for their zeal in establishing schools.[33] In a letter to the bishops of Bavaria he also stated: "We have had many noble examples of religious generosity from Catholics who have established and maintained, with the greatest burden and expense, schools of their own religious conviction in those places where only neutral schools exist. It is to be fervently hoped that these glorious and secure asylums for youth will be established in larger numbers as circumstances and local conditions allow." [34]

Well known, finally, is the zeal of the American episcopacy in establishing a school in every parish, as well as the endeavors of the Dutch hierarchy who, after long and difficult controversies, have gained the juridical and financial equality of their schools as compared with the State schools.[35]

This obligation rests on the local ordinaries, and more particularly on the residential bishops, who are the proper and immediate pastors of the dioceses entrusted to them.[36] As successors of the Apostles they received the direct command to "teach all nations." [37] They were given the care of souls in their respective dioceses. One of the primary and most efficacious means to these ends is the Catholic training of youth.[38] By the fact, however, that the Code says that it concerns primarily local ordinaries to require Catholic schools to be established, the cooperation of others is not excluded. Rather, it implicitly obliges others also, such as priests—more particularly those who have the care of souls as pastors, quasi-

[33] *AAS*, XVIII (1885-86), 305.

[34] Ep. *Officio sanctissimo*, 22 dec. 1887, n. 9—*Fontes*, n. 596.

[35] Cf. *Das holländische Schulgesetz* (Düsseldorf, 1921)—Schulpolitik und Erziehung: Zeitfragen, Heft 11; Scharnagl, *Religionsunterricht und Schule*, p. 21.

[36] Canon 334, § 1.

[37] Matthew, XXVII, 18-19; Mark, XVI, 18.

[38] Cf. Leo XIII, ep. encycl. *Quod multum*, 22 aug. 1889, n. 7—*Fontes*, n. 594; Pius X, litt. encycl. *Acerbo nimis*, 15 apr. 1905, n. 7—*Fontes*, n. 666.

pastors[39]—and generally all the faithful. All are obliged in the degree in which they participate more or less directly in the Apostolic ministry, and in the measure demanded by Christian charity and justice. To this effect the Plenary Council of Latin America, approved by Leo XIII, decreed: " In order to facilitate the grave obligation resting on Catholic parents concerning the education of their children, we command all pastors to found, either through themselves or others, elementary schools in the parish whenever there is at hand no convenient one, in so far as the bishop will judge it possible, and at the time and in the manner established by him."[40] Leo XIII himself mentioned the establishment of Catholic elementary schools as a work most pertinent to the diocesan organization, and of the greatest importance.[41]

Although emphasis is given in the pre-Code legislation to the foundation of elementary rather than of higher schools, the present legislation specifically recommends that both elementary and intermediate schools be established, and implies that the obligation to erect schools should not be limited to one rather than the other. That there is, moreover, an implied obligation to establish such schools is clear from the tenor of the paragraph in question (*curandum est*). It is also clear when compared with paragraph two of the same canon, in which the legislator speaking of the foundation of a Catholic university merely says: *optandum ut . . . condatur.*

Circumstances, together with the law of equity, will have to be considered in judging how far the obligation will extend of establishing in each individual locality schools for both elementary and intermediate pupils. The local ordinaries on whom the obligation primarily rests, will be the judges in particular cases.

[39] Canon 451, § 1, 2.

[40] *Acta et Decreta Concilii Plenarii Americae Latinae* (1899), n. 678.

[41] Const. *Romanos Pontifices*, 8 maii 1881, § 18—*Fontes*, n. 582.

No doubt, elementary teaching by its very nature may be considered of primary interest. Therein more lasting fruits are obtained because the primary schools are attended by children while still at an age when religious formation means most. Nevertheless the law remains, and the diocesan ordinaries have an obligation to provide a Catholic school for intermediate as well as elementary pupils if no suitable one is at hand. In strict law, therefore, a bishop could oblige his priests to build a high school within their parishes whenever necessity demands it. Since, however, many parishes have not within their territory enough children of intermediate school age to warrant the cost of the erection and support of a high school, a happy solution would be to establish one for several parishes and to have the youth from these different parishes attend it. This will, no doubt, satisfy the purpose of the law, which is to provide Catholic youth with a Catholic education in a Catholic school. The fact, moreover, that the teaching especially of higher grades is often undertaken by religious orders or congregations, whose primary purpose is the instruction of youth would considerably alleviate any further obligation on the part of a bishop or pastor to provide for similar schools. Cooperation, of course, should at all times exist between the diocesan clergy and teaching communities so that the work of either will not be impeded, but rather seconded, by the sympathetic efforts of the other.

The provisions of canon 1379 bear a striking analogy to the situation in the United States of America, where, because of the strict neutrality of the public school system, the general ecclesiastical law of the country, as well as the particular laws of each diocese, have recognized the necessity of establishing Catholic schools at any reasonable cost. The initiative taken regarding Catholic schools in this country was always commended by the Holy See in its repeated instructions to the American hierarchy, urging them to carry on the work to its fullness.[42] This courageous task was facilitated to a great extent by the attitude of the civil law of this country, which basically respects the right of both individuals and families. It thus gives them ample opportunity to establish schools, so that they may send their children to institutions of their own choice.[43]

Both the Second and Third Plenary Councils of Baltimore devoted a chapter to the question of parochial schools. The Fathers of the Second Council, after declaring that experience had proved that attendance at public schools constituted a great danger to the faith and morals of Catholic children, concluded that the erection of parochial schools was the necessary remedy.[44] The Fathers of the Third Council likewise insisted on the necessity of parochial schools; and furthermore laid down the following command regarding their erection (n. 199):

> Prope unamquamque ecclesiam ubi nondum existit, scholam parochialem intra duos annos a promulgatione huius Concilii erigendam . . . esse, nisi Episcopus ob graviores difficultates dilationem concedendam esse iudicet.

In order that this command might be fully realized, it was morever decreed:

> Sacerdotem, qui intra hoc tempus erectionem . . . scholae gravi sua negligentia impediat, vel post repetitas Episcopi admonitiones non curet, mereri remotionem ab illa ecclesia.

These decrees of the Council, although more detailed than the law of the Code, are nowise opposed to it; and therefore, con-

[42] Cf. S. C. S. Off., instr. (ad Ep. Stat. Foeder. Americae Septentrion.), 24 nov. 1875—*Fontes*, n. 1046; also the response of the Sacred Congregation for the Propagation of the Faith, Febr. 4, 1895—*Eccl. Review*, XII (1895), 341.

[43] Cf. *Pierce v. Society of Sisters*, 268 U. S. 510; also Lischka, *Private Schools and State Laws*, p. 186.

[44] *Conc. Plen. Balt. II, Acta et Decreta*, n. 430.

tinue to have their full force.[45] They were incorporated into many diocesan statutes,[46] and form the general law regulating the establishment of parochial schools in all the dioceses.

Apparently, these decrees refer only to elementary schools in the parish. The Council speaks of higher schools in n. 209, and strongly advises that as many as are required be founded. All these schools must be so equipped as to respond fully to the needs of the students and the demands of the time.

Neither the Code nor the Baltimore legislation makes direct regulations concerning the general management of these schools. The reason may be due to the variety of conditions which have to be met in various localities, and also to the influence that the civil authorities exercise on the Catholic parochial schools in the matter of standardization. The management of these schools, therefore, rests within the power of each bishop. According to the needs and conditions of the diocese he will set down the rules governing the school activities. In this work he is generally assisted by a diocesan school board composed of several priests. This board administers the affairs of the diocesan schools in the name of the ordinary and in conformity with local conditions.[47] As is evident, the power of this school board depends entirely on the degree of jurisdiction delegated to it by the local ordinary. It does not extend beyond the diocesan school system, nor beyond those schools which either by agreement or contract constitute a part of the diocesan school system. In such a case, the contract entered upon must naturally be respected. No provisions may be enacted which would pass the limits of the contract.

[45] Canon 6, 6°; Barrett, *A Comparative Study of the Councils of Baltimore and the Code of Canon Law,* The Catholic University of America, Canon Law Studies, n. 83 (Washington: The Catholic University of America, 1932), p. 180.

[46] Cf. v. g. *Constitutiones Dioeceseos Bostoniensis* (1935), tit. XIV, n. 164; *Synodus Dioecesana Richmondiensis III* (1933), caput IX, stat. 181; *Statuta Archidioecesis Sancti Francisci* (1936), tit. IV, cap. III, n. 345.

[47] Cf. *Statuta Archidioecesis Sancti Francisci* (1936), Appendix VII, p. 125.

As already stated, the establishment of schools in the dioceses is often undertaken by religious communities whose members devote a great part of their religious life to the education of youth. This work has ever been recommended by the Roman Pontiffs,[48] and it has always proved to be of valuable assistance to Catholic education in the dioceses. Apart from those schools that may be connected with parishes, or erected by diocesan, or by papal religious communities—incorporated, however, with the diocesan school system—the general management of all other schools depends on the religious authorities of the different communities. Over such schools the jurisdiction of the bishop will extend *per se* only to those cases mentioned by the law.[49]

According to canon 497 the permission to establish a religious house includes for all classes of religious the right to exercise the pious works proper to each institute, v. g., teaching. This presupposes, however, the observance of the conditions under which the permission to establish the house was granted. Moreover, for the building and opening of schools separate from the religious house—either exempt or non-exempt—the written permission of the ordinary is necessary and sufficient.[50]

A school may be separate from the religious house either formally or materially. It is formally separate, even though materially united, if the school is conducted for a purpose other than that of the institute. It is materially separate, though not formally—so long as its work is proper to the institute—if the

[48] Cf. Leo XIII, ep. *Au milieu*, 23 dec. 1900, n. 13—*Fontes*, n. 645; Wernz, *Ius Decretalium*, III, pars I, n. 77.

[49] Canons 1336, 1381, 1382.

[50] Canon 497, § 2: "Constituendae novae domus permissio facultatem secumfert . . . pro omnibus religionibus, pia opera exercendi religionis propria, salvis conditionibus in ipsa permissione appositis."

§ 3: "Ut aedificentur et aperiantur schola, hospitium vel similis rationis aedes separata a domo etiam exempta, necessaria est et sufficit specialis Ordinarii scripta licentia."

school is built or opened at a considerable distance from the religious house. The ordinary may have reasons for not permitting the opening of the school at such a distance. On the contrary, when the school is a work proper to the institute opening it (v. g. among the Piarists or Salesians), and is connected with the religious house—or so proximate to it that it must be considered morally united—no special permission is necessary. In virtue of paragraph two, the permission to open a school under such circumstances is contained in the permission to open the religious house itself.[51] In either case, whether the school be separated or not, the ordinary in granting his permission could, however, impose certain conditions which would regulate the status of these schools.[52] He could limit the number of pupils for instance, who are to be received. He could require that the establishment be restricted to certain nationalities, and so forth.[53]

Consideration should in every case be had for the constitutions and by-laws of the religious as approved by the Holy See, in order that they may be faithful to their traditions. In granting permission it seems that the bishop could hardly demand these schools to be so united to the diocesan system that their management be entirely subject to the regulations of the diocesan school board. Complete uniformity of teaching often proves injurious to the progress of science. On the contrary the juxtaposition of different educational establishments, directed by different groups—such as the secular and regular clergy, brothers and sisters—creates a real spirit of emulation, favorable to the progress of studies. Thus, apart from periods of struggle for its very existence, it can hardly

[51] Cf. Fanfani, *De Iure Religiosorum* (2nd ed., Taurini: Marietti, 1925), p. 34; Schäfer, *Compendium de Religiosis* (2nd ed., Münster: Aschendorff, 1931), p. 136; Coronata, *Institutiones Iuris Canonici*, I, 617.

[52] Coronata, *loc. cit.*

[53] Creusen, *Religieux et Religieuses* (3rd ed., Bruxelles: Dewit, 1924), p. 31.

be conceived that teaching in Catholic schools be circumscribed by stereotyped methods and programs.[54]

It may be permitted to conclude at this point that a religious congregation which has opened a house with a school attached is not free henceforth to suppress either the house or the school without the permission of the local ordinary. For suppressing a separate school, as above considered, this permission does not seem necessary *per se*.[55] Considered on this score alone the suppression of such a separate educational establishment belongs entirely to the religious superior. Since, however, this suppression may cause serious detriment to the faithful in the neighborhood, it is only just that the bishop be consulted before final action is taken. On the contrary, the ordinary may not suppress such separate establishments, without some previous understanding with the proper religious superior. By reason of the authorized erection, the institute or community has acquired a right which cannot be annulled without the consent of both parties. The religious however can forfeit their right, through abuse. In case of conflict either of the parties has freedom of recourse to Rome. In certain cases the permission to open a school supposes an agreement, at least tacit, that it will not be suppressed without the authorization of the ordinary. Should the bishop have refrained, for instance, from the establishment of a school himself in order to allow the religious to add such a school to their other enterprises, it is hard to see how the religious could, later on, suppress the school without the bishop's authorization. Otherwise, because of the divergent interests of the diocese or of the parish on the one hand, and of the institute on the other, very serious conflicts might later arise.[56]

[54] Creusen, "L'École catholique," *NRT*, LIII (1926), 193-194.

[55] Vermeersch-Creusen, *Epitome*, I, n. 562.

[56] Creusen, *Religieux et Religieuses*, p. 33.

3. SUPPORT OF CATHOLIC SCHOOLS

> Canon 1379, § 3: Fideles ne omittant adiutricem operam pro viribus conferre in catholicas scholas . . . sustentandas.

What the Third Plenary Council of Baltimore urged on the Catholics of the United States for the support of their schools,[57] the Code of Canon Law makes a duty of all the faithful of the world for the support of their own Catholic schools.

This obligation has its basis in the natural law. Every person who devotes his time and energy to the giving of an actual and necessary service to others has a natural right to expect a recompense sufficiently large to enable him to support himself and carry out his work. The mere suggestion that a physician, for instance, should render his services gratis, and support himself and his clinic by extraneous productive labor, would be regarded as absurd. Complaints may perhaps sometimes be heard that certain classes of public officials demand a compensation entirely out of proportion to the services which they render, or that they do not give adequate service for the salary they receive. The very fact of such complaints, however, testifies to a common belief in the justice of the rule that "the laborer is worthy of his hire." [58]

The mission of the Church is to teach and to save souls. That she renders a real service thereby is acknowledged by all her members. The fact that a person remains a member of the Church can be looked upon as evidence that he considers her help necessary to attain his ultimate end—the glory of God and the saving of his own soul. The Church needs temporal means to carry on her work of teaching and saving souls. Hence, she has an undeniable right, based on the natural law, to demand that those who benefit by her services furnish her with the necessary support. Furthermore, she exercises this right as a perfect society, independently of any civil power.

[57] *Acta et Decreta Conc. Plen. Balt. Tertii*, n. 202.

[58] Luke, X, 7.

Rightfully, then, she exacts from her members the necessary support for carrying on her work,[59] not the least important part of which is carried on through her schools.

True, it is not the concern of the Church alone to erect and maintain schools. Other agencies (v. g. the family and the State) share this right. But in the case where there are no suitable Catholic schools—as the case is here considered—it becomes necessary for the Church to establish schools of her own. It then becomes the duty in justice on the part of her members to support such institutions.

Besides this obligation of natural justice, there is another reason arising from divine positive law, which obliges them to support Catholic schools. The faithful through Baptism are separated from the infidel world. They become members of the Church and are united in the mystical Body of Christ, thus forming a part of the royal priesthood,[60] partaking also of the very ministerial character of Christ.[61] Moreover, as members of Catholic Action they are bound to cooperate in the apostleship of the Church for the saving of souls. Since the school is one of the chief means of extending the Church's work in saving souls they must contribute to its establishment as well as to its support.[62]

This obligation, originating in both the natural and the divine law, rests *in solidum* on every member of the Church's society. Nor should it be said that it rests upon parents only, merely because it is they who make use in a more direct manner of the privileges afforded by Catholic schools through sending their children to them to be educated. The Catholic school affects the whole Christian community, and serves a common purpose. Therefore, the obligation of its support rests on

59 Canon 1496.

60 I Peter, II, 9.

61 St. Thomas, *Summa*, pars III, Q. LXIII, a. III.

62 Cf. Pius XI, litt. encycl. *Divini illius Magistri*, 31 dec. 1929—*AAS*, XXII (1930), 79; Civardi, *A Manual of Catholic Action*, p. 5.

every other member as well.[63] Parents indeed must contribute in a more active manner for instance, by paying a fee imposed by the school authorities. Nevertheless, the fact remains that every one of the faithful is bound by a proportionate obligation. Furthermore, since a good moral and Christian education is of greatest importance to the well-being of society at large,[64] and the purpose of society is to procure and foster a constant betterment, both material and spiritual, of the individuals and families composing it, this obligation rests also on the civil authority, especially when it professes the Catholic faith. It is, then, the duty of the State, either to establish Catholic schools, or if this is not feasible on account of the different beliefs of its citizens, at least to contribute proportionately to the erection and support of Catholic schools.[65]

When the State refuses to render support to Catholic schools, or to contribute proportionately, and makes provision for public instruction only by a neutral or mixed school system—proposing at the same time, that every one who wants an education at the public expense must make use of these schools—it commits a serious offense against distributive justice at large.[66] This case is particularly true in the United States of America, where Catholics are confronted with a double burden in order to give a proper education to their children. As citizens of the country in which they live, they must pay for the national school system which in conscience they cannot allow their children to utilize. Moreover, they are faced with the additional

[63] *Acta et Decreta Conc. Plen. Quebecensis* (1909), n. 287 *d.*

[64] Cf. Leo XIII, litt. encycl. *Sapientiae,* 10 ian. 1890, n. 2—*Fontes,* n. 605; Pius XI, litt. encycl. *Divini illius Magistri,* 31 dec. 1929—*AAS,* XXII (1930), 51.

[65] Ottaviani, *Institutiones Iuris Publici Ecclesiastici,* II, 245; cf. also art. 6 of the Concordat with Bavaria—*AAS,* XVII (1925), 45; art. 23 of the Conc. with Germany—*AAS,* XXV (1933), 402; art. 6, § 4 of the Conc. with Austria—*AAS,* XXVI (1934), 257; Restrepo, *Concordata,* p. 636, note 547.

[66] Pius XI, litt. encycl. *Divini illius Magistri,* 31 dec. 1929—*AAS,* XXII (1930), 78; Monti, *La Libertà della Scuola,* pp. 61-64.

financial obligation of supporting the schools of their own choice. The Catholic schools, by educating children who are also citizens and members of the society in which they live, are, in justice, entitled to a proportionate share in the money which is allotted for public education. In many dioceses a real struggle is going on between the ecclesiastical authorities and the members of the legislature, in order to bring about a settlement of this important question. Indeed, it is to be hoped that the Catholics of the United Staes be given a fair deal in this matter, as justice dictates and public interest demands.[67]

Passing on now to a consideration of the "*adiutricem operam*" furnished by the faithful in support of the Catholic schools, the question may be raised: how must they support the Catholic schools? The Code does not specify any particular method in this regard. It simply reminds the faithful of their obligation and insists that they contribute to the best of their ability: . . . *adiutricem operam pro viribus conferre.* The local ordinaries, on whom the obligation of establishing Catholic schools rests primarily, will be the judges to determine the method of support which is considered most fitting for the particular circumstances and needs.

The Council of Baltimore favors the idea of organizing in each parish some kind of society, the purpose of which is to solicit financial contributions, so that the parochial schools may be ever efficient in carrying on their work and, as far as possible, rendered free of charge for the pupils attending them.[68] According to some authors,[69] a gradual formation of endowment funds would seem to offer a happy solution, especially in regard to the support of higher schools. It is often difficult,

[67] For a thorough study of the question of State support for Catholic schools, cf. Gabel, *Public Funds for Church and Private Schools*, particularly pp. 750-779.

[68] *Acta et Decreta Conc. Plen. Baltim. Tertii*, n. 202.

[69] Cf. Kremer, *Church Support in the United States*, The Catholic University of America, Canon Law Studies, n. 61 (Washington: The Catholic University of America, 1930), pp. 61, 69.

indeed, to convince the faithful that they should help to support these institutions. The general attitude is that those who benefit directly from these schools should be willing to support them. These funds would dispense with the annual assessing of parishes, or the taking up of extra collections, so necessary under present conditions for the maintenance of these schools, but often also a continual source of irritation or of financial embarrassment to the parishes.

In addition to making individual proportionate contributions towards the maintenance of their institutions of learning, Catholics might also as citizens, by a discreet exercise of the franchise, bring influence to bear on the public authority to establish Catholic schools or, if already established, to make an equitable contribution towards their support. This, under a democratic form of government, even though it does not profess the Catholic faith, should not be impossible, for much of the action of the legislature is influenced by the votes of the citizens.[70] In the event that the civil laws permit the taxpayers' money to be disposed of according to their wishes either for the benefit of the State neutral schools, or for the benefit of denominational schools, Catholics would undoubtedly sin gravely by offering their money for the support of the neutral schools, in defiance of the Catholic schools.[71]

There are, indeed, various methods by which Catholics can contribute to the support of their schools. As already mentioned, the local ordinaries are the immediate judges in particular cases, according to circumstances and needs. Their directions, however, will have to be followed, and, there is no doubt, they can even proceed with penalties against grave and notorious delinquents.[72] The penalties that are to be employed, should the ordinary find it necessary to resort to force,

[70] Coronata, *Institutiones Iuris Canonici*, II, 305; Michel, *La Question Scolaire et les Principes Théologiques*, p. 131, note 2.

[71] Cf. *Acta et Decreta Concilii Plen. Quebecensis* (1909), n. 287 *e*.

[72] Cf. *Acta et Decreta Conc. Plen. Baltim. Tertii*, n. 199, III; Vromant, *Ius Missionariorum* (Bruxelles: Dewit, 1929), II, 75.

constitute a difficult question. If a delinquent in a particular case is gravely guilty and obstinate, absolution would have to be denied him, as in the case of any other unrepentent sinner. But it is generally impossible in actual life to be morally certain of the presence of grave guilt. If there is doubt about the gravity of the guilt, the confessor would have to give the penitent the benefit of the doubt and absolve him. Under these circumstances the infliction of the graver penalties, excommunication and interdict, would certainly be unjustified.[73]

As a conclusion, the words of Pius XI are worthy of study in dealing with the support of Catholic schools: "Catholics", said the Pope, "will never feel, whatever may have been the sacrifices already made, that they have done enough, for the support and defense of their schools and for the securing of laws that will do them justice. For, whatever Catholics do in promoting and defending the Catholic school for their children, is a genuinely religious work, and therefore, an important task of Catholic Action. For this reason, the associations which in various countries are so zealously engaged in this work of prime necessity are especially dear to Our paternal heart and are deserving of every commendation." [74]

[73] Canon 2218, § 3. Cf. also Kremer, *Church Support in the United States,* p. 53.

[74] Litt. encycl. *Divini illius magistri,* 31 dec. 1929—*AAS,* XXII (1930), 79.

CHAPTER X

Special Rights of the Church

1. EXCLUSIVE AND DIRECT RIGHT OF THE CHURCH

Canon 1381, § 1: Religiosa iuventutis institutio in scholis quibuslibet auctoritati et inspectioni Ecclesiae subiicitur.

The present canon reaffirms the divine right of the Church over the religious formation which is given to her children in the schools. As the Church was founded by Christ for the purpose of leading men to salvation, she was vested by Christ with a unique authority over matters of faith and morals. She was established as " the column and foundation of truth, in order to teach the divine faith to all, to direct men's actions and establish them in honesty of conduct and regularity of life according to the rules of revealed doctrine." [1]

This character of the Church is so essential to her very nature that she cannot divest herself of it without at the same time defeating the purpose for which she was established. Since this character is part of her *direct power*, no one can usurp her position whether it be an individual, a community, or the State. To no one other than to the Church was confided the power of dispensing and interpreting divine revelation.[2] The authoritative supervision of religion, when taught in the school, must fall entirely within the competence of the Church. This is true irrespective of the necessity of teaching religion in the school either as a mere subject on the curriculum, or as a vital educative element. To deny this is tantamount to im-

[1] Pius IX, ep. *Quum non sine*, 14 iul. 1864, n. 2—*Fontes*, n. 539.

[2] Cf. canon 1322; Leo XIII, ep. encycl. *Immortale Dei*, 1 nov. 1885, n. 5—*Fontes*, n. 592; ep. encycl. *Satis cognitum*, 29 iun. 1896, nn. 16, 18—*Fontes*, n. 630.

plying that the Church lacks that exclusive juridical power which, as a divinely established society she has in the field of religion and morals. It is equivalent to setting up either the individual or the State as the sole agent in matters of faith and morality. The Church by her very nature is a juridical person. She is supreme in the spiritual sphere, and empowered with all the means necessary for the exercise and performance of her mission.[3]

Individuals and families, as members of the Church by Baptism, must conform to her directions concerning the religious education of their children. The State, as promoter of the rights and duties of families, must abide by whatever the Church ordains in what constitutes her sphere of jurisdiction. To attribute to the State any control over matters touching directly the spiritual order, as for instance, the religious training of youth, would be to confuse the spheres of the two societies. Religious training, both as a subject to be taught and as a vital educative element, pertains by divine ordinance to the teaching office of the Church. As Leo XIII writes: " The Almighty has apportioned the charge of the human race between two powers, the ecclesiastical and the civil, the one being set over things divine, and the other over human things. Each in its kind is supreme, each has fixed limits within which it is contained, limits which are defined by the nature and special object of the province of each, so that there is, we may say, an orbit traced out within which the action of each is brought into play by its own native right." [4]

This right of the Church in the domain of religion is a right which implies authority, or jurisdiction, in virtue of which she has a true power to teach her members the truths of faith, and

[3] Leo XIII, ep. *Officio sanctissimo*, 22 dec. 1887, n. 13—*Fontes*, n. 596; cf. Ruffini, *La Personalità Giuridica Internazionale della Chiesa* (Isola del Liri: Soc. Tip. Macioce & Pisani, 1936), pp. 34, 64. Cavagnis, *Institutiones Iuris Publici Ecclesiastici*, I, 248.

[4] Ep. encycl. *Immortale Dei*, 1 nov. 1885, n. 6—*Fontes*, n. 592. Cf. also Jansen, *De Facultate Docendi*, pp. 63-65.

to demand that the same be accepted. Such right derives from her divine mission itself.[5] It is not a question here of a mere request, but rather of the power of exacting or demanding that religious instruction be given, and that this be done under her own control.[6]

Together with this authority which the Church exercises by divine right in matters of religion, there is intimately connected the subject of inspection. She has the right and the duty to see to it that the teaching of religion be consistent with the principles of faith and Christian morality. These two prerogatives—authority and inspection—are correlatives. The latter is the necessary consequence and completion of the former. It would avail little if one possessing authority in a certain field of knowledge, would at the same time be deprived of the right of inspection in this domain.

The ambit, furthermore, within which the Church exercises her authority and vigilance over the religious formation of youth extends to any school attended by Catholics. Catholics are her subjects. Over them she has direct jurisdiction. The mere fact that a school is founded by private individuals, communities, or by governments, does not restrict her authority. The Church alone is the competent authority in what concerns the religious formation of youth.[7]

Moreover, the schools are but agencies erected for the assistance of the three institutions: family, Church, and State, in the carrying on of the work of formal education. To deny the Church what is hers exclusively is to go against the very order of things as ordained by God.[8] It is, to say the least, an injustice both to the Church and to Christian pupils. The former has a divine commission to teach and the latter are

[5] Cavagnis, *Institutiones Iuris Publici Ecclesiastici*, I, 28.

[6] Coronata, *Institutiones Iuris Canonici*, II, 306.

[7] Wernz, *Ius Decretalium*, III, pars I, n. 69, *a*.

[8] Cf. Romans, XIII, 1.

bound by a strict obligation to learn and live according to those truths which are for them of prime importance.

The religious element in the school requires, in addition, that the teachers possess firm religious convictions which not only regulate their lives, but also are reflected in their teaching. Even in the case of a sincere and thoroughly Catholic teacher, there is need of authoritative direction and control. If the authority of the Church be denied, there is no longer any guarantee that a teacher will remain within the limits of orthodoxy. His personal sentiments though inspired by the best intentions, may lead him to ambiguity, exaggerations, and even to error in the teaching and the application of truths which, partly at least, by their very import surpass human understanding. The authority of the Church—the infallible teacher of religion—must, therefore, be absolutely accepted. For Catholics this is a matter of faith which cannot be denied without heresy.[9]

To admit religion in the school and at the same time to exclude the authority of the Church is a contradiction. Such a concept would be parallel to that of a ship without a pilot in mid-ocean left to the mercy of the winds. The results would be devastating.[10]

The Church's authority over religion in all schools belongs *in concreto* to the appropriate prelate hierarchically constituted according to the degrees of ecclesiastical jurisdiction. Primarily, therefore, and in the highest degree, it belongs to the Pope. As successor of St. Peter he has supreme power in matters of divine revelation, and has jurisdiction over the universal Church. To the bishops, under the authority of the Roman Pontiff, the same power is given within their own territory. They are, in fact, the teachers of faith and the

[9] Cf. Vatican Council, *Constitutio dogmatica I de Ecclesia Christi*, sess. IV —Denzinger-Umberg, *Enchir. Symbol.*, n. 1821.

[10] Michel, *La Question Scolaire et les Principes Théologiques*, pp. 152-153.

judges of morals by divine authority, and they rule the dioceses committed to their care.[11]

Apart from any consideration of those to be instructed, the content of the teaching of religion in the schools may be classified in the following general groups: 1) apologetics, which examines the principal truths concerning man, God, natural religion, supernatural religion, the divinity of Christ and His religion, and the Church. 2) The dogmatic truths as contained in the Apostles' Creed and in the definitions of the Church. These include a study of the unity and trinity of God, the mystery of the Incarnation, the doctrine regarding the Blessed Virgin, the public life of Christ, His death and resurrection, the action of the Holy Ghost, the Church and her distinguishing marks, the primacy and infallibility of the Pope, the episcopacy, the remission of sin, the resurrection of the dead, the communion of saints, particular judgment at death, purgatory, the general judgment at the end of the world, hell, heaven, and life eternal. 3) The moral truths, under which is grouped the consideration of the commandments of God and the Church, sin and its species, the cardinal virtues, the beatitudes, the works of mercy, the state of life, and the daily pious exercises of a good Christian. 4) The Sacraments, in which group is included a study of the nature and kinds of grace, together with an examination of each of the seven Sacraments. 5) The liturgy, which explains the various kinds of prayer, the external solemnity associated with public acts of worship—primarily the holy Sacrifice of the Mass. 6) Religious history, which includes Old Testament History, New Testament History, and a brief conspectus of Church History.[12]

[11] Conc. Trid., sess. XXIII, *de sacr. ord.*, c. 4; Bouix, *Tractatus de Episcopis et Synodo dioecesana* (Paris, 1853), p. 81.

[12] *Periodica*, XIX (1930), 202-206.

2. INDIRECT RIGHT

> Canon 1381, § 2: Ordinariis locorum ius et officium est vigilandi ne in quibusvis scholis sui territorii quidquam contra fidem vel bonos mores tradatur aut fiat.

With the direct right which the Church has over the control of religion in the schools, there is intimately connected another question which falls within the competence of each local ordinary: the right and duty to see that nothing against faith or Christian morality be taught or done within the schools of his territory. This comes from the very nature of the episcopal office.[13] It has its reason in the fact that morality cannot be detached from religion. Religion is the foundation of morality. It would be impossible to conceive even of the beneficial effects of morality without admitting the necessity of its cause—religion. The two go hand in hand. They come from the same principle. Therefore, they must be governed by the same authority.

In order that the Church may effectively exercise this right of vigilance over matters touching religion and morals in the schools, her right will have to extend to the very school curriculum. Thus, in virtue of her indirect power, she must see that the teaching of profane sciences be in keeping with revealed doctrine, and that the general disciplinary rules of the school be in conformity with Christian morality.[14]

This exercise of supervision should not be considered as a confusion of powers. Regarding the Church's power it is not difficult to distinguish two different aspects, according to the matters in which it is exercised. In spiritual things she has a proper and direct authority. In temporal things *per se* she

[13] Although the canon speaks of local ordinaries, thus including all those mentioned in canon 198, § 1, more properly, however, does the Code specify that residential bishops, who are the proper and immediate pastors of the dioceses entrusted to them, are bound to fulfill this obligation. Cf. canon 336, § 2. This obligation rests also on others, as will be seen later.

[14] Wernz, *Ius Decretalium*, III, pars I, n. 72, *b*.

exercises no direct control. Indirectly, however, in so far as things temporal often overlap the spiritual, she justly claims a certain authority in these also. This relation becomes more evident upon consideration that human acts are more or less connected with the use of temporal goods. All these goods are created for man, and he must make use of them with the view of attaining his ultimate end. There is, therefore, no human power that can with impunity absolutely ignore the supernatural order. The Church, on her part, must watch that these temporal goods as used by men do not become an obstacle to the salvation of their souls. The direct right which is hers of maintaining among Christians a respect for the laws of nature and of God has, as a correlative, a genuine, though indirect, power concerning the things of the temporal order. This indirect power consists not only in preventing any injury to the supernatural order by things temporal; but also in establishing an harmonious accord between both orders.[15]

This principle applies particularly to the relation between the supernatural order of faith and the natural order of reason. Confronted with the charges of modern rationalists, the supreme magisterium of the Church has not ceased to emphasize the Catholic doctrine. She sharply distinguishes the domain of faith from that of reason. She states that no real opposition can exist between them, for both have their origin in the eternal and immutable Truth which is God Himself. On the contrary, since they have the same origin, they must be mutually sustaining.[16]

The Church, being entrusted by Christ with the mission of teaching all truths, must teach revealed truths, and keep intact the deposit of sacred doctrine. Thus, she defends it from any

[15] Michel, *La Question Scolaire et les Principes Théologiques*, pp. 39-40.

[16] Vatican Council, *Constitutio dogmatica de fide catholica*, sess. III, cap. IV, *de fide et ratione*—Denzinger-Umberg, *Enchir. Symbol.*, n. 1797; cf. also nn. 1635, 1649.

possible attack. Logically following therefrom is her right and duty of watching over all teaching, in order to prevent even profane sciences from becoming for teachers or for pupils an obstacle to faith or morals. "The Church, having received along with the apostolic mission to teach, the command to safeguard the deposit of faith, has also from God the right and duty to condemn false science, 'lest any man be deluded by philosophy and vain deceit.'"[17] To this solemn statement, the same Vatican Council adds the following anathema: "If any one says that human learning is to be accorded such liberty that its statements, even when they are opposed to revealed doctrine, can yet be held as true; and cannot be proscribed by the Church, let him be anathema."[18]

It is, therefore, an incontestable right of the Church to watch over the whole training imparted to Catholic youth. When it is a question of religious training, her title comes from her power which is direct, independent, and absolute. When it is a question of profane teaching, her title comes from her power which is indirect, and in virtue of which she "has the right and the means to prevent the teaching of profane sciences or any bad example from becoming a detriment to the belief or practices of Catholic youth."[19]

Leo XIII, in his letter to the bishops of Bavaria, strongly vindicates this double function: "It is unjust," he says, "to exclude from the domain of letters and science the authority of the Catholic Church, because it is to the Church that God has entrusted the mission to teach religion, namely, to inculcate what every man needs to achieve eternal salvation. This mission was given to no other society. No one else but the Church can claim it. . . . Moreover, the greatest care and attention must be used in order that in those schools which

[17] Vatican Council—*op. cit.*, n. 1798.

[18] *Canones de fide catholica*, cap. IV, *de fide et ratione*, c. 2—Denzinger-Umberg, *Enchir. Symbol.*, n. 1817.

[19] Sortais, "Instruction de la jeunesse," *Dictionnaire Apologétique de la Foi catholique*, II, 919.

partly or completely freed themselves from the yoke of the Church, youth be in no peril and suffer no damage to Catholic faith and morals." [20] The Plenary Council of Latin America summarizes thus this Catholic teaching: "Because it is her right, (the Church) . . . claims jurisdiction over the religious instruction and formation of Catholic youth; and the right to prohibit anything to be taught in any subject, which is against Catholic religion and good morals." [21]

Finally, Pius XI in his encyclical on Christian education vindicates anew this same doctrine: "Again," he writes, "it is the inalienable right as well as the indispensable duty of the Church, to watch over the entire education of her children in all institutions, whether public or private, not merely in regard to religious instruction there given, but in regard to every other branch of learning and every regulation in so far as religion and morality are concerned. Nor should the exercise of this right be considered undue interference, but rather maternal care on the part of the Church in protecting her children from the grave danger of all kinds of doctrinal and moral evil. Moreover, this watchfulness of the Church not only can create no real inconvenience, but must, on the contrary, confer valuable assistance in the right ordering and well-being of families and of civil society; for it keeps far away from youth the moral poison which at that inexperienced and changeable age more easily penetrates the mind and more rapidly spreads its baneful effects." [22] The fact that the Church is forbidden to supervise the education of her children in the public schools of many countries does not deprive her of her right to do so. The possession of a right is one thing, its use is quite another.[23]

This right of vigilance in relation to secular matters in the schools is *per se* of a negative nature. It empowers the holder

[20] Ep. *Officio sanctissimo*, 22 dec. 1887, n. 9—*Fontes*, n. 596.

[21] *Acta et Decreta Concilii Plenarii Americae Latinae* (1899), n. 674.

[22] Litt. encycl. *Divini illius Magistri*, 31 dec. 1929—*AAS*, XXII (1930), 56.

[23] Pius IX, allocut. *In consistoriali*, 1 nov. 1850, n. 9—*Fontes*, n. 509; Ottaviani, *Institutiones Iuris Publici Ecclesiastici*, II, 250.

to see that nothing takes place which, in any way, is contrary to faith or morals. The Code expressly calls it a right of vigilance. The word "vigilance," from the Latin *vigilare*, indicates that quality or state which makes one tend to supervise those things for which he is responsible. From the pedagogical point of view *vigilance* includes an intervention in school affairs extending to the whole routine of the school and affecting both teachers and pupils. As it is used by the canon here, distinct also from the right of visitation referred to in canon 1382, it seems to be reduced in meaning to a mere general supervision, and to an intervention in those cases only where there is a well-founded suspicion of error concerning integrity of belief, or offence against Christian morality.[24]

Par excellence the local ordinaries are the pastors of their territories, and the constituted judges in matters of faith and morals. To them principally then, this right and its resultant duty pertain. This obligation is a personal one, in the sense that the local ordinaries are personally charged with the responsibility of preventing any departure from the truths of faith and the principles of morality in the schools within their territories. This vigilance is a part of the office of the care of souls. It touches more or less directly anyone who is connected with this ministry. The Code of Canon Law enumerates among the duties of pastors that of a particular vigilance lest in the public and private schools in their parishes anything be taught which does not correspond with faith and morals.[25] Among the pastors the residential bishops, as *Ordinarii loci,* are obliged especially by reason of their office to exercise this vigilance. They are to see that the "purity of faith and morals be preserved both among the clergy and the laity," and that "in schools, both for children and youth, the training be in conformity with the principles of the Catholic religion."[26]

[24] Blanco Nájera, *Derecho Docente*, pp. 430-431.

[25] Canon 469.

[26] Canon 336, § 2. Cf. also S. C. C., *Conimbricen.*, 18 aug., 1 sept. 1888—*ASS*, XXI (1888), 686.

3. EXTENT OR PRACTICAL APPLICATION OF THE TWO RIGHTS

> Canon 1381, § 3: Eisdem [Ordinariis locorum] similiter ius est approbandi religionis magistros et libros; itemque, religionis morumque causa, exigendi ut tum magistri tum libri removeantur.

This paragraph is an extension or rather a further practical application of the principles established in the two previous articles. Because of the direct power of the Church over religion, it also rests on her, more specifically on the local ordinaries, to approve the teachers and textbooks to be used in teaching religion. Furthermore, the local ordinaries are the recognized judges in faith and morals within their respective territories. Their power in regard to schools extends indirectly to every branch of learning and of management. Hence it follows that they have a right to demand that teachers who are in any way unfit or books which are in any way dangerous be removed, because of religion and morality.

A. *Extent arising from the direct power.* The right to approve books and teachers of religion.

a) *Books.* There can be no doubt that the books which are used for the teaching of religion must be approved by the local ordinaries. These books contain the truths of religion. Since the teaching of religion is by law subject to the local ordinaries, it is but natural that the instruments used for this purpose be equally subject to them.

The main textbook of religion is the catechism which is principally used in the elementary schools. In the intermediate schools the catechism is supplemented by other works, such as apologetical treatises, Bible and Church histories, and the like, according to the particular laws and customs, and to the aptitudes of the students.

In the instruction of youth the most important point is the adapting of the subject matter to the mental ability of the various groups of students. Prescinding from the work of the teacher, it must be admitted that this is done chiefly by the proper selection of textbooks of Christian doctrine.[27] In this regard, according to the regulation of the Code,[28] it is necessary that the local ordinary approve the texts which are to be used in the schools of the diocese. Consequently, the choice of textbooks does not belong to the school authorities.[29] This is especially true of the textbooks to be used in those schools which are not under the direct management of the Church.[30] This is true also of the schools which come under the more immediate direction of the Church. Creusen is of the opinion that in Catholic schools which are not immediately under the jurisdiction of the bishops (as, for instance, schools of regulars) the local ordinary has no authority to impose a specific textbook of religion in preference to another text which, from the doctrinal point of view, is irreproachable.[31] This, however, does not seem correct. All religious, including those that are exempt, are obliged to observe the regulations of the local ordinary in the teaching of religion generally. This applies to the prescription of textbooks also, since this phase of instruction is likewise under his supervision.[32]

[27] "Textbooks" is used advisedly in this instance in contradistinction to "catechism", which is commonly accepted to designate a question and an answer text. It is not necessary to use the latter for all groups, if teaching methods among some of them may be better served by another form.

[28] Canon 1336.

[29] Jansen, *Canonical Provisions for Catechetical Instruction*, p. 46.

[30] Wernz, *Ius Decretalium*, III, pars I, n. 76; cf. also art. 13, n. 1 of the Concordat with Lithuania—*AAS*, XIX (1927), 428; art. 36, Conc. with Italy—*AAS*, XXI (1929), 291; art. 20, § 6, Conc. with Roumania—*AAS*, XXI (1929), 450; art. 21, Conc. with Germany—*AAS*, XXV (1933), 401; art. 6, § 1, Conc. with Austria—*AAS*, XXVI (1934), 256.

[31] "L'École catholique," *NRT*, 53 (1926), 189.

[32] Canon 1336; S. C. C., decr., *Provido sane*, 12 ian. 1935—*AAS*, XXVII (1935), 151. The ordinary could even proceed to punish religious if these fail to abide by his regulations regarding the prescribed texts (canon 619).

In applying canon 619 the bishop *per se* may proceed by way of both vindictive and medicinal penalties (censures). His authority extends over both non-exempt religious and exempt religious, regulars not excepted (Wernz-Vidal, *Ius Canonicum*, III, 436). By virtue of a special privilege

A desire for uniformity, at least for catechisms printed in the same language, has frequently been expressed by the Roman Pontiffs and by many provincial councils. It was also a subject of discussion in the Vatican Council.[33] It would seem that the ordinary should demand this uniformity as well. The reasons for this may be manifold. Uniformity would be a stabilizing influence. The people, especially the parents would be enabled to teach and examine their children from the same text with which they themselves are familiar. Moreover, errors would be prevented from creeping into the catechism, and purity of doctrine would thus be more easily maintained. At the same time, the methods employed in teaching catechism would become more stabilized. A final advantage would be that a secure foundation would be given and a reliable source of Catholic literature would be established especially in the polemic and apologetic field.[34]

In the United States there still may be raised the question as to whether the Catechism of Christian Doctrine prepared and prescribed by the Third Plenary Council of Baltimore must be used, since the council decreed as follows:

> . . . hoc catechismo [a coetu R.morum Archiepiscoporum approbato] in lucem edito quamprimum uti teneantur omnes . . . praeceptores tam religiosi quam laici.[35]

This catechism, when edited, was approved by Archbishop Gibbons in 1885. There is no evidence to show that this catechism was approved by the archbishops as a body in the

granted to regulars, and to those who participate in their privileges, the bishop *per accidens* may not apply censures, except in such instances in which he is granted special authorization by way of exception to the privilege. Religious instruction seems to be one of these exceptions. Cf. Piatus Montensis, *Praelectiones Juris Regularis* (3rd ed., Tornaci, 1906), II, q. 13.

[33] Wernz, *Ius Decretalium*, III, par I, n. 46; Conc. Vat. (1869-1870)—*Coll. Lac.*, VII, 663-666.

[34] Cf. "Il Catechismo Unico," *Civiltà Cattolica*, II (1905), 385-401.

[35] *Conc. Plen. Balt. III*, n. 219.

manner which the council had expressly stipulated. As a consequence, the approbation of Cardinal Gibbons would not suffice for such a general approbation.[36] Therefore, the use of this textbook cannot be said to be obligatory. The ordinary of the diocese then is free to determine the textbook of religion to be employed. Even if this decree had been in force at any time, custom would have nullified its force. Since 1885, throughout many of the dioceses of the United States of America, other catechism texts have been used with either the explicit or at least implicit approval of the ordinaries. The conclusion is obvious, especially when it is considered that a custom of forty years' continuous duration against an ecclesiastical law abolishes such law—provided the custom itself is reasonable, and is not expressly reprobated.[37]

The teaching of religion, as of any other subject, avails little unless the matter be presented to the students in an orderly manner. This is done when a method is used whose principal aim is to adapt the content of the instruction to the mental ability of the various groups of pupils. Since the method of teaching is intimately related to the object taught, it consequently falls within the power of the ecclesiastical authority to decide the method to be followed.

A distinction must here be made. There are certain elements which are essential, and which are objectively related to the matter taught. There are other elements of a character strictly psychological. These latter are dependent upon the individual personality of the teacher. The ecclesiastical authority may hence prescribe the general method, as well as the quantity, order, and content of the matter to be taught. It can even demand that certain parts be known by heart.[38] On the contrary, if there is question of determining the particular

[36] *HPR*, XXXIII (1933), 1198-99.

[37] Canon 27.

[38] Wernz (*Ius Decretalium*, III, pars I, n. 76) remarks that the local ordinary should avoid taking measures which might possibly disturb the order of the school, especially of the common schools.

details of teaching methods, the rôle of the ecclesiastical authority has no longer the same importance. The experience of a good teacher, such as is often found in this or that teaching order or congregation would then seem to be favored.

b) *Teachers.* It is the duty of the local ordinary not only to approve the books to be used in classes of religion, and to lay down standard teaching methods, but also to approve the teachers who are employed in carrying on this teaching in the schools.[39]

Before analyzing this point, however, some remarks must be made concerning the teaching magisterium of the Church, which can be either public or private. The former belongs properly to the Church as hierarchically constituted. Relative to it Christ has given the authority to teach whilst promising at the same time His assistance. No one can assume this office unless he has been given authority to do so. The private magisterium is a prerogative of the faithful provided that they be sufficiently learned. Suarez says in this connection: " Privata instructio aut doctrina fieri potest a quocumque fideli sufficienter erudito, quando ratio charitatis et occasio id postulaverit; nam tunc locum habet illud: ' Unicuique mandavit Deus de proximo suo.' Tunc enim non est usurpata iurisdictio, quia actio illa non fit quasi ex pastorali officio, sed ex obligatione vel consilio charitatis." [40]

In order to teach in a public capacity, and thus to partake of the public magisterium, one must first receive a commission to do so. This commission, which is called the *missio canonica,* may be defined as a positive deputation, given by the proper ecclesiastical authority, to teach revealed doctrine. The necessity of the *missio canonica* arises from the nature of the teaching office as such, inasmuch as it is not to be exercised until one has been admitted into the body of authorized

[39] Cf. Jansen, *De Facultate Docendi*, p. 63.

[40] *De Fide*, disput. XVIII, sect. I, n. 5; cf. also Leo XIII, litt. encycl. *Sapientiae*, 10 ian. 1890, n. 8—*Fontes*, n. 605.

teachers.[41] In other words, teaching in a public capacity implies the right to teach. This right must be obtained from the lawful authority who, in this instance, is the local ordinary.

To participate in the private magisterium of the Church, on the contrary, there is no need of a deputation by the ordinary in the sense of the *missio canonica.* The position of those undertaking this teaching is that of private persons teaching in a private capacity. Thus, for instance, parents may, nay, must, instruct their children in religion. For this however, they do not require a *missio canonica* from the Church.[42]

Relative to the authority of the bishop over the teachers of religion, several distinctions are to be made according to the various kinds of schools. Cavagnis[43] distinguishes in this regard three types of schools: strictly private schools, public schools, and those schools which are established along the lines of the public schools.

I. Private schools are those conducted by the parents themselves, or established by the express delegation of one or more families for the purpose of training their children.

By reason of divine dispensation the Church was constituted supreme in matters of religion. According to her dictates and directions Catholic parents must educate their children while

[41] Conc. Trid., sess., XXIII, *de sacr. ordinis*, c. 7; Wernz, *Ius Decretalium*, III, pars I, nn. 26, 28.

[42] Coronata, *Institutiones Iuris Canonici*, II, 303; Sägmüller, *Lehrbuch des katholischen Kirchenrechts* (3rd ed., Freiburg im Breisgau, 1914), II, 4.

It may be said that in this case a kind of *missio canonica* is given to parents in the very celebration of their marriage. The marriage of the baptized is always and necessarily a Sacrament, and as such is subject to the jurisdiction of the Church. Parents, in so far as they are recognized by the Church as suitable for marriage, receive from her the mandate for the supernatural education of their children according to the principles of the Christian religion. In this sense parents are real mandatories of the Church and the instruments which she uses in the exercise of her ministry for the salvation of souls. Cf. Cappello, *Summa Iuris Publici Ecclesiastici*, pp. 504-505. What is spoken of here, however, is not the *missio canonica* proper.

[43] *Institutiones Iuris Publici Ecclesiastici*, III, 25-38.

at the same time these parents remain subject to her. Although this obligation of parents is a personal one, in the sense that they cannot waive it, they may delegate others to perform this duty for them. This is true especially when there is question of insufficient knowledge on their part, or of rendering the work of instruction easier and more efficacious. As the parents must be subject to the Church, so also those teachers, who take the place or carry on the work of parents, must depend upon the Church. This is true with even greater reason because their right is neither proper nor natural, but is only a delegated and circumstantial one.

Now, is there required a positive approbation of these teachers on the part of the Church? In other words, is it necessary that there be a *missio* of the Church whereby she herself designates these teachers? Or, need the Church give only a specific approbation by consenting to the appointment of the teachers designated? In the first case there is no need of a *missio,* for such teachers represent the authority of the parents which is capable of delegation. The office of teaching, in this case retaining the nature of private instruction, does not require a mission from public authority. Concerning the question whether the Church can demand a positive approbation, a distinction is necessary. Generally speaking, the answer is in the affirmative if it is morally necessary for the safe instruction of the faithful. The right of the Church is supreme. She not only may but she must see to it that there be sufficient guarantee of probity on the part of the teachers—so necessary for the safe instruction of the faithful. If it may be presumed, however, that these teachers have the necessary qualifications a negative opinion is to be preferred, since these teachers represent the proper authority of the parents which is capable of delegation. In these schools, therefore, the local ordinary has only a negative right, that is, the right to exclude as teachers those who are not fit. The right of appointing the teacher does not belong to him.[44]

[44] Cavagnis, *op. cit.*, III, 29.

II. Public schools are those erected by public authority for the general use of children and youth.

As has been seen religious training in these schools is necessary. When there is question of Catholics it is mandatory. The teacher of religion in these schools may perform his duty either independently of the other subjects taught, that is, hold a distinct position as teacher of religion, or he may hold the office both as teacher of religion and of the other subjects as well. In the former instance, this teacher is appointed by the ecclesiastical authority since his nomination is dependent solely upon that authority.[45] In the latter instance, since the appointment of all teachers depends upon the school authority, this same authority will have the right to appoint also the teacher of religion. In both cases, however, the approbation of the Church is necessary. Instruction in the schools is a public and social function. As such it is dependent upon the authority competent for the imparting of this instruction. Religion is dependent upon the ecclesiastical authority. Likewise, the teachers intended for the imparting of religious knowledge, will depend upon ecclesiastical authority, even though they instruct the pupils in other subjects also.

It may be objected here that the common schools are instituted by public authority which acts in the place of parents. Parents, though, being under the supervision of the Church, do not need a *missio* proper for the instruction of their children. According to this objection neither would the public civil authority need this *missio* in designating the teachers who hold the place of parents. This, however, is not correct, for the civil authority in instituting its own schools does not *represent* parental authority. It is one thing to *supply the insufficiency* of parental authority, and quite another to *represent* such authority. Only the former is true of the State. Similarly it is applicable to all other attributes of civil authority. In fact,

[45] Cavagnis, *op. cit.*, III, 35; cf. also art. 5, § 2 of the Concordat with Bavaria—*AAS*, XVII (1925), 44; art. 6, § 1 of the Concordat with Austria —*AAS*, XXVI (1934), 256.

civil society was instituted for the purpose of supplementing the insufficiency of families, together with their reciprocal relations. Now civil society, in supplementing this insufficiency of families, does not proceed by a delegated parental authority, but by its own. Hence, such authority is public. Provision for religious instruction proceeds from public authority. In matters of religion civil society has no proper authority. It has only a ministerial authority. The conclusion, therefore, is evident: a positive action of the Church is required regarding the teachers of religion. This action amounts to the designation of the person, if it be question of a teacher of religion *ex professo*. It amounts to simple approbation, if this teacher of religion be at the same time a teacher of other subjects.[46]

III. Finally there are schools instituted by private persons, but after the fashion of the public schools.

For purpose of law these schools are regarded as public schools, at least as to the civil effects. For the juridical effects it is indifferent whether something be first established by the public authority, or, having been established, be later recognized by it. In the latter instance it is necessary that it satisfy the conditions towards society—whether civil or ecclesiastical—previously noted. Hence, the religious element must necessarily depend upon the Church. Such dependence, considered with reference to the teachers of religion, is to be limited to approval, not strictly to designation. It is indeed within the right of private individuals to cooperate in matters touching public utility, provided they are competent.[47]

No doubt it is often hard to determine, in particular cases in which private persons establish schools, whether they wish them to be so private that they are of mere assistance to fathers of families, and have their *raison d'être* contingent upon the families alone, or whether they wish to establish them as social institutions. There is question here of principles. As

[46] Cavagnis, *Institutiones Iuris Publici Ecclesiastici*, III, 35-36.

[47] Cavagnis, *op. cit.*, III, 37.

Cavagnis remarks,[48] in practice the judgment of the Church will have to be followed.

Generally, the purpose of schools nowadays is of public character. They are established for the common education of children. Consequently, whenever religious instruction is therein imparted, it is given in a public capacity, and the teacher shares in the public magisterium. A canonical *missio* of the Church is always necessary. This may entail the designation of the person approved, as is done when the teacher of religion teaches only religion *ex professo*. Or it may be merely approbation, as in the case when the teacher appointed for the purpose of teaching other subjects teaches religion also, and had been designated by the school authorities.

In either case, however, the ecclesiastical authority has a right to see that the candidate for the office has the proper qualifications for carrying on his work. This may be done either by an examination [49] or by other means, as determined by the local ordinary. In many instances, too, the Church demands from these candidates a profession of faith, especially when they undertake the teaching of religion in the schools conducted by the civil authority.[50] In the schools of the Church, or in the Catholic schools properly so called, there will be no difficulty in this regard. The entire management of these schools, whether they be diocesan or religious, is under the control of the ecclesiastical authority, which will see to it that proper candidates for the teaching of religion be appointed.[51]

It has been mentioned elsewhere that in the primary schools it is desirable that the teacher to whom is entrusted the teaching of the other branches of knowledge, be also in charge of

[48] *Op. cit.*, III, 38.

[49] Cf. S. C. C., decr., *Provido sane*, 12 ian. 1935—*AAS*, XXVII (1935), 148.

[50] Wernz, *Ius Decretalium*, III, pars I, n. 76.

[51] Cf. S. C. de Rel., instr. 25 nov. 1929—*AAS*, XXII (1930), 28; also *Periodica*, XIX (1930), 201-206.

the religious instruction classes. Although this is not always the case in the public State schools, even if the government be Catholic, it does, however, apply to the system of parochial schools, especially as it exists in America.

Regarding the approbation of the teachers in these schools, which are of special interest here, the ecclesiastical law of this country demands that teachers receive a testimonial or certificate of fitness, to be given by the Board of Examiners, composed of one or more members, representing the bishop. This certificate is given after the candidates have proved themselves capable by a satisfactory examination. This law, moreover, is to be observed by all who are to teach in the parochial schools, whether the teachers be secular, or whether they be religious of diocesan right.[52] While this will comply with the demand of the Code that teachers of religion be approved by the local ordinary, it also offers an opportunity for the bishop to see that every teacher has the proper qualifications for the office.

In the parochial schools, entrusted by the local ordinary to religious orders or congregations not immediately under the jurisdiction of the bishop, generally the management of the school as well as the appointment of the teachers is left entirely to the religious school authorities. The approval of the teacher of religion in this case is given by the local ordinary indirectly. That is to say, the religious superior designates the person, who thereby receives the approval of the bishop. This is true insofar as the bishop is usually understood to approve

[52] *Conc. Plen. Balt. III*, n. 203. The law of the council dealing with the Board of Examiners in reference to schools is *praeter codicem* and therefore still binding. The function of the Board is exercised by a superintendent of schools, among whose duties is that of approving as well as of ascertaining in the name of the bishop the competence of the parochial school teachers. This method is quite in keeping with the Baltimore legislation, especially in view of the present-day educational system, with its credits, diplomas, and degrees. Cf. Barrett, *A Comparative Study of the Councils of Baltimore and the Code of Canon Law*, p. 182; *Stat. Arch. S. Francisci* (1936), Appendix, VII.

whomsoever the religious superior designates. Moreover, if some contract with these religious has been entered upon by the local ordinary, concerning the appointment or removal of teachers in the parochial schools assigned to them, the same contract will have to be observed. In the visitation of these schools [53] the bishop or his representative will have ample opportunity to see whether these teachers have the necessary qualifications for their office.

B. *Extent arising from the indirect power.* The right to demand that teachers and books be removed because of religion and morality.

This right is derived from that which the Church has over religion and morality. Faithful to the divine mission given her by Christ,[54] and loyal to the trust of safeguarding the deposit of His revelation which was entrusted to her to guard and preserve intact, and to teach all men till the end of time, the Catholic Church defends this divine treasure against all attacks, in whatever form or from whomsoever they may come.[55]

The right and the duty of the Church to defend the faith and to safeguard the morality of her subjects everywhere has a special import in the schools. There children and youth have their minds and hearts formed for the years to come. Much, if not all, of their future life will depend upon the education that they have received in school.[56] Wisely, therefore, the Church desires that in those schools where Catholic children are educated only those books be used, and only such teachers be employed as are in keeping with Christian faith and morality. If books, however, were to be found, the content of which is deleterious from the standpoint of either belief or

[53] Canon 1382.

[54] Matthew, XXVIII, 18-20; John, XX, 21.

[55] Cf. d'Herbigny, *Theologica de Ecclesia* (3rd ed., Paris: Beauchesne, 1927-1928), II, n. 388.

[56] Leo XIII, const. *Romanos Pontifices*, 8 maii 1881, § 18—*Fontes*, n. 582.

behaviour to those who use them, or if teachers were to be employed whose conduct or teaching is detrimental to the students for the same reason, then the Church has a right to demand that such books or teachers be removed. This right of the Church, though coming from her indirect power, is proper to her. Being part of her mission of saving souls, she cannot renounce it.[57] The reason, however, for her intervention in these matters will always concern either faith or morals (*religionis morumque causa*). In these alone she has direct authority independent of any other. Only by reason of them does her indirect authority in other matters arise.

This prerogative of the Church extends, indeed, to every school and to every matter taught. Nevertheless, it seems that certain limitations are to be made. These affect primarily those subjects and teachers that have, more or less, a direct relation in their content or teaching to the truths of faith and the principles of morality. Thus, for instance, the teaching of arithmetic, grammar, and writing, *per se* has no point of contact with either religion or morality. The teachers of these subjects, too, are directed by pedagogical methods alone, which have nothing to do with religion. Here, therefore, the Church will not intervene. But in the teaching, for instance, of history, literature, biology, and the like, may be found numerous contacts with revealed doctrine and the rules of morality. The attitude of the teachers, too, in these subjects will have a tremendous influence on the minds of the pupils. In such cases the demands of the Church will naturally be more insistent and precise. She will demand, for instance, that the teaching of these subjects be entrusted as far as possible to Catholic teachers.[58] If this is not possible, the teachers employed should then, at least limit their teaching to a mere

[57] Leo XIII, ep. encycl. *Caritatis providentiaeque*, 19 mart. 1894, n. 3—*Fontes*, n. 623; Coronata, *Institutiones Iuris Canonici*, II, 307.

[58] Cf. S. C. de Prop. Fide, instr. (ad Arch. Hibernae), 7 apr. 1860—*Collect. S. C. de P. F.*, n. 1190.

exposition of facts, without particular comment or criticism based upon their private beliefs or personal views.[59] In the use of classics or other literary works, moreover, only expurgated editions should be used.[60] No books which are listed in the Index or otherwise condemned, either by the general law of the Church or by the bishop, may be used in the schools. Least of all may books which are condemned by the natural law itself be used.[61]

Again, the different kinds and gradations of schools will compel the Church to make additional demands according to their needs. Since the schools exist for the purpose of imparting an education, and since this cannot be separated from religion and morality, the Church will always have the right to require that in schools attended by her members the principles of faith and morality must be respected. If circumstances warrant, she may also demand that teachers or books offensive to these principles be removed. As already mentioned, this right arises from her position as custodian of revealed truth and morality. No Christian government can take exception to her in the performance of her duty.[62]

The particular representatives of this right and duty of the Church are, as the canon expressly states, the local ordinaries. For the practical execution of these provisions, however, the bishops, through instructions and statutes, could well leave it to their pastors and rural deans. On the one hand, there is nothing against this procedure. It may even be more advan-

[59] C. S. de Prop. Fide, instr. (ad Vic. Ap. Sin.), 18 oct. 1883, n. XI, 5—*Fontes*, n. 4903.

[60] S. C. S. Off., instr. (ad Ep. Iassen.), 22 aug. 1900—*Collect. S. C. de P. F.*, n. 2093; Leo XIII, const. *Officiorum ac munerum*, 25 ian. 1897, art. X—*Fontes*, n. 632.

[61] Canons 1395-1405; Pernicone, *The Ecclesiastical Prohibition of Books*, The Catholic University of America, Canon Law Studies, n. 72 (Washington: The Catholic University of America, 1932), p. 173; Langasco, *De Institutione Clericorum in disciplinis inferioribus*, p. 45, note 1.

[62] Cf. Leo XIII, letter to President Grévy of France, May 12, 1883—Nègre, *Les Écoles—Les Documents du Saint-Siège* (Paris, 1911), pp. 149-151.

tageous. Often the management of the common schools depends, to a great extent, upon the discretion of the local civil authority with whom the pastors or rural deans may have greater influence.[63]

There is no difficulty in applying the provisions of the canon to the schools of the Church. Difficulty, however, may arise when dealing with the State schools, even in Christian nations. Because of the claims that civil governments sometimes make in the field of education, it is not always possible for the Church to demand the full recognition of all her rights. In such circumstances she endeavors to enter upon some kind of agreement with those governments which are still Christian. Thereby, she tries to bring about a settlement for the use of at least her inherent rights. The settlements thus made have been known by various names. The most common of these are Concordats and Conventions. It is not the purpose of the present work to enter into a specific treatise on such agreements.[64] It is, however, deemed necessary as well as sufficient to consider the following points.

In the Concordats prior to the World War the right of the Church to safeguard the whole education of youth is generally well provided for, particularly in Catholic countries.[65] The

[63] Cf. Coronata, *Institutiones Iuris Canonici*, II, 307.

[64] For a detailed study of such Conventions, cf. Doyle, *Education in Recent Constitutions and Concordats* (Washington: The Catholic University of America, 1933), pp. 92-124.

[65] Cf. art. 5, 7 of the Concordat with Bavaria (1817)—Mercati, *Raccolta di Concordati su Materie Ecclesiastiche tra la Santa Sede e le Autorità Civili* (Roma: Tipografia Poliglotta Vaticana, 1919), pp. 593-594; art. 1, 2 of Conc. with Sicily (1818)—Mercati, *op. cit.*, p. 621; art. 1, 2 of Conc. with Spain (1851)—Mercati, *op. cit.*, p. 771; art. 2 of Conc. with Costa Rica and Guatemala (1852)—Mercati, *op. cit.*, pp. 800, 810; art. 2 of Conc. with Honduras and Nicaragua (1861)—Mercati, *op. cit.*, pp. 937, 949; art. 2 of Conc. with San Salvador and Venezuela (1862)—Mercati, *op. cit.*, pp. 961, 971; art 7 of Conc. with Würtemberg (1857), and Baden (1859)—Mercati, *op. cit.*, pp. 857, 885.

Concordats with Ecuador (1862),[66] moreover, and with Colombia (1887)[67] make special provision for safeguarding the right of the local ordinary to exclude from the common schools books which are not in conformity with faith and morals. The Concordat with Montenegro (1886),[68] furthermore, stipulates that in those places where the population is exclusively or overwhelmingly Catholic, there shall be employed as teachers in the public schools only those persons who are acceptable to the ecclesiastical authority.

In the Concordats following the World War, which have reference to schools,[69] with the exception possibly of Bavaria,[70] Lithuania,[71] and Austria,[72] these two rights are not dealt with. In the Concordat with Italy [73] they are expressly not recognized. This, however, should not be cause for wonderment. The Church is a tender mother, who is willing at times to sacrifice in part some of her rights for the purpose of avoiding greater evils, and with the hope of obtaining a fuller recognition of her rights later on. Hence, a perfect settlement of the school question cannot be found in any of the Concordats. The very fact that a Concordat is entered into presupposes a condition which falls short of the ideal. If there were perfect

[66] Art. 3, 4—Mercati, *op. cit.*, p. 984; cf. also p. 1002 for a new revision of the same Concordat in 1881.

[67] Art. 13—Mercati, *op. cit.*, p. 1054.

[68] Art. 8—Mercati, *op. cit.*, p. 1049.

[69] Latvia, art. 10—*AAS*, XIV (1922), 578; Poland, art. 13—*AAS*, XVII (1925), 277-278; Italy, art. 35-36—*AAS*, XXI (1929), 291; Roumania, art. 19-20—*AAS*, XXI (1929), 449; Baden, art. 11—*AAS*, XXV (1933), 187; Germany, art. 21-25—*AAS*, XXV (1933), 401-403. As to the Concordat with Prussia, of particular interest is the correspondence between the Apostolic Nuncio, Archbishop Pacelli (now Pius XII), and Dr. Braun—*AAS*, XXI (1929), 536-541.

[70] Art. 8, § 2—*AAS*, XVII (1925), 46.

[71] Art. 13, n. 4—*AAS*, XIX (1927), 428.

[72] Art. 6, § 2—*AAS*, XXVI (1934), 257; cf. also *protocollo addizionale*—*AAS*, *op. cit.*, p. 276.

[73] Coronata, *Institutiones Iuris Canonici*, II, 307, note 1.

agreement between the Church and the State, if the State were disposed to grant to the Church the use of all her rights, rarely enough would there be any need to enter into such negotiations.[74]

4. RIGHT OF VISITATION

> Canon 1382: Ordinarii locorum sive ipsi per se sive per alios possunt quoque scholas quaslibet, oratoria, recreatoria, patronatus, etc., in iis quae religiosam et moralem institutionem spectant, visitare; a qua visitatione quorumlibet religiosorum scholae exemptae non sunt, nisi agatur de scholis internis pro professis religionis exemptae.

As a corollary of canon 1381, as well as of the whole treatise on schools, the present canon confirms the right of local ordinaries to visit the schools within their territorial jurisdiction and to examine them in what concerns the religious and moral formation of youth.

Visitation of itself is primarily an administrative procedure. It offers to the visitor an opportunity of collecting information more reliable than might otherwise be obtained. The visitor is thus enabled to become personally acquainted with the real status of religious and moral training in the schools, and to provide remedies which will be well adapted to the concrete situation. The old canonists were fond of repeating the saying that he to whom visitation belongs fulfills the Scriptural precept: "Diligenter agnosce vultum pecoris tui, tuosque greges considera."[75] Ordinarily, the visitor's inquiries, and, if conditions warrant, his corrections, are to be paternal in form, dispensing with the technical rules of judicial proceedings. Judicial duties are, in fact, a secondary aspect of the visitor's office. This is particularly true of the visitation of

[74] Ottaviani, *Institutiones Iuris Publici Ecclesiastici*, II, 278, 287-288.

[75] Prov., XXVII, 23.

schools which, either public or private, are in their general management not dependent upon the Church.[76]

The canon, besides schools, mentions also *oratoria, recreatoria, patronatus*. *Oratoria* and *recreatoria* are almost similar. They are places destined for the poor or the aged. They are likewise conservatories for boys and girls. In *oratoria*, however, among the other practices, pious and intellectual exercises take place. In *recreatoria* (from the Italian *ricreatori*) the main feature is honest recreation and relaxation. *Patronatus* is generally understood of orphanages. In many instances though, its meaning is similar to *oratoria*.[77] From the content (*De scholis*), and from the fact that these various institutions are enumerated together with the schools, it would appear that the legislator primarily intended to designate here all such institutions where youth are admitted for the purpose of obtaining an intellectual as well as a moral and religious training.[78]

The legislation of the Code concerning the visitation of such institutions by the local ordinary is not new. Already the Council of Trent upheld this right of the bishops. It empowered them to visit within their territories all institutions such as hospitals, colleges, and schools, even though these were under the direction or the care of laymen, or enjoyed the privilege of exemption. No custom or contrary privilege was recognized as having sufficient effect to overrule this right of the bishop. The only exception was in the case of those institutions which enjoyed an immediate royal protection.[79] Benedict XIV in his constitution "*Ad militantis*" of March 30, 1742, renewed these same regulations and added that by this law no appeal was to be allowed.[80]

[76] Cf. Pius XI, litt. encycl. *Divini illius Magistri*, 31 dec. 1929—*AAS*, XXII (1930), 56.

[77] Coronata, *Institutiones Iuris Canonici*, II, 312; Augustine, *A Commentary on the New Code of Canon Law*, VI, 426, note 31.

[78] Cf. Vermeersch-Creusen, *Epitome*, II, n. 718; Cocchi, *Commentarium*, VI, 133; De Meester, *Compendium*, III, pars I, 241.

[79] Sess. XXII, *de ref.*, c. 8.

[80] §§ 5, 31—*Fontes*, n. 326.

The present legislation, since it primarily concerns schools, does not depart altogether from the former law. It does, however, make an important change: it restricts the right of visitation to matters concerning religious and moral training, and extends its scope to all schools, no matter what their status may be. *Per se,* therefore, it is not required that such institutions be erected or approved by the ecclesiastical authority, in order that they be submitted to this jurisdiction of the local ordinaries. It is sufficient that they be destined for the intellectual and moral training of the faithful. It happens, however, in many countries which are influenced by an exclusive State monopoly, that the right of visitation *de facto* cannot be exercised outside those schools which depend directly upon the ecclesiastical authority.[81]

The reason for this right of visitation is the same as the one considered in the arguments advanced under canon 1381. Since the bishops are the judges in all matters pertaining to faith and morals, theirs is a doctrinal superintendence which they cannot divide with civil governments or with individuals. Thus, in order to be faithful to their divine mission and mandate, they must so supervise religious and moral formation that it be in conformity with the intentions of the Church. This work evidently cannot be carried out to its fullest extent unless the bishops have free access to teaching institutions. Neither the State nor private organizations should, therefore, oppose this right by restricting or conditioning it. They have no jurisdiction in matters pertaining to faith and morals. Such matters are preeminently the concern of the Church. By virtue of divine authority the bishops are given charge over these matters. However, since the right of visitation implies *per se* something more than mere supervision, the canon demands that

[81] Blanco Nájera, *Derecho Docente,* p. 440; Coronata, *Institutiones Iuris Canonici,* II, 312; cf. *Acta et Decreta Primi Concilii Prov. Torontini* (1876), decr. IX, n. 4, p. 23.

the exercise of the right be carried out only in what concerns the religious and moral training.[82]

The question of visitation receives a special emphasis when applied to the Catholic school system, properly so called. Leo XIII in a letter to the bishops of Hungary in 1893, urged them to appoint school inspectors in each diocese and deanery, so as to ensure a more complete supervision of school conditions. These inspectors were to present a report every year to the bishop.[83]

The Third Plenary Council of Baltimore enacted similar legislation in regard to the parochial schools of this country. It ordered that there be appointed, according to the diversity of place and language, several school boards composed of one or more priests, for the purpose of investigating conditions in urban and rural schools. These were to visit once or twice a year, every school of their district. An accurate report, following their visitation, was to be submitted to the chairman of the Diocesan Board. The results were to be transmitted to the bishop, who might thereupon take action.[84] This law, as far as the Code is concerned, is regarded as *praeter codicem*. As was the case with regard to the Board of Examiners, here too, each bishop establishes in his diocese a diocesan school

[82] The right of vigilance and visitation, as the terms are used in the Code, while not the same, are very similar. The precise distinction between them is difficult to define. Both rights imply a certain amount of jurisdiction. A person or a place may be subject to vigilance or visitation, even though in a general sense exempt (canons 1491, § 1; 344, § 1). Visitation, however, is the broader term. The right of visitation signifies that one may go to a place (or person) and subject the place (or person) to an investigation. The right of vigilance does not extend so far. When the Code wishes to include visitation along with vigilance, the former is expressly mentioned (canon 1515, § 2). However, when one has the right of visiting a place with regard to certain matters, it is legitimate for him, while there, to exercise also the right of vigilance possessed in regard to other points. In such cases it is at times all but impossible to show wherein visitation and vigilance differ.

[83] Ep. encycl. *Constanti Hungarorum*, 2 sept. 1893, n. 6—*Fontes*, n. 620.

[84] *Acta et Decreta Conc. Plen. Balt. Tertii*, n. 204.

board for the purpose of administering, in the name of the ordinary, and according to the best pedagogical methods, the affairs of the parochial schools. The superintendent of schools, as the immediate representative of the bishop, is given among his other duties that also of visiting the schools of the diocese. The office of the superintendent conforms to the requirements of the Baltimore legislation. With equal conformity it corresponds to canon 1382, which empowers the local ordinary to visit, either personally or through another, the schools of the diocese.

Concerning the extent of the right of visitation, as exercised by the bishop or his delegate over Catholic schools properly so called, a distinction must be made. There are those schools, elementary or intermediate, which *per se* come directly under the jurisdiction of the bishop, either because founded by him, or because, after their foundation by others, they were incorporated into the diocesan school system. On the other hand, there are schools owned or held by religious institutes, whether orders or congregations. At the head of such schools there is a superior, a director, or a subordinate superior named by his higher superior.[85]

The authority of the bishop over the first type of schools is evidently unquestionable. His right of visitation extends to the religious and moral formation therein imparted. His jurisdiction, moreover, extends also to the entire scholastic administration and pedagogical system. These schools, since they form an integral part of the work of the bishop in the diocese, are subject to him as to their chief superior. The same may be said of schools maintained by religious institutes of diocesan right. As such these schools are entirely subject to the jurisdiction of the local ordinary.[86] If the schools,

[85] Among this latter type of schools could also be mentioned other institutions founded by groups of individuals. The same principle applies regarding the right of the bishop's visitation of these schools as is the case for the common schools.

[86] Canon 492, § 2.

however, are not incorporated into the diocesan school system, but are conducted by religious institutes which enjoy exemption—and therefore are not subject directly to the bishop's jurisdiction—the extent of the right of visitation assumes a different aspect as will be explained below.

The primary consideration here concerns schools of regulars, since they enjoy the greatest exemption. There will be no difficulty in applying the general principle to other schools held by religious congregations enjoying a like or similar exemption.

Already before the Code, the question of episcopal visitation of schools held by regulars received consideration. It was at the time of the reestablishment of the ecclesiastical hierarchy in England. This country up to that time had been directed by the discipline peculiar to missionary countries. When the hierarchy was again regularly constituted, difficulties arose between the bishops of England and the religious orders with regard to the jurisdiction of each, in the schools. In order to settle this matter, Leo XIII, on May 8, 1881, promulgated the constitution "*Romanos Pontifices.*" Speaking of the formation of youth, the Pope makes a very definite distinction. He distinguishes primary or elementary schools—in England called schools of the poor—from other establishments of education conducted by religious men for the instruction of adolescents, according to the rules and constitutions of their institute. He quotes numerous regulations of special councils, and gives arguments from reason. He shows that primary schools are in themselves, chiefly a religious work, over which the local ordinaries must exercise a constant vigilance and expend their greatest solicitude. Since, therefore, such schools are to be considered among the works which belong inherently to the diocese, the bishops have the right to visit these schools with regard to all matters, both in localities of regulars and of seculars. As regards the other schools, however, the same Pontiff declares it to be the demand of reason and also his will that the privileges granted to religious by the Holy See remain intact.[87]

The present law no longer mentions this distinction. It simply states that the local ordinary can visit any schools in matters concerning the religious and moral training. An analysis of canon 1382, in the light also of the other canons on schools already considered, shows that there is here no real departure from the former law. The old law, on this point, considered specifically, or more in detail, what the present canon states generally *i. e.,* after the fashion of a general principle. On the one hand, there is no express revocatory clause in canon 1382 against privileges acquired before the Code which exempted schools from the visitation of the bishop. If such privileges were still in use, and not revoked up to the time of the promulgation of the Code, they still remain in force.[88] On the other hand, the nature of the Catholic primary schools is today as it was of old. Religion is the principal subject, taking precedence over all other subjects taught. These latter, indeed, are taught primarily in reference to religion. The very work of such schools is so preeminently connected with religion that it gives them predominantly a religious character. Hence it must be concluded that they fall within the scope of the diocesan activities over which the local ordinary has full power of visitation. True, as Pius XI remarks, religious and moral training should be the crown of the whole school curriculum, not merely in the elementary schools, but also in the higher ones.[89] In the primary schools, however, such training is to be so emphasized as to become the central, and almost exclusive interest of the curriculum. To

[87] §§ 18-20—*Fontes,* n. 582. The Third Plenary Council of Baltimore asked that this constitution be extended to the United States. By a decree of the Sacred Congregation for the Propagation of the Faith (Sept. 25, 1885), approved by Leo XIII, this request was granted. *Acta et Decreta Conc. Plen. Baltim. Tertii,* p. cv.

[88] Canon 4.

[89] Litt. encycl. *Divini illius Magistri,* 31 dec. 1929—*AAS,* XXII (1930), 77.

use the words of Pius IX: "In hisce potissimum scholis . . . religiosa praesertim doctrina ita primarium in institutione et educatione locum habere ac dominari debet, ut aliorum cognitiones, quibus iuventus ibi imbuitur, adventitiae appareant." [90]

Thus the evident meaning of the canon is none other than its literal import:—the bishop is the visitor for all schools in matters concerning religious and moral training. Where such training, because of the very nature of the schools, constitutes its main purpose (as is the case in primary schools), the visitation of the bishop will extend to the entire curriculum. Where, on the contrary, this training, although the "crown" of all other subjects, is nevertheless distinct from them by the very nature of the school as well as of the subjects taught (as is the case in the intermediate schools), the right of visitation will include only the religious and the moral elements. However, a right of vigilance over the other matters still remains.

Aside from cases where privileges may possibly have been obtained from the Holy See, the Code of Canon Law makes all schools without exception subject to the visitation of the bishop, in what pertains to religious and moral formation. It makes no distinction as to the nature of the schools as such. The only exception made refers to the *scholae internae,* namely, those schools destined for the professed members of an exempt religious institute.

The exception is granted by the law *taxative.* It precludes the fact that any other schools, even though *de iure* exempt, could be subject to the visitation of the bishop concerning the points enumerated. Vermeersch [91] would include among the *scholae internae* mentioned by the canon, also schools for novices, since novices, in virtue of canon 567, § 1, participate in the privileges of the institute to which they belong. His interpretation, however, is merely arbitrary. The very wording of canon 1382 contradicts it. Moreover, it is uncanonical

[90] Ep. *Quum non sine,* 14 iul. 1864, n. 4—*Fontes,* n. 539.

[91] *Summa Iuris Novi,* n. 544.

to speak of schools for novices. Novices are not to attend schools properly so called. They must spend their novitiate rather in pious exercises, such as meditation, and the like.[92] The very history of canon 1382 confirms the fact that the only exception allowed by the law, and intended by the legislator is found in the reference to the domestic schools for professed members of exempt religious institutes. Therefore, scholasticates, schools for postulants, apostolic schools, etc., are excluded.

The preparatory edition of the Code (1912) under canon 655 stated that the local ordinary could visit any school in matters concerning religious training; and that from such a visit the schools of regulars were not exempt.[93] Some of the generals of religious orders in their critical remarks upon this text, suggested adding the following: "nisi agatur de scholis pro postulantibus ad propriam religionem praeparandis." The editions which followed (in 1913-1914, under canon 1381, and again in 1916, under canon 1382) were changed to read that the local ordinary either personally or through others may visit any school, oratory, etc., in matters concerning religious training. The schools of regulars were not to be exempt from this visitation, unless it be a question of schools for postulants who were being prepared to enter the institute.[94] It seemed at this time that the desire expressed by exempt religious was fulfilled. However, the legislator, in the definitive draft of the Code which was authentically promulgated, changed the

[92] Canon 565; cf. also S. C. Rel., instr. 3 nov. 1921—*AAS*, XIII (1921), 539.

[93] "Ordinarii loci possunt quoque scholas quaslibet in iis quae religiosam institutionem spectant visitare; a qua visitatione Regularium scholae exemptae non sunt."

[94] "Ordinarii locorum sive per se sive per alios possunt quoque scholas quaslibet, oratoria, recreatoria, etc., in iis quae religiosam institutionem spectant visitare: a qua visitatione Regularium scholae exemptae non sunt nisi agatur de scholis internis pro postulantibus ad propriam religionem praeparandis."

phraseology to the form it has today by merely saying: *nisi agatur de scholis internis pro professis religionis exemptae.*[95]

The main purpose of the present work is concerned with schools where children and youth are received in order to obtain a common Christian education. Therefore, it is not concerned with schools which train members or aspirants for life in certain religious institutes. Hence, no further consideration of this latter type of school seems necessary. Regarding the first mentioned schools, however, there is to be found also in some of the other canons a certain conformity with the prescriptions found in canon 1382. Thus, for instance, canon 1491, which deals with hospitals, asylums, orphanages, and similar institutions for the works of religion and Christian charity, expressly mentions that the local ordinary has a right and an obligation to visit all such institutions. Even institutions which are erected as legal persons and howsoever exempt, are here included. When these institutions have not been created legal persons, and have been entrusted to a religious community, they are entirely subject to the jurisdiction of the local ordinary, if the institute in charge be of diocesan right. If the institute be of papal right, the institutions in question are subject to the supervision of the local ordinary in all matters

[95] Cf. Goyeneche, "Consultationes," *CpR*, IV (1923), 224-225. It may be noted here that since the local ordinary may visit these schools, the privilege of exemption is not destroyed nor the character of the school changed. The privilege of exemption is given primarily to regulars and their novices. Secondarily it is given to their houses and churches. Though it allows of exceptions, the same privilege substantially remains whether it be personal or local. The fact that the Code gives to the bishop the power to visit such schools merely proves that the religious houses to which these schools are connected, or of which they form a part, are not so exempt, as otherwise they would be. This is true because the students therein are not yet professed religious, or rather because of the general principle contained in canons 1336 and 1381, § 2. There is, therefore, a limitation of the privilege of exemption. This limitation, however, does not affect the juridical character of the schools as such. Cf. Langasco, *De Institutione Clericorum in disciplinis inferioribus*, p. 158.

pertaining to the teaching of religion, moral conduct, exercises of piety, and the administration of the Sacraments.[96]

Canon 344, furthermore, rules that all pious places, even though exempt, are subject to the visitation of the bishop of the diocese. This holds unless one can prove that a special exemption from the bishop's visitation was obtained from the Holy See. The scope of such visitation, when there is question of schools, is determined by canon 1382. It extends to everything which concerns the religious and moral formation of youth. Since exemption implies a restriction of the bishop's jurisdiction, it is evident that the fact of this exemption must be proved. It may be that some of the religious orders have obtained from the Holy See a direct exemption, even in what pertains to faith and morals. As already seen, canon 1382 does not destroy acquired privileges. However, express proof must be shown, since a claim for exemption from the bishop's visitation is contrary to a right which belongs to the bishop by law.

Vermeersch [97] is of the opinion that exempt clerical religious have a long-standing privilege of exemption from the bishop's visitation in their schools, even in what concerns faith and morals. According to canon 63, § 2, moreover, possession of a privilege for one hundred years or from time immemorial justifies the presumption that a privilege has been granted.

[96] Although the latter part of canon 1491, § 2, speaks only of supervision, it does not exclude visitation in the points mentioned (Coronata, *Institutiones Iuris Canonici*, II, 433, note 5). The main trend of title XXVI is concerned practically with works of charity apart from schools. Of these the Code already speaks in title XXII. Whenever there is question of schools properly so called, namely, where an intellectual, religious, and moral education is imparted, canon 1382 rules. Cf. Langasco, *De Institutione Clericorum in disciplinis inferioribus*, p. 154, note 3. In the other institutions, a charitable work, and not the imparting of an intellectual, religious, and moral formation is the primary aim. This perhaps explains the somewhat greater liberty of the legislator in demanding *per se* only vigilance when these charitable institutions are attached to a religious house of papal right.

[97] "De permanente vi C. *Romanos Pontifices*, 8 maii 1881, post c. 1382," *Periodica*, XV (1926-27), (57), (61).

This is so true, he says, that Leo XIII in the constitution "*Romanos Pontifices*" (§ 20) supposed and confirmed such a privilege, hence removing any further question of its acquisition. Vermeersch, however, does not seem to prove his argument. He merely asserts the fact of exemption and corroborates his contention with an argument from the wording of the constitution of Leo XIII.

Apart from the fact that the canons used by Vermeersch refer to privileges to be acquired after the promulgation of the Code only [98]—and therefore do not apply to the case at issue—the following may be noted.

If a privilege which had been obtained, was still in use, and was not revoked, up to the time of the promulgation of the Code, it is but logical that such privilege would still endure, since no express revocation of it is found in canon 1382.[99] Whether, however, such a privilege was actually given is another question. None is known to the present writer.[100] Nevertheless there is no intention of denying the possibility of the acquisition of any such privilege. In each and every privilege one must respect the free exercise of the granter's authority.

Leo XIII in his constitution mentioned above, neither confirms nor grants privileges against the bishop's right of visitation in matters of faith and morals. It is true that paragraph 20 of the constitution says that privileges granted to religious orders must be respected and be considered as still in force. But in paragraph 19 the submission to the bishop's visitation of the entire elementary schools is precisely due to the predominant religious and moral element in them. By contrast, therefore, with paragraph 20 it seems that any privileges considered in the latter would refer only to the general management of the school, and to the profane subjects, apart

98 Cf. also Blanco Nájera, *Derecho Docente*, pp. 445-446; canon 1509, n. 2.

99 Canon 4.

100 Cf. also "L'Evêque a-t-il droit de visite sur les écoles tenues par les Ordres religieux?," *Ami du Clergé*, V ser., L (1933), 253-254.

from religion and morality taught therein. Such a deduction is warranted, since these two phases of instruction are not, in the higher schools, an integral and exclusive part of the curriculum.

A similar conclusion can also be drawn from a later response of the Sacred Congregation for the Propagation of the Faith under date of January 18, 1886. In order to bring about a settlement of difficulties between the Society of Jesus and the Vicars Apostolic, the Sacred Congregation was asked: "Se la giurisdizione sui collegi o convitti nelle loro missioni spetti al Superiore regolare o al Vicario Apostolico." The answer was: "Quoad collegia et collegiorum scholas atque convictus, in quibus religiosi viri secundum Ordinis sui praescripta iuventuti instituendae operam dare solent, et recta ratio postulat et S.S. vult firma atque integra privilegia Regularibus concessa manere, adeoque tum regimen eorum Institutorum, tum personarum in iis destinatio ad Superiores regulares spectat, iuxta Societatis constitutiones, et, quatenus opus sit, verbo facto cum Sanctissimo." [101] In virtue of its last words, this reply remedies all defects both of form and argument. Therefore, even if the privilege cannot be directly demonstrated, the fact remains that such schools of regulars are not subject to the jurisdiction of the bishop. It must be noted, however, that *per se* this refers only to colleges and higher schools where adolescents are educated. It does not refer to elementary schools. Furthermore, nothing is said here about faith and morals. Reference on the contrary, is explicitly made to the *regimen institutorum* and *designatio personarum,* namely, to the management of these schools as such. It seems, then, that a further privilege is necessary in order that the privilege of exemption from the visitation of the bishop in matters pertaining to the religious and moral formation of youth may be claimed. Since this privilege is against the very right that the bishops have by common law it must be proved.

[101] S. C. de Prop. Fide, 18 ian. 1886 (C. G.), ad 4—*Collect. S. C. de P. F.*, n. 1651.

CONCLUSION

THE right as well as the various prerogatives of the Church in reference to schools have been expounded in the foregoing pages. As a conclusion there may well be inserted here the words of Saint Augustine which Pius XI himself used in concluding the encyclical letter on Christian Education: " 'O Catholic Church, true Mother of Christians! Not only dost thou preach to us, as is meet, how purely and chastely we are to worship God Himself, Whom to possess is life most blessed; thou dost moreover so cherish neighborly love and charity, that all the infirmities to which sinful souls are subject, find their most potent remedy in thee. Childlike thou art in molding the child, strong with the young man, gentle with the aged, dealing with each according to his needs of mind and body. Thou dost subject child to parent in a sort of free servitude, and settest parent over child in a jurisdiction of love. Thou bindest brethren to brethren by the bond of religion, stronger and closer than the bond of blood. . . . Thou unitest citizen to citizen, nation to nation, yea, all men, in a union not of companionship only, but of brotherhood, reminding them of their common origin. Thou teachest kings to care for their people, and biddest people to be subject to their kings. Thou teachest assiduously to whom honor is due, to whom love, to whom reverence, to whom fear, to whom comfort, to whom rebuke, to whom punishment; showing us that whilst not all things nor the same things are due to all, charity is due to all and offense to none.' "[1]

[1] *De moribus Ecclesiae catholicae*, lib. I, c. 30; litt. encycl. *Divini illius Magistri*, 31 dec. 1929—*AAS*, XXII (1930), 85-86.

PARTICULAR CONCLUSIONS

1) One of the first well authenticated evidences of the existence of Catholic primary schools is the school of Protogenes at Antinone in the latter part of the fourth century.

2) The first canonical enactment of legislation dealing with this subject is the first canon of the Council of Vaison in the year 529.

3) The assertion that the Church exercised and claimed for herself an exclusive monopoly in education in the Middle Ages is, to say the least, prejudiced, and based on a distorted view of documents and history.

4) The right of the Church to maintain schools is proper and native (although indirect), partial and cumulative, that is, not exclusive, but nevertheless independent.

5) The Church has a right as well as a duty to see to it that the principles of faith and morality be respected and practiced in all schools.

6) The local ordinaries have the right and duty to inspect any and all schools in matters pertaining to the religious and moral formation of youth.

7) The Catholic elementary schools, since they must primarily be a religious work, come directly under the supervision of the local ordinaries. They, therefore, have a right of visitation over them in their entirety.

8) No privilege is found which would preclude any school of general learning from being subject to the visitation of the bishop in matters of religious and moral training. Indirectly the local ordinaries have a right to survey the entire training of Catholic youth.

ABBREVIATIONS

AAS—Acta Apostolicae Sedis.
AJP—Analecta Juris Pontificii.
AKKR—Archiv für katholisches Kirchenrecht.
ASS—Acta Sanctae Sedis.
C—Codex (Justinianus).
CpR—Commentarium pro Religiosis.
C. Th.—Codex (Theodosianus).
Fontes—Codicis Iuris Canonici Fontes.
HPR—Homiletic and Pastoral Review.
IER—Irish Ecclesiastical Record.
MGH—Monumenta Germaniae Historica.
MPG—Migne, *Patrologia, Series Graeca.*
MPL—Migne, *Patrologia, Series Latina.*
NRT—Nouvelle Revue Théologique.
RSR—Revue des Sciences Religieuses.

BIBLIOGRAPHY

Sources

Acta Apostolicae Sedis, Commentarium Officiale, Romae, 1909—.

Acta et Decreta Concilii Plenarii Americae Latinae (1899), Romae, 1902.

Acta et Decreta Concilii Plenarii Baltimorensis Tertii (1884), Baltimorae, 1886.

Acta et Decreta Concilii Plenarii Quebecensis (1909), Quebeci, 1912.

Acta et Decreta Concilii Provincialis Mechliniensis Quarti (1922), Mechliniae: Dessain, 1923.

Acta et Decreta Primi Concilii Provincialis Torontini (1875), Toronto, 1882.

Acta et Decreta Sacrorum Conciliorum Recentiorum (*Collectio Lacensis*), 7 vols., Friburgi Brisgoviae, 1870-1890.

Acta Sanctae Sedis, 41 vols., Romae, 1865-1908.

Bullarium Romanum, 24 vols., Editio Taurinensis, 1857-1872.

Bullarii Romani Continuatio, 13 vols., Prati, 1845-1854.

Canones et Decreta Sacrosancti Oecumenici Concilii Tridentini, Romae: Typographia Polyglotta S. C. de Propaganda Fide, 1882.

Codex Iuris Canonici Pii X Pontificis Maximi iussu digestus Benedicti Papae XV auctoritate promulgatus, Typis Polyglottis Vaticanis, 1917.

Codicis Iuris Canonici Fontes cura E.mi Petri Card. Gasparii editi, 8 vols., Typis Polyglottis Vaticanis, 1923-1938. (Vol. VII et VIII ed. cura et studio E.mi Iustiniani Card. Serédi.)

Codex Theodosianus (Krueger, Mommsen-Meyer), 3 vols., Berolini, 1905.

Collectanea S. Congregationis de Propaganda Fide, 2 vols., Romae: Typographia Polyglotta S. C. de Propaganda Fide, 1907.

Concilii Plenarii Baltimorensis II (1866), *Acta et Decreta*, Baltimorae, 1894.

Concilii Provincialis Portlandensis in Oregon Quarti, Acta et Decreta, Portlandiae, 1932.

Constitutiones Dioeceseos Bostoniensis (*in Synodo Dioecesana VI 1919*), Boston, 1935.

Corpus Iuris Canonici, ed. Lipsiensis 2, Aemilius Ludouicus Richter-Aemilius Friedberg, ed. anastatice repetita, 2 vols., Lipsiae: Tauchnitz, 1928.

Corpus Iuris Civilis (Krueger-Mommsen-Schoell-Kroll), 5th ed., 3 vols., Berlin: Weidman, 1928.

Decreta Concilii Provincialis Burdigalae habiti, sub RR.DD. Ant. P. Sansaco, Bordeaux, 1623.

Denzinger, H., et Umberg, J. B., *Enchiridion Symbolorum, Definitionum et Declarationum de Rebus Fidei et Morum*, 18th et 20th ed., Friburgi Brisgoviae: Herder, 1932.

Hardouin, J., *Acta Conciliorum et Epistolae Decretales ac Constitutiones Summorum Pontificum*, 12 vols., Parisiis, 1715.

Hartzheim, J., *Concilia Germaniae*, 11 vols., Coloniae Augustae Agrippinensium, 1759-1790.

Jaffé, Philippus, *Bibliotheca Rerum Germanicarum, Monumenta Carolina*, Tom. IV, Berolini, 1867.

Las siete Partidas del Rey D. Alfonso el Sabio, cotejadas con varios códices antiguos por la real Academia de la historia, Madrid, 1807.

Mansi, Joannes, *Sacrorum Conciliorum Nova et Amplissima Collectio*, 53 vols., Parisiis, 1901-1927.

Martène-Durand, *Veterum Scriptorum et Monumentorum Historicorum Dogmaticorum Amplissima Collectio*, 2nd ed., 9 vols., Paris, 1724-1733.

Martène, E., *Thesaurus novus anedoctorum seu Collectio monumentorum, complectens regum ac principum aliorumque virorum illustrium epistolas et diplomata bene multa*, Paris, 1717.

Migne, Jacques Paul, *Patrologia Cursus Completus, Series Graeca*, 161 vols., Parisiis, 1856-1866.

——, *Patrologia Cursus Completus, Series Latina*, 221 vols., Parisiis, 1844-1864.

Monumenta Germaniae Historica, Legum Sectio II, Capitularia Regum Francorum, Tom. I, ed. A. Boretius, Hannoverae, 1883.

Potthast, A., *Regesta Pontificum Romanorum*, Berolini, 1874.

Statuta Archidioecesis Sancti Francisci (in Synodo Dioecesana Secunda 1936), San Francisco: The Monitor Publishing Co., 1936.

Wilkins, David, *Concilia Magnae Britanniae et Hiberniae*, 4 vols., Londini, 1737.

Reference Works

Aertnys, Josephus, et Damen, Cornelius, *Theologia Moralis secundum Doctrinam S. Alfonsi de Ligorio*, 11th ed., 2 vols., Taurinorum Augustae: Marietti, 1928.

Aichner, Simon, *Compendium Iuris Ecclesiastici*, 6th ed., Brixinae, 1887.

Albers, P., *Manuale di Storia Ecclesiastica*, New Italian translation from the 2nd Dutch ed. by S. M. Berardo, 2 vols., Torino, 1913.

Allain, L'Abbé, *L'Église et l'enseignement populaire sous l'ancien Régime*, Paris, 1901.

——, *L'Instruction primaire en France avant la Révolution*, Paris, 1881.

Aquinas, St. Thomas, *Opera Omnia*, ed. Vivès, 32 vols., Parisiis, 1871-1879: *De Eruditione Principum*; *De Regimine Principum*; *Summa Theologica*.

[Bachofen], Charles Augustine, *A Commentary on the New Code of Canon Law*, 4 ed., 8 vols., St. Louis: Herder, 1921-1929.

Ballerini-Palmieri, *Opus Theologicum Morale*, 3rd ed., 7 vols., Prati, 1898-1901.

Barrett, John, *A Comparative Study of the Councils of Baltimore and the Code of Canon Law*, The Catholic University of America, Canon Law Studies, n. 83, Washington: The Catholic University of America, 1932.

Blat, Albertus, *Commentarium Textus Codicis Iuris Canonici*, 6 vols., Romae: Collegio "Angelico," 1921-1927.

Bondini, Aloisius, *De Privilegio Exemptionis*, Romae: Desclée, 1919.

Bouix, *Tractatus de Episcopis et Synodo dioecesana*, Paris, 1853.

Buison, M. F., *Dictionnaire de Pédagogie et d'Instruction Primaire*, Paris, 1882.

Cabrol, F., et Leclercq, H., *Dictionnaire d'Archéologie Chrétienne et de Liturgie*, Paris: Librairie Letouzey et Ané, 1924—.

Cappello, Felice M., *Summa Iuris Publici Ecclesiastici*, 2nd ed., Romae: apud Aedes Universitatis Gregorianae, 1928.

Casotti, Mario, *Maestro e Scolaro - Saggio di Filosofia dell'Educazione*, Milano: Società Ed. "Vita e Pensiero," 1930.

Catholic Encyclopedia, The, 16 vols., New York, 1907-1914.

Cathrein, Victor, *Moralphilosophie*, 2nd ed., 2 vols., Freiburg im Breisgau, 1893.

Cavagnis, Felix, *Institutiones Iuris Publici Ecclesiastici*, 3 vols., Romae, 1883.

Civardi, Luigi, *A Manual of Catholic Action*, Tr. by C. C. Martindale, New York: Sheed and Ward, 1936.

Cocchi, Guidus, *Commentarium in Codicem Iuris Canonici*, 7 vols., Taurinorum Augustae, 1922-1930; Vol. VI, *De Rebus*, 2nd ed., Taurinorum Augustae: Marietti, 1927.

Compayré, J., *Storia della Pedagogia*, Tr. by A. Valderini, Torino, 1919.

Coronata, Matthaeus Conte a, *Institutiones Iuris Canonici*, 5 vols., Taurini (Italia): Marietti, 1928-1936; Vol. II, *De Rebus*, 1931.

Costa-Rossetti, Julius, *Philosophia Moralis*, Oeniponte, 1886.

Creusen, J., *Religieux et Religieuses d'après le Droit Ecclésiastique*, 3rd ed., Bruxelles: Dewit, 1924.

D'Alès, A., *Dictionnaire Apologétique de la Foi Catholique*, 4 vols., Paris: Beauchesne, 1911-1922.

Das holländische Schulgesetz, Düsseldorf, 1921, in *Schulpolitik und Erziehung: Zeitfragen*, Heft 11.

de Beaurepaire, *Recherches sur l'Instruction publique, dans le diocèse de Rouen, avant 1789*, 3 vols., Evreux, 1872.

De Hammerstein, Ludovicus, *De Ecclesia et Statu Juridice Consideratis*, Treviris, 1886.

De Hovre, Franz, *Philosophy and Education*, Tr. by E. Jordan, New York: Benziger Brothers, 1931.

Delisle, Leopold, *Études sur la condition de la classe agricole et l'état de l'agriculture en Normandie au moyen-âge*, Paris, 1903.

De Luca, M., *Institutiones Iuris Publici Ecclesiastici*, 2 vols., Romae, 1904.

De Meester, Alphonsus, *Juris Canonici et Juris Canonico-Civilis Compendium*, Nova ed., 3 vols in 4, Brugis: Desclée, De Brouwer, 1921-1928.

Demeuran, J. Louis, *L'Église - Constitution - Droit public*, Paris, 1914.

Denifle, Heinrich, *Die Enstehung der Universitäten des Mittelalters bis 1400*, Berlin, 1885.

Denk, V. M. Otto, *Geschichte des Gallo-Frankischen Unterrichts und Bildungswesens, von den ältesten Zeiten bis auf Karl den Grossen*, Mainz, 1892.

de Resbecq, M., *Histoire de l'Instruction primaire dans les Communes qui ont formé le departement du Nord*, Paris, 1878.

De Rossi, Giovanni, *La Roma Sotterranea*, 3 vols., and *Tavole*, Roma, 1867.

d'Herbigny, Michael, *Theologica de Ecclesia*, 3rd ed., 2 vols., Paris: Beauchesne, 1927-1928.

Doyle, J., *Education in Recent Constitutions and Concordats*, Washington: The Catholic University of America, 1933.

Drane, Mother Augusta, *Christian Schools and Scholars*, 2 vols., London, 1867.

Dupanloup, M., *L'Éducation*, 3 vols., Paris, 1861.

Fanfani, Ludovicus, *De Iure Religiosorum*, 2nd ed., Taurini et Romae: Marietti, 1925.

Fumi, *Documenti di Storia Italiana*, Firenze, 1884.

Gabel, R. J., *Public Funds for Church and Private Schools*, Toledo, 1937.

Gasquet, Francis A., *Henry VIII and the English Monasteries*, London, 1906.

Gerson, J., *Tractatus de visitatione praelatorum et curatorum*, ed. E. L. de Pin, *Gersonii Opera*, Antuerpiae, 1706.

Godts, *Les droits en matière d'éducation*, 5 vols., Bruxelles, 1900-1901.

Gredt, Joseph, *Elementa Philosophiae Aristotelico-Thomisticae*, 7th ed., 2 vols., Friburgi Brisgoviae: Herder, 1937.

Healy, John, *Insula Sanctorum et Doctorum: Ireland's Ancient Schools and Scholars*, Dublin, 1893.

Hefele, Karl, *Conciliengeschichte*, 2nd ed., 9 vols., Freiburg im Breisgau, 1873-1890.

Heimbucher, Max, *Die Orden und Kongregationen der katholischen Kirche*, 2 vols., Paderborn: Verlag F. Schöningh, 1933-1934.

Hinschius, Paul, *Das Kirchenrecht der Katholiken und Protestanten in Deutschland*, 6 vols., Berlin, 1869-1897; Vols. I-IV, *System des katholischen Kirchenrechts*, 1869-1888.

Histoire littéraire de la France - ouvrage commencé par des religieux Bénédictins de la Congregation de Saint-Maur, et continue par des Membres de l'Institut, 33 vols., ed. Palmé, Paris, 1733-1898.

Ireland, John, *The Church and Modern Society - Lectures and Addresses*, Chicago, 1897.

Jansen, Alphonsus, *De Facultate Docendi seu de Scholis Institutiones Juridicae*, Parisiis, Buscoduci et Zwollae, 1885.

Jansen, Raymond J., *Canonical Provisions for Catechetical Instruction*, The Catholic University of America, Canon Law Studies, n. 107, Washington: The Catholic University of America, 1937.

Johnson, George, *The Curriculum of the Catholic Elementary Schools*, Washington, 1919.

Joly, Claude, *Traité Historique des Écoles Épiscopales et Ècclésiastiques*, Paris, 1678.

Juliani Imperatoris opera quae supersunt, graece et latine, Lipsiae, 1875-1876.

Jullien, E., *Les professeurs de littérature dans l'ancienne Rome et leur enseignement depuis l'origine jusqu'à le mort d'Auguste*, Paris, 1885.

Kandel, J. L., *History of Secondary Education*, Boston: Houghton Mifflin Co., 1930.

Krabbe, C. F., *Obligatio parochi instruendi juvent. et de scholis parochialibus*, Münster, 1842.

Kremer, Michael, *Church Support in the United States*, The Catholic University of America, Canon Law Studies, n. 61, Washington: The Catholic University of America, 1930.

Lalanne, J. A., *Influence des Pères de l'Église sur l'éducation publique pendant les cinq premiers siècles de l'ere chrétienne*, Paris, 1850.

Lämmer, H., *Institutionen des katholischen Kirchenrechts*, 2nd ed., Freiburg im Breisgau, 1892.

Langasco, Agathangelus a, *De Institutione Clericorum in disciplinis inferioribus*, Typis Polyglottis Vaticanis, 1936.

Laurie, S. S., *Rise and Early Constitution of Universities*, New York, 1898.

Leach, A. F., *English Schools at the Reformation*, Westminster, 1896.

Lexikon der Pädagogik der Gegenwart, hrg. vom Deutschen Institut für wissenschaftliche Pädagogik, Münster i. W., Freiburg im Br., 1930-1932.

Lischka, Charles N., *Private Schools and State Laws*, Washington: The National Catholic Welfare Conference, 1926.

Mabillon, J., *Praefationes in Acta Sanctorum Ordinis Sancti Benedicti conjunctim editae*, Venetiis, 1740.

——, *Traité des études monastiques*, Bruxelles, 1672.

McCormick, P. J., *Education of the Laity in the Early Middle Ages*, Washington, 1912.

——, *History of Education*, Washington, 1915.

Maître, Leon, *Les écoles épiscopales et monastiques de l'occident*, Paris, 1866.

Manacorda, Giuseppe, *Storia della Scuola in Italia*, 1 vol. in 2, Palermo, 1913.

Manitius, Max, *Geschichte der lateinischen Literatur des Mittelalters*, München, 1911.

Marion, L., *Histoire de l'Église*, 3 vols., Paris, 1905-1906.

Marion, Marie-Albert, *Le Problème Scolaire étudié dans ses principes*, Ottawa: Impr. de l'*Ottawa Printing Co.*, 1920.

Marique, Pierre J., *History of Christian Education*, 3 vols., New York: Fordham University Press, 1924-1932.

Mercati, Angelo, *Raccolta di Concordati su Materie Ecclesiastiche tra la Santa Sede e le Autorità Civili*, Roma: Tipografia Poliglotta Vaticana, 1919.

Merkelbach, Benedictus Henricus, *Summa Theologiae Moralis ad Mentem D. Thomae et ad Normam Iuris Novi*, 3 vols., Parisiis: Desclée, 1931-1933.

Michel, A., *La Question Scolaire et les Principes Théologiques*, Paris: Desclée, De Brouwer, 1921.

Montalambert, Count de, *Monks of the West*, 5 vols., Boston, 1872.

Monti, Giuseppe, *La Libertà della Scuola*, Milano: Soc. Ed. "Vita e Pensiero," 1928.

Moore, Ernest Carroll, *The Story of Instruction - The Church, the Renaissances, and the Reformations*, New York: Macmillan, 1938.

Mullinger, J. Bass, *The Schools of Charles the Great and the Restoration of Education in the Ninth Century*, New York, 1911.

Muratori, L. A., *Antiquitates Italicae*, Mediolani, 1740.

Muteau, Charles, *Les écoles et collèges en Provence*, Dijon, 1882.

Nájera, Francisco Blanco, *Derecho Docente de la Iglesia, la Familia y el Estado*, Linares: Impr. "El noticiero," 1934.

Nègre, M., *Les Écoles - Les Documents du Saint-Siège*, Paris, 1911.

Oddone, Andrea, *La Costituzione Sociale della Chiesa e le sue Relazione con lo Stato*, Milano: Soc. Ed. "Vita e Pensiero," 1932.

Ojetti, Benedictus, *Commentarium in Codicem Iuris Canonici*, 4 vols., Romae: apud Aedes Universitatis Gregorianae, 1927-1931.

Ottaviani, Alaphridus, *Institutiones Iuris Publici Ecclesiastici*, 2nd ed., 2 vols., Typis Polyglottis Vaticanis, 1935-1936.

Paquet, Louis Adolphe, *Droit Public de l'Église - L'Église et l'éducation à la lumière de l'histoire et des principes chrétiens*, Québec, 1909.

Paré, G., Brunet, A., Tremblay, P., *Le Renaissance du XIIe Siècle - Les Écoles et l'enseignement*, Ottawa, Inst. d'études Médiévales, 1933.

Paulsen, F., *German Education, Past and Present*, Tr. by Lorenz, New York, 1908.

Pernicone, Joseph, *The Ecclesiastical Prohibition of Books*, The Catholic University of America, Canon Law Studies, n. 72, Washington: The Catholic University of America, 1932.

Piatus Montensis, *Praelectiones Juris Regularis*, 3rd ed., 2 vols., Tornaci, 1906.

Ratherius, *Opera Omnia*, ed. Ballerini, Verona, 1765.

Ravelet, Armand, *Blessed John Baptist de la Salle*, with an Introduction by Mons. D'Hulst, Paris, 1888.

Reiffenstuel, Anacletus, *Jus Canonicum Universum*, 5 vols., Parisiis, 1864-1870.

Rendu, E., *De l'Instruction populaire dans l'Allemagne du Nord*, Paris, 1855.

Reques, *Derechos de la Iglesia, del Estado y de la Familia*, Barcelona, 1868.

Restrepo, Joannis M. Restrepus, *Concordata regnante Sanctissimo Domino Pio PP. XI Inita*, Romae: apud Aedes Pont. Universitatis Gregorianae, 1934.

Ruffini, Edoardo, *La Personalità Giuridica Internazionale della Chiesa*, Isola del Liri: Soc. Tip. Marcioce e Pisani, 1936.

Sägmüller, I. B., *Lehrbuch des katholischen Kirchenrechts*, 3rd ed., 2 vols., Freiburg im Breisgau, 1914.

Sandys, John Edwin, *History of Classical Scholarship*, 3 vols., Cambridge, 1906.

Scarascia, Giuseppe, *Le Scuole Parrocchiali e degli Istituti Religiosi e l'Istruzione Elementare in Italia*, Torino: Soc. Ed. Internazionale, 1936.

Schäfer, Timotheus, *Compendium de Religiosis*, 2nd ed., Münster: Aschendorff, 1931.

Scharnagl, A., *Religionsunterricht und Schule nach dem neuen kirchlichen Gesetzbuch*, 2nd ed., M. Gladbach, 1923, in *Schulpolitik und Erziehung: Zeitfragen*, Heft 15.

Scherer, Rudolf Ritter von, *Handbuch des Kirchenrechtes*, 2 vols., Graz und Leipzig, 1886-1898.

Schmalzgrueber, Franciscus, *Jus Ecclesiasticum Universum*, 5 vols., Romae, 1843-1845.

Schmid, K. A., *Geschichte der Erziehung vom Anfang an bis auf unsere Zeit*, 3 vols., Stuttgart, 1884-1892.

Schroeder, H. J., *Disciplinary Decrees of the General Councils*, St. Louis: Herder, 1937.

Schröteler, Josef, *Das Elternrecht in der katholisch-theologischen Auseinandersetzung*, München: Neuer Filser-Verlag, 1936.

Schultes, Reginaldus Maria,—Prantner, Edmundus, M., *De Ecclesia Catholica - Praelectiones Apologeticae*, 2nd ed., Parisiis: Lethielleux, 1931.

Schulz, H., *Die Schulreform der Sozialdemokratie*, 2nd ed., Berlin, 1919.

Schwickerath, Robert, *Jesuit Education: its History and Principles in the light of modern educational problems*, St. Louis, 1903.

Sertillanges, A. D., *La Famille et L'État dans l'éducation*, Paris, 1907.

Solieri, Franciscus, *Institutiones Iuris Ecclesiastici*, 2nd ed., Romae: Pustet, 1921.

Spalding, J. L., *Means and Ends of Education*, 3rd ed., Chicago, 1901.

Steffes, Johann, *Religion und Politik*, Freiburg im Breisgau: Herder, 1928.

Stöckl, Albert, *Geschichte der Pädagogik*, Mainz, 1876.

Suarez, Franciscus, *Opera Omnia*, ed. J. Cardon, 15 vols., Lugduni, 1617-1632; Vol. XI, *De Triplici Virtute Theologica.*

Taparelli, Luigi, *Saggio Teoretico di Diritto Naturale*, 2nd ed., 2 vols., Prato, 1883.

Tarquini, Camillus, *Iuris Ecclesiastici Publici Institutiones*, 4th ed., Romae, 1875.

Thomassinus, Ludovicus, *Vetus et Nova Ecclesiae Disciplina circa Beneficia et Beneficiarios*, 10 vols., Moguntiaci, 1787.

Van Hove, A., *De Legibus Ecclesiasticis*, Mechliniae et Romae. Dessain, 1930.

Vermeersch, A., et Creusen, J., *Epitome Iuris Canonici*, 4th ed., 3 vols., Mechliniae et Romae: Dessain, 1930-1931.

Ville, Cirot de la, *Histoire de l'abbaye de la Sauve*, 2 vols., Bordeaux, 1844.

Vromant, G., *Ius Missionariorum*, 5 tomes, Louvain: Éditions du Museum Lessianum, 1929-1931; Tome II, *De Personis*, 1929.

Wernz, Franciscus X., *Ius Decretalium*, 6 vols., Romae et Prati, 1906-1913; Tomus III, *Ius Administrationis Ecclesiae Catholicae*, 2nd ed., Romae, 1908.

Wernz-Vidal, *Ius Canonicum*, 7 vols., Romae: apud Aedes Universitatis Gregorianae, 1923-1938.

Willmann, Otto, *Didaktik als Bildungslehre nach ihren Beziehungen zur Sozialforschung und zur Geschichte der Bildung*, 2nd ed., 2 vols., Braunschweig, 1894-1895.

Zech, F. X., *De Iure Rerum Ecclesiasticarum*, Ingolstadii, 1758.

PERIODICALS

Acolyte, The, Huntington, Indiana, 1925—.

Ami du Clergé, L', Langres, 1883—.

Analecta Juris Pontificii, Rome, 1855-1866; Paris, 1867-1888.

Annuaire International de l'Éducation et de l'Enseignement, Genève: Bureau Intern. d'Éducation, 1933—.

Apollinaris, Romae, 1928—.

Archiv für katholisches Kirchenrecht, Innsbruck, 1857-1861; Mainz, 1862—.

Civiltà Cattolica, La, Roma, 1850—.

Commentarium pro Religiosis, Romae, 1920—; ab anno 1935: *Commentarium pro Religiosis et Missionariis*.

Documentation catholique, La, Paris, 1919—.

Ecclesiastical Review, The [originally *The American Ecclesiastical Review*], Philadelphia, 1889—.

Études classiques, Les, Namur, 1932—.

Homiletic and Pastoral Review, The, New York, 1900—.

Irish Ecclesiastical Record, The, Dublin, 1864—.

Monitore Ecclesiastico, Il, Roma, 1876—.

Nouvelle Revue Théologique, Tournai, 1869—.

Osservatore Romano, L', Roma, 1861-1929; Città del Vaticano, 1929—.

Periodica de Re Canonica et Morali utili praesertim Religiosis et Missionariis, Brugis, 1905—; ab anno 1927: *Periodica de Re Morali, Canonica, Liturgica*.

Questions ecclésiastiques, Lille, 1908—.

Revue Apologétique, Paris, 1905—.

Revue de l'Université d'Ottawa, Ottawa, 1931—.

Revue des Sciences Religieuses, Paris, 1921-1924; Strasbourg, 1925—.

ALPHABETICAL INDEX

BIBLIOGRAPHICAL NOTE

Conrad Humbert Boffa was born in Susa (Turin-Italy) on February 26, 1913. He completed his elementary and higher studies in Europe. In 1932 he came to America and after four years of Theology was ordained to the priesthood by the Most Rev. John T. McNicholas, Archbishop of Cincinnati. In September of 1936 he was enrolled in the school of Canon Law of the Catholic University of America.

CANON LAW STUDIES

1. Freriks, Rev. Celestine A., C.PP.S., J.C.D., Religious Congregations in Their External Relations, 121 pp., 1916.
2. Galliher, Rev. Daniel M., O.P., J.C.D., Canonical Elections, 117 pp., 1917.
3. Borkowski, Rev. Aurelius L., O.F.M., J.C.D., De Confraternitatibus Ecclesiasticis, 136 pp., 1918.
4. Castillo, Rev. Cayo, J.C.D., Disertacion Historico-Canonica sobre la Potestad del Cabildo en Sede Vacante o Impedida del Vicario Capitular, 99 pp., 1919 (1918).
5. Kubelbeck, Rev. William J., S.T.B., J.C.D., The Sacred Penitentiaria and Its Relations to Faculties of Ordinaries and Priests, 129 pp., 1918.
6. Petrovits, Rev. Joseph J. C., S.T.D., J.C.D., The New Church Law on Matrimony, X-461 pp., 1919.
7. Hickey, Rev. John J., S.T.B., J.C.D., Irregularities and Simple Impediments in the New Code of Canon Law, 100 pp., 1920.
8. Klekotka, Rev. Peter J., S.T.B., J.C.D., Diocesan Consultors, 179 pp., 1920.
9. Wanenmacher, Rev. Francis, J.C.D., The Evidence in Ecclesiastical Procedure Affecting the Marriage Bond, 1920. (Printed 1935.)
10. Golden, Rev. Henry Francis, J.C.D., Parochial Benefices in the New Code, IV-119 pp., 1921. (Printed 1925.)
11. Koudelka, Rev. Charles J., J.C.D., Pastors, Their Rights and Duties According to the New Code of Canon Law, 211 pp., 1921.
12. Melo, Rev. Antonius, O.F.M., J.C.D., De Exemptione Regularium, X-188 pp., 1921.
13. Schaaf, Rev. Valentine Theodore, O.F.M., S.T.B., J.C.D., The Cloister, X-180 pp., 1921.
14. Burke, Rev. Thomas Joseph, S.T.D., J.C.D., Competence in Ecclesiastical Tribunals, IV-117 pp., 1922.
15. Leech, Rev. George Leo, J.C.D., A Comparative Study of the Constitution "Apostolicae Sedis" and the "Codex Juris Canonici," 179 pp., 1922.
16. Motry, Rev. Hubert Louis, S.T.D., J.C.D., Diocesan Faculties According to the Code of Canon Law, II-167 pp., 1922.
17. Murphy, Rev. George Lawrence, J.C.D., Delinquencies and Penalties in the Administration and the Reception of the Sacraments, IV-121 pp., 1923.

18. O'Reilly, Rev. John Anthony, S.T.B., J.C.D., Ecclesiastical Sepulture in the New Code of Canon Law, II-129 pp., 1923.
19. Michalicka, Rev. Wenceslas Cyrill, O.S.B., J.C.D., Judicial Procedure in Dismissal of Clerical Exempt Religious, 107 pp., 1923.
20. Dargin, Rev. Edward Vincent, S.T.B., J.C.D., Reserved Cases According to the Code of Canon Law, IV-103 pp., 1924.
21. Godfrey, Rev. John A., S.T.B., J.C.D., The Right of Patronage According to the Code of Canon Law, 153 pp., 1924.
22. Hagedorn, Rev. Francis Edward, J.C.D., General Legislation on Indulgences, II-154 pp., 1924.
23. King, Rev. James Ignatius, J.C.D., The Administration of the Sacraments to Dying Non-Catholics, V-141 pp., 1924.
24. Winslow, Rev. Francis Joseph, O.F.M., J.C.D., Vicars and Prefects Apostolic, IV-149 pp., 1924.
25. Correa, Rev. Jose Servelion, S.T.L., J.C.D., La Potestad Legislativa de la Iglesia Católica, IV-127 pp., 1925.
26. Dugan, Rev. Henry Francis, M.A., J.C.D., The Judiciary Department of the Diocesan Curia, 87 pp., 1925.
27. Keller, Rev. Charles Frederick, S.T.B., J.C.D., Mass Stipends, 167 pp., 1925.
28. Paschang, Rev. John Linus, J.C.D., The Sacramentals According to the Code of Canon Law, 129 pp., 1925.
29. Piontek, Rev. Cyrillus, O.F.M., S.T.B., J.C.D., De Indulto Exclaustrationis necnon Saecularizationis, XIII-289 pp., 1925.
30. Kearney, Rev. Richard Joseph, S.T.B., J.C.D., Sponsors at Baptism According to the Code of Canon Law, IV-127 pp., 1925.
31. Bartlett, Rev. Chester Joseph, M.A., LL.B., J.C.D., The Tenure of Parochial Property in the United States of America, V-108 pp., 1926.
32. Kilker, Rev. Adrian Jerome, J.C.D., Extreme Unction, V-425 pp., 1926.
33. McCormick, Rev. Robert Emmett, J.C.D., Confessors of Religious, VIII-266 pp., 1926.
34. Miller, Rev. Newton Thomas, J.C.D., Founded Masses According to the Code of Canon Law, VII-93 pp., 1926.
35. Roelker, Rev. Edward G., S.T.D., J.C.D., Principles of Privilege According to the Code of Canon Law, XI-166 pp., 1926.
36. Bakalarczyk, Rev. Richardus, M.I.C., J.U.D., De Novitiatu, VIII-208 pp., 1927.
37. Pizzuti, Rev. Lawrence, O.F.M., J.U.L., De Parochis Religiosis, 1927. (Not Printed.)
38. Bliley, Rev. Nicholas Martin, O.S.B., J.C.D., Altars According to the Code of Canon Law, XIX-132 pp., 1927.
39. Brown, Mr. Brendan Francis, A.B., LL.M., J.U.D., The Canonical Juristic Personality with Special Reference to its Status in the United States of America, V-212 pp., 1927.
40. Cavanaugh, Rev. William Thomas, C.P., J.U.D., The Reservation of the Blessed Sacrament, VIII-101 pp., 1927.

41. Doheny, Rev. William J., C.S.C., A.B., J.U.D., Church Property: Modes of Acquisition, X-118 pp., 1927.
42. Feldhaus, Rev. Aloysius H., C.PP.S., J.C.D., Oratories, IX-141 pp., 1927.
43. Kelly, Rev. James Patrick, A.B., J.C.D., The Jurisdiction of the Simple Confessor, X-208 pp., 1927.
44. Neuberger, Rev. Nicholas J., J.C.D., Canon 6 or the Relation of the Codex Juris Canonici to the Preceding Legislation, V-95 pp., 1927.
45. O'Keefe, Rev. Gerald Michael, J.C.D., Matrimonial Dispensations, Powers of Bishops, Priests, and Confessors, VIII-232 pp., 1927.
46. Quigley, Rev. Joseph, M.A., A.B., J.C.D., Condemned Societies, 139 pp., 1927.
47. Zaplotnik, Rev. Johannes Leo, J.C.D., De Vicariis Foraneis, X-142 pp., 1927.
48. Duskie, Rev. John Aloysius, A.B., J.C.D., The Canonical Status of the Orientals in the United States, VIII-196 pp., 1928.
49. Hyland, Rev. Francis Edward, J.C.D., Excommunication, Its Nature, Historical Development and Effects, VIII-181 pp., 1928.
50. Reinmann, Rev. Gerald Joseph, O.M.C., J.C.D., The Third Order Secular of Saint Francis, 201 pp., 1928.
51. Schenk, Rev. Francis J., J.C.D., The Matrimonial Impediments of Mixed Religion and Disparity of Cult, XVI-318 pp., 1929.
52. Coady, Rev. John Joseph, S.T.D., J.U.D., M.A., The Appointment of Pastors, VIII-150 pp., 1929.
53. Kay, Rev. Thomas Henry, J.C.D., Competence in Matrimonial Procedure, VIII-164 pp., 1929.
54. Turner, Rev. Sidney Joseph, C.P., J.U.D., The Vow of Poverty, XLIX-217 pp., 1929.
55. Kearney, Rev. Raymond A., A.B., S.T.D., J.C.D., The Principles of Delegation, VII-149 pp., 1929.
56. Conran, Rev. Edward James, A.B., J.C.D., The Interdict, V-163 pp., 1930.
57. O'Neil, Rev. William H., J.C.D., Papal Rescripts of Favor, VII-218 pp., 1930.
58. Bastnagel, Rev. Clement Vincent, J.U.D., The Appointment of Parochial Adjutants and Assistants, XV-257 pp., 1930.
59. Ferry, Rev. William A., A.B., J.C.D., Stole Fees, V-136 pp., 1930.
60. Costello, Rev. John Michael, A.B., J.C.D., Domicile and Quasi-Domicile, VII-201 pp., 1930.
61. Kremer, Rev. Michael Nicholas, A.B., S.T.B., J.C.D., Church Support in the United States, VI-136 pp., 1930.
62. Angulo, Rev. Luis, C.M., J.C.D., Legislacion de la Iglesia sobre la intencion en la applicacion de la Santa Misa, VII-104 pp., 1931.
63. Frey, Rev. Wolfgang Norbert, O.S.B., A.B., J.C.D., The Act of Religious Profession, VIII-174 pp., 1931.

64. ROBERTS, REV. JAMES BRENDAN, A.B., J.C.D., The Banns of Marriage, XIV-140 pp., 1931.
65. RYDER, REV. RAYMOND ALOYSIUS, A.B., J.C.D., Simony, IX-151 pp., 1931.
66. CAMPAGNA, REV. ANGELO, PH.D., J.U.D., Il Vicario Generale del Vescovo, VII-205 pp., 1931.
67. COX, REV. JOSEPH GODFREY, A.B., J.C.D., The Administration of Seminaries, VI-124 pp., 1931.
68. GREGORY, REV. DONALD J., J.U.D., The Pauline Privilege, XV-165 pp., 1931.
69. DONOHUE, REV. JOHN F., J.C.D., The Impediment of Crime, VII-110 pp., 1931.
70. DOOLEY, REV. EUGENE A., O.M.I., J.C.D., Church Law on Sacred Relics, IX-143 pp., 1931.
71. ORTH, REV. CLEMENT RAYMOND, O.M.C., J.C.D., The Approbation of Religious Institutes, 171 pp., 1931.
72. PERNICONE, REV. JOSEPH M., A.B., J.C.D., The Ecclesiastical Prohibition of Books, XII-267 pp., 1932.
73. CLINTON, REV. CONNELL, A.B., J.C.D., The Paschal Precept, IX-108 pp., 1932.
74. DONNELLY, REV. FRANCIS B., M.A., S.T.L., J.C.D., The Diocesan Synod, VIII-125 pp., 1932.
75. TORRENTE, REV. CAMILO, C.M.F., J.C.D., Las Processiones Sagradas, V-145 pp., 1932.
76. MURPHY, REV. EDWIN J., C.PP.S., J.C.D., Suspension Ex Informata Conscientia, XI-122 pp., 1932.
77. MACKENZIE, REV. ERIC F., M.A., S.T.L., J.C.D., The Delict of Heresy in its Commission, Penalization, Absolution, VII-124 pp., 1932.
78. LYONS, REV. AVITUS E., S.T.B., J.C.D., The Collegiate Tribunal of First Instance, XI-147 pp., 1932.
79. CONNOLLY, REV. THOMAS A., J.C.D., Appeals, XI-195 pp., 1932.
80. SANGMEISTER, REV. JOSEPH V., A.B., J.C.D., Force and Fear as Precluding Matrimonial Consent, V-211 pp., 1932.
81. JAEGER, REV. LEO A., A.B., J.C.D., The Administration of Vacant and Quasi-Vacant Episcopal Sees in the United States, IX-229 pp. 1932.
82. RIMLINGER, REV. HERBERT T., J.C.D., Error Invalidating Matrimonial Consent, VII-79 pp., 1932.
83. BARRETT, REV. JOHN D. M., S.S., J.C.D., A Comparative Study of the Third Plenary Council of Baltimore and the Code, IX-221 pp., 1932.
84. CARBERRY, REV. JOHN J., PH.D., S.T.D., J.C.D., The Juridical Form of Marriage, X-177 pp., 1934.
85. DOLAN, REV. JOHN L., A.B., J.C.D., The Defensor Vinculi, XII-157 pp., 1934.
86. HANNAN, REV. JEROME D., M.A., S.T.D., LL.B., J.C.D., The Canon Law of Wills, IX-517 pp., 1934.

87. Lemieux, Rev. Delisle A., M.A., J.C.D., The Sentence in Ecclesiastical Procedure, IX-131 pp., 1934.
88. O'Rourke, Rev. James J., A.B., J.C.D., Parish Registers, VII-109 pp., 1934.
89. Timlin, Rev. Bartholomew, O.F.M., M.A., J.C.D., Conditional Matrimonial Consent, X-381 pp., 1934.
90. Wahl, Rev. Francis X., A.B., J.C.D., The Matrimonial Impediments of Consanguinity and Affinity, VI-125 pp., 1934.
91. White, Rev. Robert J., A.B., LL.B., S.T.B., J.C.D., Canonical Ante-Nuptial Promises and the Civil Law, VI-152 pp., 1934.
92. Herrera, Rev. Antonio Parra, O.C.D., J.C.D., Legislacion Ecclesiastica sobra el Ayuno y la Abstinencia, XI-191 pp., 1935.
93. Kennedy, Rev. Edwin J., J.C.D., The Special Matrimonial Process in Cases of Evident Nullity, X-165 pp., 1935.
94. Manning, Rev. John J., A.B., J.C.D., Presumption of Law in Matrimonial Procedure, XI-111 pp., 1935.
95. Moeder, Rev. John M., J.C.D., The Proper Bishop for Ordination and Dimissorial Letters, VII-135 pp., 1935.
96. O'Mara, Rev. William A., A.B., J.C.D., Canonical Causes for Matrimonial Dispensations, IX-155 pp., 1935.
97. Reilly, Rev. Peter, J.C.D., Residence of Pastors, IX-81 pp., 1935.
98. Smith, Rev. Mariner T., O.P., S.T.Lr., J.C.D., The Penal Law for Religious, VII-169 pp., 1935.
99. Whalen, Rev. Donald W., M.A., J.C.D., The Value of Testimonial Evidence in Matrimonial Procedure, XIII-297 pp., 1935.
100. Cleary, Rev. Joseph F., J.C.D., Canonical Limitations on the Alienation of Church Property, VIII-141 pp., 1936.
101. Glynn, Rev. John C., J.C.D., The Promoter of Justice, XX-337 pp., 1936.
102. Brennan, Rev. James H., S.S., M.A., S.T.B., J.C.D., The Simple Convalidation of Marriage, VI-135 pp., 1937.
103. Brunini, Rev. Joseph Bernard, J.C.D., The Clerical Obligations of Canons 139 and 142, X-121 pp., 1937.
104. Connor, Rev. Maurice, A.B., J.C.D., The Administrative Removal of Pastors, VIII-159 pp., 1937.
105. Guilfoyle, Rev. Merlin Joseph, J.C.D., Custom, XI-144 pp., 1937.
106. Hughes, Rev. James Austin, A.B., M.A., J.C.D., Witness in Criminal Trials of Clerics, IX-140 pp., 1937.
107. Jansen, Rev. Raymond J., A.B., S.T.L., J.C.L., Canonical Provisions for Catechetical Instruction, VII-153 pp., 1937.
108. Kealy, Rev. John James, A.B., J.C.D., The Introductory Libellus in Church Court Procedure, XI-121 pp., 1937.
109. McManus, Rev. James Edward, C.SS.R., J.C.D., The Administration of Temporal Goods in Religious Institutes, XVI-196 pp., 1937.
110. Moriarty, Rev. Eugene James, J.C.D., Oaths in Ecclesiastical Courts, X-115 pp., 1937.

111. Rainer, Rev. Eligius George, C.SS.R., J.C.D., Suspension of Clerics, XVII-249 pp., 1937.
112. Reilly, Rev. Thomas F., C.SS.R., J.C.D., Visitation of Religious, IX-195 pp., 1938.
113. Moriarty, Rev. Francis E., C.SS.R., J.C.D., The Extraordinary Absolution from Censures, XV-334 pp., 1938.
114. Connolly, Rev. Nicholas P., J.C.D., The Canonical Erection of Parishes, X-132 pp., 1938.
115. Donovan, Rev. James Joseph, J.C.D., The Pastor's Obligation in Prenuptial Investigation, XII-322 pp., 1938.
116. Harrigan, Rev. Robert J., M.A., S.T.B., J.C.D., The Radical Sanation of Invalid Marriages, VIII-208 pp., 1938.
117. Boffa, Rev. Conrad H., J.C.L., Canonical Provisions for Catholic Schools, 1939.
118. Parson, Rev. Anscar J., O.M.Cap., J.C.L., Canonical Elections, 1939.
119. Reilly, Rev. Edward M., J.C.L., The General Norms of Dispensation, 1939.
120. Ryan, Gerald A., J.C.L., Principles of Episcopal Jurisdiction, 1939.

www.ingramcontent.com/pod-product-compliance
Lightning Source LLC
LaVergne TN
LVHW050242080826
844660LV00012B/584

* 9 7 8 0 8 1 3 2 2 3 0 6 3 *